Who needs the Old Testament?

Its enduring appeal and why the New Atheists don't get it

KATHARINE DELL

CASCADE *Books* · Eugene, Oregon

WHO NEEDS THE OLD TESTAMENT?
Its Enduring Appeal and Why the New Atheists Don't Get It

Copyright © 2017 Katharine Dell. All rights reserved. Except for brief quotations in critical publications or reviews, no part of this book may be reproduced in any manner without prior written permission from the publisher. Write: Permissions, Wipf and Stock Publishers, 199 W. 8th Ave., Suite 3, Eugene, OR 97401.

Cascade Books
An Imprint of Wipf and Stock Publishers
199 W. 8th Ave., Suite 3
Eugene, OR 97401
www.wipfandstock.com

ISBN 13: 978-1-5326-1964-9

First published in Great Britain in 2017 by SPCK, 36 Causton Street, London, SW1P 4ST. First US edition published by Cascade Books under license from SPCK, 2017.

Manufactured in the U.S.A.

'Dell confronts the "New Atheists" head-on, demonstrating how their reading of the Old Testament ignores its cultural context and misrepresents its account of God, the world and humankind. With equal rigour, she examines the conflicted intersection between Church and academy, where scholarly scepticism seeds a growing clerical reluctance to preach and teach the Old Testament . . .With the skill of a scholar and the passion of one committed to the work of the Church in the modern world, Dell demonstrates why and how the Old Testament offers a rich and realistic account of life in all its messiness. As she puts it, the Old Testament "can be our friend, even if a rather challenging and contrary one at the end of the day".'
Samuel E. Balentine, Professor of Old Testament
Union Presbyterian Seminary, Richmond, Virginia

'Katharine Dell is bold, both in naming real difficulties posed by Old Testament texts and in showing how misleading are the widely publicized claims of ill-informed critics. She does not give simple answers but, rather, better ways to live with hard questions. This is the kind of deeply informed yet plain speaking about the Bible that the Church needs from its best scholars and teachers.'
Ellen F. Davis, Professor of Bible and Practical Theology
Duke Divinity School, Durham, North Carolina

'If you've ever wondered how relevant the Old Testament is today or worried about how to defend the God of the Old Testament against the many criticisms aimed at him, then this is the book for you! It is a careful, thoughtful and clear exploration both of the issues raised by New Atheists and by the Old Testament itself. I can't recommend it highly enough.'
Paula R. Gooder, Theologian in Residence, Bible Society

Contents

Preface vii

Introduction ix

Part 1
BREAKING THE NEW ATHEIST SPELL

1 From Dawkins to Marcion: countering scepticism and atheism	3
2 The character and scope of the Old Testament: countering a bad press	27
3 Meeting Dawkins head-on: texts in Genesis	49
4 Homing in on Hitchens (and Dawkins): Exodus, Numbers and legal texts	76
5 Countering Dawkins: texts in the 'histories'	99

Part 2
ENGAGING WITH THE OLD TESTAMENT

Introduction	119
6 The Writings: a neglected corner of the Old Testament	121
7 The Prophets: a more convincing source of morality?	144
8 Back to the Pentateuch and historical books: the power of story	162

9 Questioning the history of Israel: scepticism within the academy	187
10 A Christian perspective on the Old Testament	204
Notes	221
Further reading	241
Index of biblical references	243
Index of authors and subjects	249

Preface

This book has evolved over a number of years, starting with a commitment to spreading the message of the value and worth of the Old Testament to theology students and ordinands in training, to churchgoers, readers, clergy and the wider public. I am grateful for the many opportunities that I have had to speak at courses for readers and clergy in a number of dioceses and to preach in churches and college chapels. Encountering the work of the New Atheists along that path has led to a particular interest in seeking to defend these varied, difficult and yet endlessly fascinating texts in a book that would bring together those two elements.

My thanks go to my graduate student Luke Wisley for his helpful comments, to Philip Law of SPCK for his encouragement to write this book and for his arresting title, and to Steve Gove for his careful copy-editing. I would particularly like to thank my husband, Douglas, for putting up with my occasional 'Dawkins rants' and keeping me focused, and to our son, James, for putting up with Mummy being 'in her study' yet again. Our younger cats, Tabitha and Miriam, have also offered many purrs and lap comforts during this time.

I wish to dedicate this book to the churches with which I have been associated in my life – St Andrew's Chesterton, Cambridge where my father was vicar, Derby Cathedral where he was a canon and archdeacon, the University Church in Oxford where I worshipped as a student, All Saints, Cuddesdon where I attended as one of the Ripon College, Cuddesdon staff, St Benet's, Cambridge and St Peter and St Paul, Kings Sutton, where I mainly worship today. I would also like to mention the chapels of Oriel

Preface

College, Oxford, and St Catharine's College, Cambridge, where I have heard many inspiring sermons and anthems. May their clergy, be it in church or chapel, continue to nourish their congregations in the faith, and occasionally – even only 'just' occasionally – preach on the Old Testament!

Introduction

The idea for this book first arose when, on a beautiful summer's day, I sat in the garden in a deckchair and read a book that I had just bought at my local supermarket – *The God Delusion* by Richard Dawkins. Reading his chapter on the Old Testament made my blood boil, not only because I disagreed with it, but because it was full of misrepresentation, inaccuracy and empty diatribe. Since then I have felt that no real apology specifically for the Old Testament/Hebrew Bible in direct response to the New Atheist attack has been made in Church or academy, although wider refutations of Dawkins' approach have appeared.

This frustration is accompanied by two others. The first is the revolution in biblical studies, largely in relation to method but also with reference to history and archaeology. The agenda of some scholars seeks to undermine many of the claims made by the biblical text and by many subsequent generations of Christians and Jews. While I am a wholehearted supporter of questioning, there is, in my view, a movement here seeking to undercut serious scholarly endeavour. The second frustration is the way in which the Old Testament/Hebrew Bible tends to be marginalized in Christian circles, notably in church life. Furthermore, the God of the Old Testament is severely misunderstood and remembered for 'the bad elements' rather than the good. Christians often have little more than a nodding acquaintance with the Old Testament – what they glean is little more than a decontextualized reading on a Sunday morning in church or a carefully chosen lectionary selection, the main purpose of which is to complement the central New Testament reading or gospel. The sermon that follows may well build on this pairing of texts, but seldom is a sermon preached entirely on an Old Testament text. Even Bible study groups rarely have time to connect the whole Old Testament together, getting a sense of its history, its rich literary connections and profound theological ideas. Rather, one key text is chosen and explored, but not in particular depth.

This book is an attempt to counter such developments and to foster a clearer understanding of these texts and the picture(s) of God within them. It is, in that sense, an initial introduction to the Old Testament, its nature, its value, its contents and its enduring appeal. In that service some chapters are designed to give an overview of the diversity and character of a broad range of texts. While I may have 'cherry-picked' the more instructive and nurturing parts of the Old Testament in Part 2, it is done deliberately to counter the relentless 'cherry-picking' of abhorrent texts by its critics, as demonstrated in Part 1. I make no apology for choosing texts – we all do it, and my aim in this book is to counter the one-sided selection of difficult texts that gives the impression that these are all that the Old Testament contains. Moreover, it is a call to the Church for a deeper engagement with the Old Testament, with its message and its themes, and to the New Atheists at the very least to stop mischaracterizing and misrepresenting its contents.

Part 1

BREAKING THE NEW ATHEIST SPELL

1

From Dawkins to Marcion: countering scepticism and atheism

> The God of the Old Testament is arguably the most unpleasant character in all fiction: jealous and proud of it; a petty, unjust, unforgiving control-freak; a vindictive, bloodthirsty ethnic cleanser; a misogynistic, homophobic, racist, infanticidal, genocidal, filicidal, pestilential, megalomaniac, sadomasochistic, capriciously malevolent bully.
> (Richard Dawkins, *The God Delusion*)[1]

The God of the Old Testament has recently had a bad press from the New Atheists, as the above quotation from Richard Dawkins makes clear. Indeed it is more than just a bad press, it is a character assassination. First, Dawkins suggests that the Old Testament is a work of fiction rather than of holy writ, and second, he draws out all the bad characteristics of any person he can think of and applies them wholesale to God. It is interesting that, despite his atheism, Dawkins has more pleasant things to say about the God of the New Testament. He states that, compared to the 'cruel ogre' of the Old Testament, Jesus is a huge improvement. The New Testament 'undoes the damage and makes it all right. Doesn't it?' he asks sarcastically.[2]

Let us be clear here that he is talking about ethics – the ethics of Jesus is more palatable to him than that of God in the Old Testament. Ethics is Dawkins' starting point and his main criterion for judging the two 'Gods' to be so different. This raises first of all the question whether there is any continuity between the 'Gods' of the Old and New Testaments, and why that might matter; and second, the further question of how Christians can 'read' the Old Testament in a nurturing way if a very different kind of God lurks within its pages.

The questioning of the place of the Old Testament, both in Christian life and thought and in the canon, is an old chestnut. The characterization of very different 'Gods' as portrayed by the two Testaments is also an ancient concern. It takes us back to Marcion, that famous first critic of the value of the Old Testament for Christians.[3] He took a radical stance in sweeping away the old Scriptures to make way for the new, and, even more radically, focusing on St Paul and the Gospel of Luke alone for the Christian message. This may be because Luke was the Gospel of which he had knowledge – we are speaking here of pre-canonical times, where individual Gospels seem to have been known and popular in certain areas. But the writings of St Paul were where the real newness of the Christian message lay for Marcion, in the gospel to the Gentiles and the consequent leaving behind of the Jewish heritage. This led him to reject the Old Testament and its God, whom he described as the Demiurge, a different God, creator and redeemer of the Jews, who had no place in the Christian proclamation. Indeed he excised from Luke passages citing the Old Testament in order to show that Jesus was indeed a fulfilment of the promises made by the Old Testament prophets. He disliked the God of the Old Testament almost as much as Dawkins does. Marcion has had a number of followers over the years, most famously Adolf Harnack,[4] and in modern times Eric Seibert, who takes a very Marcionite line in his recent work.[5]

Clearly the Old Testament with the God it portrays is easily open to attack and, as with most accusations, however exaggerated, there is some justification; evidence abounds of God's less savoury characteristics, as Dawkins makes us aware. It is interesting, however, that Dawkins can cite passages only from the narrative sections of the Old Testament to be found in the Pentateuch and in the historical books. Large swathes of the Old Testament, notably the Prophets and the Writings, are entirely left out of account, along with their portrayals of God. It is of course the books of the Prophets to which the early Christians turned for prophecies of the coming, life and significance of Jesus; and the New Testament, especially the Gospel of Matthew, is a witness to the way they viewed prophecy and fulfilment in the person of Jesus. But surely the Writings deserve a mention too? The Psalms, a key book within the Writings, have long been cherished in Christian liturgy and thought and are also part of the 'fulfilment in Christ' motif for the New Testament; and an alternative system of ethics resides in the wisdom literature, notably in Proverbs.

The present book seeks to counter these 'Dawkinsite' and Marcionite accusations about God and the Old Testament. It does not seek entirely to exonerate a God who does at times behave in an opposite manner to expectation, but it seeks to understand the context of God's actions as far as possible. I try in the book to draw out the 'other side of the coin' when it comes to texts in the Old Testament, and to indicate the diversity and richness of their textual offering. While I will spend much of the book countering such critics as Dawkins on a passage-by-passage basis, I will also seek to indicate the broader context of the Old Testament as canon and as a rich historical, literary and theological document, essential for understanding its successor, the New Testament. In this chapter I want to explore further the New Atheist and Marcionite attacks and seek to understand where the critiques are coming from, before I turn in subsequent chapters to my own characterization of the Old Testament in response to these critiques.

The New Atheist movement: a brief outline

The so-called 'New Atheists' are a group of four writers and scholars – dubbed, in a reference to the book of Revelation, the 'four horsemen of the non-Apocalypse' – who have pioneered a fresh attack on religion for the twenty-first century. It was the events of September 11 2001 that inspired Sam Harris to write *The End of Faith: Religion, Terror, and the Future of Reason* (2004), and this was swiftly followed by publications by Richard Dawkins (*The God Delusion*, 2007, following his 2006 television documentary *The Root of All Evil?*), Daniel Dennett (*Breaking the Spell: Religion as a Natural Phenomenon*, 2006) and Christopher Hitchens (*God Is Not Great: How Religion Poisons Everything*, 2007).[6] There is some question as to whether this is really a new movement – it builds on a secular humanism that has its roots in the humanism of the Renaissance and on ideas from utilitarianism, ethical naturalism and evolutionary biology. It is a particularly strong brand of atheism, even anti-theism, that springs also from a scientific perspective which does not simply ignore the 'God hypothesis' but sees it as false. According to the New Atheists, the answers to our questions about the world we inhabit and the wider universe are entirely answerable by naturalism rather than by any appeal to the supernatural.

The New Atheists as a group are not particularly concerned with the Bible, especially with the Old Testament. Two of them, however – Dawkins and Hitchens – do engage with it, so it is with these two that I will interact in this book as I seek to evaluate the Old Testament from both a scholarly and a Christian perspective.

Richard Dawkins, *The God Delusion*

Dawkins' starting point in his chapter on 'The "Good" Book and the changing moral *Zeitgeist*' is, as I have said, the use of the Old Testament as a source of morality.[7] There is some question as to whether this is the only reason people read it, but that is his line. He argues that there are two channels for morality: direct instruction from God, as exemplified in the Ten Commandments (Exod. 20; Deut. 5), and the idea of God as a role model to emulate. He goes on to identify stories in the Old Testament that he deems 'morally appalling' (as he says of the story of Noah) to show that the role-model argument quickly finds God seriously lacking. He jibes at the view of the Flood as bound up with human sin by saying, 'We humans give ourselves such airs, even aggrandizing our poky little "sins" to the level of cosmic significance!'[8] And if the retort of the theologian is that we don't take the Flood story literally, then he questions how one can take some parts of the Bible literally and not other parts (see below, Chapter 2).

He then scours the first five books (the Pentateuch or Torah) of the Old Testament for the worst stories he can find. He goes on into the 'historical books' of Joshua and Judges to find more evidence. So we come across the stories of Abraham and Lot in Genesis 19, and of the Levite's concubine in Judges 19, which he paraphrases in a mocking tone. He picks on Abraham in particular – he retells the story of his passing off his wife as his sister and has a field day with Abraham's near sacrifice of Isaac, which he views as child abuse. These examples demonstrate to him that 'We do not, as a matter of fact, derive our morals from scripture', or, if we do, they are just derived from the 'nice bits'.⁹

He then turns to Judges 11, the story of Jephthah's daughter – another very difficult text, identified by biblical scholar Phyllis Trible as a 'text of terror'.[10] He repeatedly asks the question what kind of God expects loyalty to the point of sacrificing one's own offspring, and what kind of morality that conveys. Because these stories are so raw and unpalatable to modern sensibilities, he is easily able to jibe and mock with no understanding of the context in which the stories arose. He accuses the God of the Old Testament of sexual jealousy of the worst kind, with the indictment of the people for their 'going after other gods'. An example is found in Exodus 32 with the story of the golden calf and its often forgotten aftermath when 3,000 people are killed to 'assuage God's jealous sulk',[11] followed by God sending a plague.

Moses as well as Abraham comes in for a character assassination from Dawkins – the attack on the Midianites in Numbers 31 is cited as evidence. Rival gods and rival peoples that provoke God's jealousy are at the centre of concern here: 'The tragi-farce of God's maniacal jealousy against alternative gods recurs continually throughout the Old Testament.'[12] Joshua and his attack on Jericho (Josh. 6) comes under discussion as 'xenophobic relish',[13] as does the 'invasion' of the promised land (Deut. 20). Dawkins asks, 'Do those people who hold up the Bible as an inspiration to moral rectitude have the slightest notion of what is actually written in it?'[14] Again, he is establishing his point that modern morality and the Old Testament are poles apart (a fact that no one is challenging) – the issue here is whether the Old Testament has anything to teach us, on the question of morality or otherwise, or whether it is simply to be 'binned' with the rest of the Christian faith, as Dawkins would have us do.

The laws of the Old Testament, which also were clearly designed for a very different context, are then held up for ridicule – why the death penalty for offences that seem to us to be minor? He points out that, when we turn to the New Testament, Jesus defined himself against such laws as this one about Sabbath-keeping: 'Jesus was not content to derive his ethics from the scriptures of his upbringing. He explicitly departed from them.'[15] So Jesus himself is used in the argument against the 'morality' of the Old Testament.

A Christian too might use appeal to the morality of Jesus as an argument against following the morality of the Old Testament, but this is a choice that Christians are not actually being asked to make. What I am calling for here is at least an understanding of the cultural context of that morality and a fair evaluation of the nature of the stories and other texts that we find in the Old Testament, rather than a wholesale rejection on moral grounds.

Lest we think Dawkins is going soft on us when he gets to Jesus, though, he points out some more shadowy features of Jesus' ministry. He critiques Jesus' 'family values', and how he was 'short, to the point of brusqueness, with his own mother',[16] for which viewpoint he cites no evidence. My immediate response would be that the Gospels simply do not relate much about their relationship and do not specifically give us any reflection on Jesus' treatment of his mother. Furthermore, says Dawkins, Jesus demanded his disciples abandon their families to follow him, a request Dawkins regards as reminiscent of modern 'brainwashing' cults.

Dawkins can find little fault with Jesus's ethical teaching,[17] but he has a field day with the doctrine of original sin, which after all is a somewhat later interpretation (going back to the early Church Father Augustine)[18] of the links between sin in the Garden of Eden and Jesus' atonement for that sin. Adam and Eve come in for a good jibe here:

'The symbolic nature of the fruit (knowledge of good and evil, which in practice turned out to be knowledge that they were naked) was enough to turn their scrumping escapade into the mother and father of all sins.'[19] He then airs the point that if this story is symbolic – as many theologians maintain – rather than real, then what on earth was the view of Jesus' atonement? Here is one of his most vicious sentences (comparable with the one cited at the beginning of this chapter): 'So, in order to impress himself, Jesus had himself tortured and executed, in vicarious punishment for a *symbolic* sin committed by a *non-existent* individual? As I said, barking mad, as well as viciously unpleasant.'[20] While I, and many Christians, might accuse Dawkins of being 'viciously unpleasant' here in his diatribe, he quite clearly misses the point of symbolism. Even if the story is symbolic, the truth that it represents about the human condition is not (see below).

I have probably paraphrased enough of Dawkins' vitriolic chapter to give you a flavour of his argument and concerns, and I will come back to many of his points and to the texts that he lampoons. To sum up, Dawkins, in little more than half a chapter devoted to the Old Testament, grounds his discussion primarily in the context of how Scripture might be a source of morals or rules for living, either in terms of laws such as the Ten Commandments or of role models that devotees might follow. Either route he terms 'obnoxious' to any civilized modern person, particularly in the light of the fact that the Bible is 'not systematically evil but just plain weird',[21] but 'unfortunately it is this same weird volume that religious zealots hold up to us as the inerrant source of our morals and rules for living'.[22]

The word 'zealots' is very telling: Dawkins gives the impression that all religious people of any persuasion are extremists who take the Bible literally and reject all scientific explanations for natural disasters in the belief that they are payback for human misdemeanours. He comments on the human egocentricity that places human concerns at the centre, asking 'Why should a divine being, with creation and eternity on his mind, care a fig for petty human malefactions?'[23] Dawkins' main point in his half-chapter is to say not that we shouldn't get our morals from Scripture but that in fact, when we study Scripture closely, we find that we don't. I agree with him that we do not get our modern morality from his selection of texts, but I would not go so far as to say that there is no morality in Scripture at all.

Dawkins continues to argue that neither is God a good role model, nor are the laws relevant to today, so we have no need of this 'weird' and outdated set of 'textually unreliable' and confused documents called the Old Testament. His claim is that the 'good book' gives us no nourishment, moral or otherwise. There is no doubt about what his convictions are. I will attempt to show that the Old Testament is of a diverse nature and that such sweepingly general comments cannot be fairly applied to its contents. It has enduring appeal for those who engage seriously with it and seek to understand its cultural context and for those who explore its variety and appreciate the development of its ideas over the many centuries before it reached its final form.

Alister McGrath, *The Dawkins Delusion?*

Before turning to another New Atheist, I want to pause for a moment to consider the response of Alister McGrath, who in his books *The Dawkins Delusion? Atheist Fundamentalism and the Denial of the Divine* (2007, with Joanna Collicutt McGrath)[24] and *Why God Won't Go Away: Engaging with the New Atheism* (2011, see below) is virtually alone in mounting a solid defence of the Christian faith against

Dawkins' attack.[25] McGrath's concern is less biblical than theological, but he does point out the superficial engagement with the Bible, with its core themes, ideas and texts that Dawkins displays.[26] It is my concern in this book to dig below this superficiality. McGrath acknowledges the unpalatability of many Old Testament texts, but also highlights the cultural distance of the times (from 2500 BCE to 1 BCE). This means that one can neither attempt to find a direct moral link between then and now, nor understand the texts properly, without some serious attempt to contextualize them and possibly extrapolate for our own time. He writes, 'These texts arose within a group fighting to maintain their identity. They were gradually evolving their understanding of the nature of God.'[27] The ideas that God's concerns may alter over time and that his character may be multifaceted and changing, and that human perception of God also develops over time, do not seem to be taken into account at all by Dawkins. McGrath makes the point that many of these biblical texts were at first circulated in oral form, which is probably the reason they appear to be less well organized than a written-only text would be. In fact, McGrath suggests, a careful editing and re-editing process is evident within the Bible's pages. He also points out that the kinds of shocking passages to which Dawkins has drawn our attention often appear alongside more acceptable passages, such as 'the laws urging hospitality towards strangers (Deuteronomy 10:17–19), setting limits on acts of revenge (Exodus 2), prohibiting slavery (Leviticus 25), declaring a Jubilee for debt (Leviticus 25), and forbidding infant sacrifice (Leviticus 18:1; 20:2)'.[28] McGrath also makes the observation that I made at the outset, that large swathes of the Old Testament are simply not featured in Dawkins' account: 'He [Dawkins] also ignores the Prophets and wisdom literature, in which the heights of Jewish moral insight are expressed – insights that continue to shape and nourish the human quest for moral values.'[29] McGrath's analysis is christocentric in that he sees Jesus as the 'external criterion for dealing with the interpretation of these texts',[30] texts and commands that were not to be abolished, or even 'corrected' by Jesus, but fulfilled and so transformed (Matt. 5.17). He cites Dawkins on the Sabbath law – of course Christians have never obeyed Sabbath-keeping to the letter, leading to executions. This is not Christian morality, and so to suggest that we take this moral from the Old Testament is misguided and out of touch.

The Old Testament when it is used as a guide to Christian morality is filtered through the lens of Jesus Christ and his teachings. The issue of looking for morality in these texts comes up again – it is posing this question, rather than simply attacking God's existence in an atheistic manner, that muddies the waters of the debate. Of course one might reject the idea that God exists, and the nature of God in the Old Testament might be one among other arguments for doing so. But if it is modern, essentially Christian, morality that is under attack, a simple portrayal of negative aspects of the Old Testament God is not going to satisfy the argument. The God of the Old Testament has to be discussed within a Christian context that accepts Jesus and the New Testament as the authoritative guide to its ethics. But, as I have already indicated, ethics is not the only aspect of the Old Testament that is of interest and concern. These arguments, and more, will be explored below.

Christopher Hitchens, *God Is Not Great*

Let us now turn to another New Atheist, Christopher Hitchens, whose book, *God Is Not Great*, also features a chapter on 'The Nightmare of the Old Testament'.[31]

Hitchens characterizes the Old Testament as a 'nightmare', full of 'horrors, cruelties and madnesses'.[32] He has a problem with the random selection by God of 'unlettered and quasi-historical individuals in regions of Middle Eastern wasteland that were long the home of idol worship and superstition',[33] to whom different and contradictory revelations were given at different times, thus leading to religious wars over the legitimacy of one or the other. He highlights a discrepancy in that sometimes divine instruction happens once and 'to an obscure personage whose lightest word then becomes law'[34] and yet at other times, one revelation needs to be followed by another to reinforce it, 'with the promise of a further but ultimate one to come'.[35] He writes:

> We ought to be glad that none of the religious myths has any truth to it, or in it. The Bible may, indeed does, contain a warrant for trafficking in humans, for ethnic cleansing, for slavery, for bride-price and for indiscriminate massacre, but we are not bound by any of it because it was put together by crude, uncultured human mammals . . . none of the gruesome, disordered events described in Exodus ever took place.[36]

Hitchens focuses in his chapter on the Ten Commandments, which he misguidedly describes as the 'foundation story of all three faiths',[37] Judaism, Christianity and Islam, characterizing them as follows:

> There is, first, the monarchical growling about respect and fear, accompanied by a stern reminder of omnipotence and limitless reverence, of the sort with which a Babylonian or Assyrian emperor might have ordered the scribes to begin a proclamation. There is then a sharp reminder to keep working and only to relax when the absolutist says so.[38]

He describes them as the 'pitiless teachings of the god of Moses, who never mentions human solidarity and compassion at all',[39] and goes on to discuss what the commandments do not say. But then, were they ever meant to be an exhaustive ethical system? Like Dawkins, he wants more from them than they were ever intended to convey. He asks whether this means that before the time concerned murder, adultery and so on were permissible, suggesting that Moses insulted the people by imagining that they did not know these things already, but he fails to see that the Ten Commandments are probably a summary to be remembered, not exhaustive and not simply dreamt up at a single moment in time. He then tries to assert that these laws are nothing special, that they are self-evident, indeed, to all societies and clearly man-made – as evidenced by the wife being listed under property in the final commandment (Exod. 20.17).[40]

He then cites other, less palatable laws, such as Exodus 33.2, where God gives Moses instructions for buying and selling slaves, as well as commands to drive other peoples out of their homes. He sees all the events of the exodus wanderings as 'made up at a much later date' and characterizes them as 'Mosaic myths'.[41] Here he is engaging with some of the efforts of biblical scholars and archaeologists[42] to present us with ever later datings of texts and artefacts (as will be discussed in Chapter 9). He dwells on the paucity of archaeological evidence despite Jewish and Christian efforts and writes, in his cynical and amusing style, that in the nineteenth and early twentieth centuries such was Christian zeal to uncover 'evidence' that 'you could hardly throw away an orange peel in the Holy Land without hitting a fervent excavator'.[43] He also attacks the idea that Moses (described as 'commandingly authoritarian and bloody'[44] rather than the 'very meek' of Num. 12.3) himself wrote the Pentateuch, although he seems unaware that this idea went out of fashion in biblical scholarship in the nineteenth century. He describes all the events of the accounts as 'nonevents' described neither 'convincingly' nor 'even plausibly',[45] and of course cites further pronouncements by Old Testament characters that are out of line with modern sensibilities (although not unknown in modern times). These include Moses ordering parents to have their children stoned to death for indiscipline – one of his 'demented pronouncements' (but one which luckily was never carried out, he says, since the Bible is a fiction) and Numbers 31, also cited by Dawkins, which he describes as 'lascivious', the women who are saved being rather obvious 'rewards of a freebooting soldier'.[46]

Hitchens condemns the whole Old Testament when he writes:

> One could go through . . . book by book, here pausing to notice a lapidary phrase . . . and there a fine verse, but always encountering the same difficulties. People attain impossible ages and yet conceive children. Mediocre individuals engage in single combat or one-on-one argument with god or his emissaries, raising afresh the whole question of divine omnipotence or even divine common sense, and the ground is soaked forever with the blood of the innocent.[47]

Of course this list is a massive generalization – no two books are the same and I would contend that there are many fine verses. But then if you dismiss the Old Testament as a 'hopelessly knotted skein of fable',[48] presumably you would not want to spend much time with it. Interestingly he cites 'Man is born to trouble as the sparks fly upward' from the book of Job as an occasional 'fine verse' of Scripture.

He also slates the context of the Old Testament as 'confined and *local*' (his italics). Is being 'local' a crime? Of course the events described happened to and originated among small communities – 'provincial yokels', to use

Hitchens' language[49] – but that is the context we are dealing with: many aspects of human life start at a local level. Hitchens maintains that God was simply made in the image of humans and not the other way around, so that human 'locality' is reflected in the sphere of the godhead.

Unlike Dawkins, when Hitchens turns to the New Testament, he believes that its 'evil' exceeds that of the Old. He finds 'odd' the way the New Testament looks back to the Old for the foretelling of the life of Jesus and writes, 'Just like the OT, the "new" one is also a work of crude carpentry, hammered together long after its purported events, and full of improvised attempts to make things come out right.'[50] He calls these 'reverse engineered' stories. He makes a naïve attempt to critique the Gospels for being separate and often not agreeing with each other (for example, on the place of Jesus' birth). No one has ever said, though, that the Gospels did not come together in a less than systematic way – different Gospels were known in different areas in the early centuries of Christian life, as Marcion (see below) attests. He also attacks the process of canonization – in other words the way the groupings of biblical books came together – saying that 'orthodox Christianity is nothing if it is not a vindication and completion of that evil story'.[51]

Hitchens questions whether the disciples were even Christians, since they clearly could not have read books written after their time – which suggests that Christians are simply 'of the book' and that Christianity has no life apart from its Scriptures. He accuses the disciples of illiteracy, even though, if that is indeed verifiable (which is doubtful), they could well have stood at the head of a strong oral tradition. He also accuses the New Testament of an absurd belief in magic:

> Just as the script of the Old Testament is riddled with dreams and with astrology (the sun standing still so that Joshua can

complete his massacre at a site that has never been located), so the Christian Bible is full of star-predictions (notably the one of Bethlehem) and witch doctors and sorcerers.[52]

There is no acknowledgement here of the very different cosmic worldview of the time. Jesus is at best for Hitchens a 'deranged prophet', a figure whose historical existence is highly questionable. He takes the same line as Dawkins on issues of contradiction, notably differences between Jesus' own teaching and that of the early Church: 'The most glaring of these . . . concern the imminence of his [Jesus'] second coming and his complete indifference to the founding of any temporal church.'[53]

The issue of development of ideas over time is not dealt with by Hitchens here. And he agrees with Dawkins on the way Jesus 'undermines' the laws of the Pentateuch to present his own alternative, although he questions Jesus' authority to do so and mocks the idea that only 'non-sinners' might punish offenders. He tries to cite New Testament scholars to support his position, but takes the whole issue of interpretation too literally to offer anything of real value. A 'late' story in a Gospel is not proof of the 'early Church' meddling in the transmission, it could well simply be an older oral story that was left out of the earlier account and incorporated at a later stage. He reduces serious New Testament study to a joke.

Alister McGrath, *Why God Won't Go Away*

Let us pause for a moment to go back to McGrath, this time to his second book on the New Atheist attacks. McGrath pays what I see as a compliment to Dawkins in his comment: 'if there's an atheist equivalent to C. S. Lewis' Mere Christianity, this is it'.[54] I wonder if that compliment is really deserved. In this book he also mounts a critique of Hitchens which I shall focus on here. Though deciding that Hitchens' book is the 'by far the most entertaining of the New Atheist works', with 'its quickfire aphorisms and finely honed insults',[55] he accuses Hitchens of a shallow approach to arguments in general. I would add that such an approach is what Hitchens also takes in his specific chapters on the Bible. McGrath writes:

> For example, the chapter boldly entitled 'The Metaphysical Claims of Religion Are False' skims the surface of a potentially interesting debate, leaving us unsure what those metaphysical claims might be or what's wrong with them. But at least we come away knowing that Hitchens thinks they're merely so much donkey poo along the road of life. It's not exactly an argument, is it?[56]

Hitchens also, says McGrath, 'cherry-picks' historical anecdotes, as in the New Testament chapter when he cites C. S. Lewis and Bart Ehrmann, the New Testament fundamentalist scholar turned questioner,[57] a strange choice from the full range of New Testament interpreters on offer.

Marcion, *Antitheses*

I said at the outset that the kinds of difficulties that the New Atheists have with the Old Testament, and which come out particularly in the writings of the two New Atheists I am concerned with here, are not new. Various people in history have had a problem with it, and have either attacked it or left it out of account. The most famous attacker of the Old Testament is the early Church thinker Marcion, and so it is on him that I want to focus next in this chapter, taking us back to a very different context and set of concerns. The question is raised, why did Marcion so dislike the Old Testament and wish to excise it from the emergent Christian Scriptures that he knew? Furthermore, why did he reject wholesale the God of the Old Testament, not from an atheistic stance but with the idea that an entirely different God had been revealed by Jesus?

Marcion's work *Antitheses* is no longer extant; we only know of him through the writings of other contemporaries who were critics – Justin Martyr, Epiphanius and Tertullian in particular.[58] In that sense then we have a third-hand view of him, and yet such was his influence and so many were the number of churches that regarded themselves as Marcionite, that his views are fairly simple to glean.

Marcion was born in the late first or early second century CE and lived in the Roman province of Pontus in northern Asia Minor. There is an inherent dualism in his thought. For Marcion, the revelation of God in Jesus was so completely different from anything that had come before that it led him to reject the God of the Old Testament. His main commitment was to the writings of St Paul, the famous apostle to the Gentiles, which also led him to reject the Jewish heritage of Jesus in the form of Jesus' Bible. He took up Paul's critique of 'the curse of the Law' (Gal. 3.13) in particular, Christ being 'the end of the Law' (Rom. 10.4). He seems to have known only the Gospel of Luke (probably in truncated form and possibly not under the name 'Luke'), which is unsurprising since there is evidence that certain Gospels circulated only in certain areas in the second century CE and that they had not as yet been brought together as a group. But he also had the letters of Paul, ten of them at this stage – Galatians, 1 and 2 Corinthians, Romans, 1 and 2 Thessalonians, Laodiceans (our Ephesians), Colossians-Philemon, and Philippians in that order – which he regarded as the main authority of genuine Christian teaching. Marcion's emphasis on the completely different character of the God of the emergent New Testament as a God of love and goodness led him to reject the God of the Old, the creator and lawgiver whom he described as 'the Demiurge'. He did not, then, deny the existence of the God of the Jews, but thought him an inferior being who created the world and had a legalistic attitude to human actions. This contrasted with the saving grace of the God proclaimed by Jesus, who was a universal saviour and not the Jewish Messiah (who was still expected).

This led Marcion to engage with the Old Testament rather than ignore it, for he had to show how lacking its God was. A debate was already taking place among his contemporaries about the continuity of Christianity with Judaism and how far the Scriptures were authoritative. Jesus' clear overturning of some aspects of Jewish law and observance were discussed, and on the agenda too was what might be the appropriate response of an increasingly Gentile Christianity to its Jewish roots. For Marcion there was a total incompatibility between the 'high' God of Christianity and his 'low' Jewish counterpart. He saw a conspiracy against the truth of the gospel from 'Judaizers' shortly after Jesus' ascension, a conspiracy that deceived even the apostles and meant that Christ had to appoint another apostle – St Paul – to begin the preaching of the gospel again. Marcion refused to accept an allegorical reading that eased certain difficult interpretations, preferring instead a literal approach. He spent a lot of time expunging passages from his 'canon' that he thought to be secondary interpolations. This largely involved taking out any reference to the Old Testament, to its characters, its promises and its prophecies.

In Marcion's textual version of the Epistle to the Galatians, which he amended in various places, all quotations from the Old Testament were omitted except in 4.22–31. In his Gospel of Luke, the birth and pre-birth stories about Jesus and his Jewish genealogy were all omitted. Jesus' baptism and temptation were also omitted and the connection with Nazareth obscured. Marcion had no scruples about tailoring the text to his viewpoint and making additions and excisions where needed. He disliked taking verses out of context and so again kept to a literal interpretation; so he took 2 Samuel 7.12 – 'I will raise up your offspring after you ... and I will establish his kingdom [for ever]' – to refer only to Solomon rather than as a messianic prophecy in relation to David's line. For him there was no prophecy leading to Christian conversion.

He held the Prophets in a certain esteem – when Luke 7.26, citing Malachi 3.1, calls John the Baptist a prophet he does not excise the reference, and he retains Luke 16.29 with its view of Moses and the Prophets as moral guides. But he was against the idea that prophecy was fulfilled in the New Testament, so he omitted Luke 18.31 and did not see prophecy as inspired by the high God in any sense. Indeed the prophecies of a Jewish messiah were not yet fulfilled, largely because they were national, temporal hopes. Jesus, by contrast, was a universal saviour.

The high God of Christian faith was not seen by Marcion as ruler of the world, for he was above the world and entirely unknown to the creator of the world until his appearance in Christ. The redemption to be found in the high God is about eternal life rather than life in this world, and hence there is no judgement for the evil deeds done in this world. The Creator-God is ruler of the world and the Old Testament is his book – any promises therein do not refer to Christ, and the Old Testament cannot have been quoted as authoritative either by Christ or the Gospel writers or by Paul. The Creator-God is not Jesus' 'father'. Christ brought to light the contrast between law and gospel – the Creator-God was God of the law and the prophets, of flesh rather than spirit.

Marcion's dualism led him to hatred for the world, such was his perception of the evil of humankind. Creation was negatively evaluated. The law was also evil, the image of God as judge a cruel one, and so 'the Demiurge' is not truly divine – this God has too many human flaws. 'The Demiurge' changes his mind about people – for example, Saul was first chosen as king, then later rejected; he lacks omniscience – for example, God didn't know where Adam was in the Garden of Eden (Gen. 3.9); and God is often inconsistent about laws, as when the Hebrews fled Egypt with spoils of gold and silver, which contradicted laws against stealing in Exodus 12.35–36, and when Moses made a bronze serpent in direct contradiction of the command to reject images in Numbers 21.9.[59] God is also, according to Marcion, 'weak, unreliable, self-contradictory, given to irrational acts of anger and wanton cruelty'.[60] Thus 'an evil God created a miserable world with weak creatures, gave them a burdensome Law and judges them cruelly'.[61] What a contrast with a good God who spites the creator and frees humankind. No wonder Marcion rejected the Old Testament!

This kind of contrast between two Gods was not mainstream and was not accepted by the principal Christian writers of the time. Some saw the Old Testament as 'good in parts', especially the Prophets, but noted that its ethics often fell below Christian standards. But most maintained the right of the Old Testament to the dignity of Christian Scripture. Ignatius, for example, saw no conflict between Old and New and valued the Prophets as 'disciples in spirit'.[62] The gospel was the completion of the Old Testament in that the 'one covenant' was rejected by the Jews but given to Christians. Texts were reinterpreted, often non-literally, for example, ritual commands in the Old Testament were turned into ethical commands. Justin Martyr saw God as one.[63] He had no problem with laws, even if they were often interpreted allegorically – Christ's summary of the law in Matthew 22.37–39 showed how central and necessary law was for salvation. There was a distinction to be made between temporal law and eternal law.

Most of Marcion's contemporaries, then, found the redeeming God of Jesus Christ in the Old Testament, despite its rather different character from the New Testament and its preparatory role. It is interesting, though, that there were such heated debates about the place of the Old Testament in the early centuries, even before the formation of the canon of the New. It is equally interesting that the citation of the Old was already widespread in the Christian writings, so that even Marcion had to excise texts. His critics decided Marcion was wrong and in the end his strong anti-Old Testament line and dualistic view of God died a death.

Harnack wrote the definitive book about Marcion, and it is notable that his line was that Marcion had been wrong to reject the Old Testament but that nevertheless later Protestant emphasis upon it has not been altogether healthy.[64] How highly or otherwise to value the Old Testament is a question for this book. How is it different from other ancient writings? Do we only value it because it formed the context into which Christianity was born? Do we need to reject wholesale its morality? Does it have the same quality of revelation as the New Testament? Most significantly, is its God, Yahweh, one and the same as the God revealed in Jesus Christ? And, if so, how are we to view a changing God who develops in human understanding over time?

A synthesis: Marcion and the New Atheists

You might wonder why I have brought Marcion and the New Atheists together in this chapter. I see some interesting connections. While the agendas are very different – one from within faith, albeit with a rather warped view of Christianity and so outside the Christian mainstream, and the other atheistic – their attacks on the Old Testament have some very similar resonances. The authority of this set of texts is attacked by both, on grounds of the apparent inferiority of their portrayal of God and because of the presence within them of less than ethically edifying stories. While Marcion's attack contains the subtlety of a deeper knowledge of texts, his extensive revisions to the New Testament in order to exclude the Old are a precursor to Dawkins' affirmation of the ethics of Jesus while rejecting wholesale Jesus' 'Bible'. More significantly, their attacks on God and the nature of God have similar overtones. While for the New Atheists God does not exist, for Marcion such is the different God revealed in the pages of the Old Testament that he is other and inferior. This leads Marcion to an attack on God as creator and lawgiver, which in turn leads him to despise this world. This is very different from Dawkins, who does not despise this world but basically despises the Christian attitude to sin that in his view has 'warped' our more natural relationship with the world. Although Marcion would not have accepted this, he has a very other-wordly view of God that is much more spiritual than material; such a dimension is lacking in the New Atheists' worldview, which denies a spiritual level to life.

So where do we go from here? In Chapters 3, 4 and 5 of this book I intend to meet head-on the attack on the Old Testament from the New Atheists, Dawkins and Hitchens, as I examine the main passages that have been the object of that attack and attempt to characterize the nature of the Old Testament in a different way. I then wish to present in Part 2, and as a main emphasis of this book, a more balanced view of the character both of the Old Testament and its God. A supplementary issue, meanwhile, is that of the relevance of the Old Testament within Christianity, an old debate from Marcion that needs to be revisited in the present day and in the context of the modern Church.

2

The character and scope of the Old Testament: countering a bad press

> To be fair, much of the Bible is not systematically evil but just plain weird, as you would expect of a chaotically cobbled-together anthology of disjointed documents, composed, revised, translated, distorted and 'improved' by hundreds of anonymous authors, editors and copyists, unknown to us and mostly unknown to each other, spanning nine centuries.
> (Dawkins, *The God Delusion*)[1]

In this chapter I wish, in the main, to move away from the New Atheist critique and introduce aspects of the Old Testament. However, I will begin with Richard Dawkins' critique as a link to more traditional critical concerns. The aspect of Dawkins' attack that I have saved for this chapter is his characterization of the Bible as 'chaotic'. This is a very cursory nod in the direction of biblical scholarship which has for the past two hundred years sought to understand the processes by which the Bible came together, its possible stages of compilation, its issues of translation and relationship to other ancient versions and ultimately its social context spanning many centuries (although possibly not as few as nine centuries, as 'low chronology' dating would have us believe . . .).[2] Of course the Bible is, on one level, a human construction, subject to the messiness, contradiction and inadequacy of human effort in conveying perceived truth.

Whether this makes it 'weird' is another matter – there is a mixing here of value judgement with the literary issue of how the texts came together. Clearly Dawkins' statement needs unpacking. Christopher Hitchens says similar things when he condemns the Old Testament laws as 'manmade' and decides that the stories of the exodus wanderings (and probably more) were made up at a later date and are to be treated as 'myths'. How far we are dealing with myth, involving symbols or allegories, or with history seems also to be a muddled issue for the New Atheists; Dawkins describes it as 'picking and choosing which bits of scripture to believe'.[3] We have already seen (p. 10) how Dawkins slanders the idea of symbolism in Genesis, notably in the story of the Fall.

In this chapter then I wish to take a first look at the nature of the Old Testament. There is no doubt that there is some justification for the 'bad press' parts of it have engendered. But if we choose only those parts, as Dawkins has done, we end up with a very warped view of the whole. We need to look at the character of that whole and at the context of its production. If the Old Testament really is as chaotic a document as Dawkins makes out, how do we make sense of that – and can we find order amid the chaos?

The 'canon' of Scripture

For Marcion there already existed some concept of an Old Testament canon, which is why he could refer to it and pick and choose from it, but at his time the New Testament canon was still emergent. This point – that canonization only happened gradually – gives us an insight into the nature of the process, and of how decisions were made as to which books to retain and which versions to use as authoritative. The way the two canons came together was in fact very different – that of the Old Testament was

The character and scope of the Old Testament

compiled over a much longer period than the new[4] – and whether certain books should be included or not generated some debate among both the rabbis and Christian councils of the Church.[5] Issues of canonicity moreover raise issues of authority. By what authority are books made canonical and by what authority do we read them today? What is the role of church or synagogue in the presentation of religious belief through texts such as these? Do we end up picking and choosing? Is selectivity inevitable?

The Old Testament as we have it today consists of 39 books in the Hebrew Bible and Protestant canon and 46 books in the Catholic.[6] This difference already indicates that we are dealing with a complex canonical process within which there is some lack of certainty as to where to place the boundaries. In this book I am going to deal with the Old Testament/Hebrew Bible in the Protestant canon, that being my own faith tradition.

The traditional Jewish approach to the Hebrew Bible is to divide it into three groups, Torah, Prophets and Writings, each book being assigned to one of these. I shall use this tripartite division in later chapters when discussing the Old Testament material. In the Christian Old Testament the order of the books (following the Septuagint, the Greek translation of the Bible) is different, the main changes being that the historical books of Chronicles, Ezra and Nehemiah are put, in chronological order,[7] with the other histories, Samuel and Kings (rather than in the Writings) and the Prophets are placed at the end. Clearly this latter move was made because prophecy was regarded as the most important part of the Old Testament for Christians, in that it looked forward to Christ's coming. This is why the Prophets are the section of the Old Testament most often cited in the New and why they are still cherished in the Church today. We will look later at the book of Isaiah, often regarded as Christianity's 'fifth gospel', such is its importance to the Christian faith and message. This is interesting because it shows how the presentation of the order of books is itself a way of promoting a message – advertising was alive and well in ancient times!

The Old Testament was starting to come together as a canonical set by the third century BCE and was finalized in the first century BCE, so that by the time of Jesus it was a fairly fixed set of texts (see Luke 24.44). This would have been Jesus' Bible, the only written source of his knowledge of God.

A God-inspired history?

I recently appeared on the radio programme *Woman's Hour*, ostensibly to talk about Elizabeth Cady Stanton and her *Women's Bible*, but at the end of the interview I was asked, 'Is the Bible not the word of man but the word of God?' A rather large question with which to end a five-minute interview! I had to think quickly. My answer was a qualified yes, in that the Bible is compiled by humans but inspired by God and is in that sense God's 'word'. The Bible is clearly on one level a human production, and yet if it is not God-inspired then it has no real authority for believers. At every point of the process of the formation of the Bible, its authors were God-inspired, even for the difficult bits, because they were writing down an expression of their faith and an account of what God was doing for them or their people. However, the way much of the Bible is written is as a narrative account of historical events, and this raises the further question of the relationship between the word of God and the nature of the Bible as a historical record

In a sense, the Bible is not strictly a history, it is a history shaped by faith. But the word 'history' opens up another can of worms, for it is quite clear that, while many historical elements appear in its narrations (and we might assess some accounts as more historical than others), there is also a large element of story and literary styling that detracts from the strictly historical content. In many ways the Bible is as much a literary production as a historical record and its genres extend beyond narrative to poetry, aphorisms, laments and hymnic praise, to name but a very few. So we have to approach the Bible with three levels of interpretation in mind – the literary, the historical and the theological. These three elements come together to form the complex and varied text that is the Bible – and in particular my concern in this book, the Old Testament.

The prehistory of these texts – that is, the period before their canonization – is complex, maybe even 'chaotic', but it is not nonsensical. In order to reconstruct the processes by which texts came together we have a number of tools at our disposal. There is evidence in the considerable variation in style between texts that arises when different genres of material, some of which may well have had an oral prehistory, are put together. There is also evidence of different worldviews within specific portions of material that leads biblical scholars to speak of 'sources' that are layers of production of the text. The variety of genres is huge – we have laws of various types, some of them direct moral commands like the Ten Commandments and some more circumstantial. We have maxims and proverbs whose ethical content is taken largely from everyday life and observation of the world. We have stories, some short and pithy, others long and stretching over many chapters. We have poetry in the form of laments, offerings of thanksgiving, expressions of suffering, prophetic oracles of both doom and hope. The diversity of genres is overwhelming and exciting. This is no monochrome document – it needs to be carefully explored.

The issue of symbolism, myth or allegory is raised by those involved in Old Testament criticism as an alternative to 'history'. Are these texts purely 'history'? they ask. Well, clearly not. A story often contains a truth, but is not necessarily literally historically true in all its details. A maxim or law is a general principle that may or may not contain historical elements. Any historian will tell you that history is a construct made by those who relate it. The decision that a story is primarily symbolic or a myth is in the same category – it is not a matter of its not containing truth because it is symbolic. Whether Adam and Eve existed does not matter in the light of the truth the story conveys – that humankind fell away from an ideal state due to their sinful behaviour and became estranged from a close personal relationship with God. That is first and foremost a theological message, and the story itself is so lost in the mists of time that we can never know whether there was actually a couple called Adam and Eve. The lack of historicity does not detract from the story.

In other instances, though, historicity might be more important – the long lists of genealogies or the details of a battle are an attempt to put the reader in the picture historically. Even these might be constructs, and yet the detail sometimes gives us a glimpse into the biblical world that is historically verifiable just as it is theologically reliable. As readers, we need to make these decisions. The principle of 'odd is true' often holds. An example might be mentioning that x was y's brother/sister/parent (e.g. Mark 3.17). Why would one put such 'odd' details in if not for the reason that they were known to have been the case? Sometimes stories run less smoothly than they might or unnecessary details detract from the main narrative – why include those details unless they were already an inherent part of the tradition? An oral tradition in which these tales had been heard many times may well have acted as some kind of check on the authors of the Old Testament. The stories could not be substantially changed without someone making a fuss.

This might account for editorial changes and redactions – people wanted the text to speak what they knew to be true, and that perception of truth changed over time. So editors got to work adapting texts, just as we might adapt texts to our own context. This is what Marcion was doing – changing the authoritative text itself to fit what he wanted to say, what he perceived as truth.

That process might have continued indefinitely had it not been for the closing of the canon, which indicated that a fixed set of books in a particular form were going to become 'Scripture'. However, the history of interpretation shows how the process continued over the centuries in many different circles, even though the texts themselves could not be changed. There were always new translations of texts, new versions, new interpretations. This is what Dawkins critiques, and yet they are the lifeblood that makes the text relevant in ever-changing situations. In that sense the whole production of the Bible is agenda-driven, and so is the subsequent interpretation of it, and that agenda is not historical precision or literary artistry, or even theological exploration. These things are key elements, but the main agenda is human relationship with God, humankind's evolving understanding of the divine and the revelation that is believed to have been imparted through the pages of Scripture. Even if all the stories were myths, that would not detract from the truths that are being conveyed. And not all stories are life-affirming, morally acceptable or even particularly interesting to us today – we *need* to pick and choose just as our forbears did.

Cultural distance

I want here to pick up the points raised by McGrath in his countering of Dawkins about cultural distance and context. Of course if we are dealing, as we are in the Old Testament, with texts that gradually came together over hundreds of years, and were gathered together as a whole before the Christian era, we are talking of a much more ancient and primitive society than our own. While one could argue that human nature is essentially the same, then and now, and hence that there is much with which we can sympathize (for example, the laments and rejoicings of the psalms or the proverbial maxims of the wisdom literature), there is clearly much that reflects the norms of a very different culture. That is the problem when we come to many of the Pentateuchal texts that Dawkins condemns. We can find similar 'ancient' cultures in our own time, largely in primitive tribal society, and we often condemn their practices roundly. So bridging that gap between ancient and modern cultural and ethical sensibilities is an issue, especially if the Bible is an authoritative document for us, and even more so if we seek ethics within its pages, moral norms by which we can live our lives. This is where the point about contextualization comes in – we cannot just extrapolate moral issues with no recognition of the context in which the ancient writers were formulating their ideas. To cite McGrath again, 'These texts arose within a group fighting to maintain their identity.'[8] The cradle of the Old Testament is the story of a small group of beleaguered people fighting for freedom within the confines of a despotic Egyptian state. It was a question of identity – of their people and of their God. They asked questions such as, how could they find their place in the world, cease being subject to slavery and make their way to the freedom of their own homeland where they could live in peace, prosper and multiply? These issues are the context of much of the early material of the exodus and Sinai wanderings in the Pentateuch, of the laws that were used by the people in the wilderness and of the hopes that they had of settlement and peace.

The character and scope of the Old Testament

McGrath goes on, 'They were gradually evolving their understanding of the nature of God.'[9] This is a second important point. Many of us have the experience of a deeper understanding coming to us over the course of our lives and through our experiences. The 'children' of Israel were no exception – children is an apt word for them at the early stages as they learned about their relationships with God, with each other, with the world. At first, the context was a very particular one – a small group's fight for freedom with the support of what seemed to be their own personal God, Yahweh. But gradually, as the centuries wore on, the awareness of a larger world stage and a more universal God emerged and their wider experience showed them that their initial view of God was too restricted.

The Christian revelation too, in Jesus, is another step in the progressive revelation of God. In the New Testament the claim of divine authority is taken further with the expression of the belief that God is incarnate in the person, life and words of Jesus. Revelation itself, like the development of ideas, happens at a number of moments in time, and is gradual rather than sudden. The ever-changing context of the Old Testament 'revelation' is of key importance both within the pages of the Old Testament and in relation to further revelation in the New.

Contextualizing this material is not to explain away the difficulties it presents. While context helps us to understand people's motivations for doing things, it does not always exonerate those actions. When God commits deeds or condones actions that we find morally difficult we must seek to understand the context, but we may not wish necessarily to extrapolate that context to our own. One question is whether God's character changes over time. It appears to do so from the human side, but it is arguable that in fact God is simply revealing different aspects of his character at different times. If we look at the intricate tapestry of the books of the Old Testament, we will also see that a rich picture of God's character emerges across different texts, and that God is far from monochrome. It is simply not true that the God of love appears for the first time in the New Testament, whatever Marcion would have us believe.

Selectivity

It is a challenging task to read the Old Testament, in the way one would a novel, as a continuous book. People sometimes try, starting with Genesis, and they soon nod off when they reach the social and sacrificial laws of Leviticus. It even proves difficult for the modern Church, which prefers to pick its way through the Old Testament with the help of a lectionary. There are Bible study guides and commentaries that enable us to access any book, chapter or verse.[10] The Old Testament is made up of a large and complex set of texts, and when we lose the context of their original conception and production we struggle to comprehend their relevance. When a snippet is read out in church in parallel with a Gospel reading from the New Testament, we are being encouraged not only to understand the original context of that Old Testament passage but also to read it in conjunction with the New Testament, in the same way that the New Testament has 'read' Old Testament texts from early times. This process of assimilation is an interpretative challenge first thing on a Sunday morning, and is what the preacher might hopefully shed light upon. But it is difficult, even after many years of engagement with the lectionary, for Christians to have a real 'handle' on the Old Testament. This is why I wrote my book *Opening the Old Testament*, to which I refer the reader now.[11]

The point I wish to stress here is that selectivity is inevitable. Just as the Gospel writers chose those parts of prophecy that seemed to point to Christ rather than other parts of the Old Testament, or Christian writers stressed those parts of the Old Testament that affirmed a loving God, so we nowadays tend to select the parts of Scripture that speak to us. Marcion did exactly the same – he chose not just the Scripture he preferred, by excising most Old Testament references from Luke and Paul, but he even chose the version of God who spoke to him. This tendency towards selection may be channelled through our experience of listening to texts that are read to us in church, this too being done on a selective basis. Selection is exactly what Dawkins too has done in finding all the 'bad bits' of the Old Testament. Selection, as we are about to see, is what those who have sought over the years to find ammunition for racist and sexist attitudes have also done. And ultimately selection is what the canonizers did when they sought to differentiate authoritative from non-authoritative texts, orthodoxy from heresy.

Ways of reading the Bible

Recent developments in biblical studies have taken us away from a focus solely on the origins of texts, their original context and the processes by which they came to us. All these approaches are still valid, but interest has refocused, in postmodern vein, on the reader of texts.[12] The identity of the reader affects interpretation and understanding not just for that one individual but also for those he or she seeks to influence. The reader has a context in time and place and culture just as an author does. When I read a text my background impinges upon my reading and the original text impinges in turn on me – it is a two-way process.[13] In a sense all readings contain bias, but there are different levels of bias.

One can easily find justification for different ethical positions – within Genesis 1—3 alone one can find support in one text for the inferiority of women (Gen. 2.21–24) and in another for equality, 'male and female he created them' (Gen. 1.27b). One can find support for slavery in that it was a 'given' of the time, but also a generous attitude towards slaves (e.g. Exod. 21.2); support for loving relationships of all types (e.g. Song of Songs), but also condemnation of same-sex relationships (Lev. 18.22); support for racism (Gen. 9.18–27) and for the destruction of all enemies that stand in one's way (Deut. 7); and evidence of universal salvation for all peoples (Isa. 66.18). One could go on enumerating examples, and I will draw out further examples in the chapters that follow. Any reader, teacher or preacher has to be selective, and there is nothing wrong in that – what is wrong is when the selection is somehow presented as 'fundamental' or as the only authority. Departure from the breadth and variety of the Old Testament easily leads to narrowness and partisan readings. This takes me back to Hitchens' critique of the local – to be 'confined and local' is deemed a crime. And yet, this is in a sense how the Old Testament is best understood – there are many small, local engagements with God and with other people, and although localness can be confining, the bigger picture, the sum of all the 'locals', gradually and imperceptibly reveals a more complex, more varied and ultimately more satisfying experience of understanding God and the world. Local encounters sometimes have life-changing consequences not just for the individual but also for ever widening circles of believers.

As I said earlier, many critics (including Dawkins) make the false assumption that we look at biblical texts only for a source of ethics.[14] This may be the reason that many people read the Bible, but it is not the only one. We read the Bible on many levels – as literature, appreciating its poetry perhaps, or enjoying some of its 'ripping yarns'; as history, offering evidence of ancient cultures, customs, places, ideas; or for the development of theological ideas about the relationship between God and humans or the nature of God. We are back to the three key interpretative levels: the literary, the historical and the theological. An ethical standpoint cuts across these levels, because in a modern context we have divided morality from religion, whereas we are in fact looking at a text where morality and religion were inseparably bound. In this sense we are doing a 'reading' that is alien to the nature of the text. Hence the literary, historical and theological levels of interpretation get confused in Dawkins' attack. He mentions the chaotic presentation of texts, their symbolic nature and their theological elements all in the service of 'looking for ethics'; unsurprisingly, he finds little that is pleasing to the modern eye.

Development along a timeline

Before moving on to specific texts and books in the chapters that follow, I want to present the unfolding story on a developmental line that helps us to understand the progression of the Old Testament. One of the problems of the current presentation of the Old Testament in terms of 'books' is that the different time periods and the development of ideas are obscured by the arrangement. Although the Protestant Christian canon of the Old Testament attempts to rectify this by rearranging texts out of the threefold Jewish canonical division into a reconstructed historical scheme, this obscuring is still the case. In the Old Testament I hold in my hand, the book of Ruth has been taken out of its position in the Writings and its sub-position among the Megilloth or 'Five Scrolls' and put into the 'historical' ordering between Judges and 1 Samuel. This was done because conclusions were made by Protestants about the historical context of Ruth, thought to belong to the period of the Judges before the monarchy. In fact it breaks up the series of books that make up the early narrative 'history' of Israel in terms of their settlement in the promised land and eventual establishment of a monarchy (known in scholarly circles as the Deuteronomistic history),[15] but that did not trouble the canonizers who placed it there.

If we try to reconstruct the Old Testament according to a historical timeline we are inevitably imposing on the text something foreign to its nature, because it was not written simply to reflect history, nor was it ever ordered in that way. Furthermore, as previously mentioned, what are we to say is 'history', and who are we to reconstruct it? These are the kinds of problems that modern scholarship encounters, and among contemporary scholars there has been much criticism of 'earlier' scholarly positions that were quite definitive about giving a historical timeline for the Old Testament.[16] These early scholars confidently backed up their historical conclusions with archaeology, but that too has been proven slippery to say the least. One example will suffice. Were the walls of Jericho uncovered by archaeologists the product of the eleventh century BCE, when the events of the book of Joshua and the battle that caused them to fall down are purported to have taken place? If the archaeological evidence does not match – as in this case, where the walls found are later in date – how do we cope with that? Do we say the archaeologists are wrong, or that perhaps they haven't found the earliest walls? Or do we say that the account is wrong and grew in the telling, and that perhaps there weren't any walls to come down anyway? Or do we redate the whole

The character and scope of the Old Testament

event to a later period and decide that the historical timeline is at fault? It is the last option that is often favoured in modern scholarship, which seeks to question the timeline, indeed even to question that these accounts have any historical veracity at all.[17] Perhaps it is all fictional – but then why would anyone trouble to make such details up? If it is a fabrication, it is a very elaborate one.

Many theologians seeking to characterize the Old Testament find the kernel in the exodus, in liberation from slavery and the story of the flight of the tribe of Israel from Egypt.[18] One might look for other models of Old Testament theology, but in historical terms, rather than in terms of the history of ideas, this emphasis on the exodus seems to be a reasonable assumption. At this point in their history, the God of the Israelites was revealed to the Israelites, but this God, Yahweh, was simply their God rather than the God of others. There was no attempt to suggest that other gods did not exist for other nations, and their loyalty and allegiance to this God led the Israelites to expect a two-way relationship – they would worship God, while God would help them to win their battles. This nationalistic view of God persisted for some centuries, and the early parts of the Old Testament are full of stories that are partisan, nationalistic and racist. Of course enemies had to be destroyed, and those opposed to 'their God' were the first in line. This does not make killing people in general morally acceptable (as the Ten Commandments make clear), but it puts the bloodshed of early parts of the Old Testament into some kind of context. This was a nationalistic approach by a nationalistic people who saw God in confined terms as fighting their particular battles for them.

While this story of liberation and eventual arrival in the promised land is central, there are earlier stories about the ancestors of Israel that have been collected together as well as more reflective books that ponder the significance of these events in a fresh context. Although the central event of 'revelation' of God to his people is formative, it provides the opportunity to gather together the 'annals' of the nation, to understand their past and to point forward to a more settled, more literary and reflective future. It is also an opportunity to gather together laws, both the laws formulated in the desert and those of later, settled times. The watershed of literary activity of this type – of the gathering together of material, stories, laws, texts – is thought to have been the Israelite Exile in the sixth century BCE and possibly too the century leading up to that, the seventh, when the Israelite monarchy was well established but also under increasing threat. This is not to say that the earlier 'history' of the monarchy belonged entirely to that period, but clearly this later time was one in which earlier ideas and texts were gathered together and reflected upon, such that by the time the Exile was over (by the time of Ezra)[19] the embryo of a canon had appeared.

Diversity and authority

While this 'timeline' is key for our understanding, an aspect of the Old Testament that I also wish to stress is its diversity of ideas. This springs perhaps from my own research interest in the wisdom literature (Proverbs, Job and Ecclesiastes), books that were for many years sidelined in scholarly enquiry precisely because they did not appear to 'fit' the historical timeline of salvation history.[20] Where do ideas that are more timeless and less precisely linked to particular events fit in? The proverbs, ethical statements, poetry, laments and other questioning as encapsulated in the wisdom tradition are timeless and their relevance to our modern day is much more easily conveyed by the universal nature of the material. God to some extent takes a 'back seat' in this literature, in that God is behind the scenes rather than in the foreground and that is possibly a reason for its past sidelining. However, God is certainly profoundly there in relationship with humans as they try to understand their lives.

For those who brought the material of the Old Testament together the question of authority was a key aspect. So, for example, in some ways the historical framework given by the Old Testament for the promulgation of its laws is a false one. The idea that all the law was given by Moses at a point in time, on Mount Sinai (Lev. 26.46), is so clearly a construction that no biblical scholar would take it literally. However, it is important to understand that this packaging of the laws was an attempt to give them authority under the auspices of a significant historical figure. Collections of laws from different periods and dates have been assembled here by later editors and redactors. Their status, however, as a collection ascribed to Moses is far greater than the sum of their parts.

In the same way the proverbs probably reflect an accumulation of knowledge, experience and insight over many generations, but they have been gathered together at a particular time and attributed, for authority, to King Solomon, who had an established reputation for his wisdom. Similarly the psalms are attributed in the main to King David, but it is unlikely that he wrote any of them, let alone most of them – the ascription to his considerable authority is a way of tying essentially non-historical material loosely into the retrospective historical framework of the whole. This suggests that it was often the historical timeline that was the unifying factor in bringing together the rich tapestry of the canon. Key historical figures were selected to be the agents of this unification.

The prophetic books also contain a great deal of poetic material that does not always fit a historical situation but is mixed with narrative, autobiography and so on, that contextualizes more general material into a cohesive whole under the name of a character with prophetic authority – in this case a number of individual prophets. So when we read the prophecies attributed to a named prophet, we need to be aware of the possibility that in fact the prophecies of many may exist under the same heading, or that editors or redactors have added their own material or shaped the whole. For example, the text of Jeremiah tells us that Baruch the scribe wrote down some of Jeremiah's words (Jer. 36.4). This is what seems to make the Old Testament complex or confusing, but in fact it is simply a process of assigning authority, contextualizing within a historical framework and making material relevant within a long timeframe.

Theological richness

It has been said by proponents of the historical model that the 'heartbeat' of the Old Testament is the covenant between Israel and her God, notably that between God and Moses on Mount Sinai. The covenant model is clearly at the core of the relationship between God and the people. However, there are different covenants in the Old Testament: the Mosaic, between Moses on behalf of the people and God, mainly seems to consist of a series of laws, notably the Ten Commandments; the Davidic, between King David and God, which involves a dynastic undertaking that David's line will rule for ever in Israel; the Noachic covenant, between Noah and God, is about the created world and promises for the continuance of the known environment and earth. There are also promises for the future couched in the language of everlasting covenant, dealing with the relationship between

The character and scope of the Old Testament

a 'new' Israel, a wider world and a more universal God. The concept is handled in different ways, with some Old Testament writers seeing the covenant as essentially generated by God and requiring passive adherence by the people and others seeing the process as more reciprocal, with obligations on the part of the people (which they found hard to keep – as a result of which they fell short of the ideal, which then was pushed into an indeterminate future). While the covenant is essentially a key theological idea, covenants (except perhaps the 'symbolic' one with Noah) originated in historical situations; and so the concept is linked to Israelite history and yet transcends that plane when it broadens out into the cosmic and the universal. Fresh understandings of covenant and different presentations of it unfold in the course of time across the Old Testament period.

This world of covenant was one into which Jesus stepped; he no doubt knew of the special relationship between God and Israel and appreciated its complexity. It is interesting that the New Testament is in fact the new covenant, inaugurated by Jesus, and both defined against the old covenant of the Old Testament and seen as its fulfilment. This point about the development of the concept illustrates well the point that both God's self-presentation and human understanding of the relationship with God change over time. The Old Testament covenant was very nationalistic to start with, but opened out into new areas to become an all-encompassing theological idea.

One aspect of covenant is the cosmic, and this broader view of the relationship between God and humans is also explored in the area of creation as a key theme of the Old Testament. Indeed it starts with creation in Genesis 1, an indication perhaps of its importance. The way the Old Testament is presented is with a 'cosmic' start, which then narrows down to a few principal characters and tribes, before gradually opening out again into an appreciation of a greater, universal God and a larger worldview. Many of these creation-orientated ideas are found in the prophetic books and in the Writings – that very part of the Old Testament that Dawkins ignores.

Those who focus only on Genesis 1—3 (the creation) and 6—9 (the Flood) for the Old Testament's account of creation are getting a one-sided idea of what it is about.[21] These are the 'symbolic' narrative texts that attempt to explain the origins of the world, of humans within it and significantly of the nature of sin. But there are many other parts of the Old Testament that reflect on the created world and God as creator (the very image of God that Marcion so disliked). The book of Job in the wisdom literature is central to that portrayal with its view of God having created everything, even the wildest animals in the furthest corners of the earth, even if no human is looking, and tending them to ensure the sustaining of the world. Here images of power and of tenderness can be found side by side. This gives us just a hint of the richness and diversity of the Old Testament and its God that the New Atheists have totally ignored, and which I shall explore in later chapters.

The Old Testament contains many theological themes, too many to number here. But we will encounter many of them in our necessarily 'selective' reading in Part 2.

A jigsaw puzzle?

The Old Testament has the character of a large jigsaw puzzle, whose different thematic areas and genres of material all ultimately fit together into the united whole that it presents in its canonical form. Inevitably as a biblical scholar one knows certain corners of it better than others. For a churchgoer, especially one who follows the patterns of reading

The character and scope of the Old Testament

prescribed by the Church authorities through the lectionaries, that is also true. It holds for different faith traditions too – in Judaism, for example, high authority is given to the Torah or Pentateuch but many other parts (e.g. the 'Five Scrolls')[22] also feature in liturgies or festivals. All faith traditions are selective in their interest in texts, and all denominations of those faiths have their own variants. This makes reading the overall jigsaw puzzle picture highly complex.

With the 'new covenant' of the New Testament the picture becomes more complex still. It is almost as if the older jigsaw puzzle now needs to be fitted in with the new. I was recently in Cordoba in Spain and saw the wonderful Mezquita. There the layers of history were apparent – an originally Christian foundation, of which evidence in the form of impressive mosaics remains under the present floor level, and which Muslims then built on to create an extensive and beautiful mosque. It was finally re-Christianized, with the central part of the mosque being replaced by an elaborate cathedral in the gothic style. The building was adapted and changed over time to accommodate different architectural styles, traditions and faiths and is now a unity, but a rather strange juxtaposition of styles and symbols. So too must the Old and New Testaments, sometimes rather awkwardly, be fitted together.

The process started early on with the attempt to understand the significance and authority of Jesus in terms of the Old Testament, notably in relation to prophetic predictions such as those contained in Isaiah and Micah. This is where Marcion with his 'excisions' got involved. Clearly, as the New Testament sees it, the continuity between Old and New was essential to the understanding of both from the start and was not a construct. St Paul is no exception, citing the Old Testament extensively. Despite what Marcion tried to do in separating Paul's letters and the Gospels, such a separation does not exist. We simply cannot understand any part of the New Testament without the Old and – as Christians at least – we cannot understand the Old without the New. The New Testament gives us a new lens through which to 'read' the Old, and however much we might wish to put any 'faith bias' aside, especially within academic circles, it is very difficult to do.

A complex, relational God

Behind the scenes of all this talk of texts, though, lies a revelation of God. It is at all stages a revelation about relationship. God wants a relationship with the world, with animals, with humankind. God is not simply the watchmaker-creator who sets the world in motion.[23] God interacts and is involved. This may lead to problems as well as benefits for human beings. It sends us, though, a message that we are not alone and that there is some purpose in our brief existence in this world.

Of course the atheist rejects entirely the premise that there is a God at all, and the New Atheist attack seems to enjoy not only challenging that premise but also countering it on the grounds of the character of the God that is revealed. In looking at this attack more closely we need to bear the following questions in mind: How is God characterized in Old Testament texts, and how far is the criticism justified? And how far can consideration of context, or broader literary, historical and theological concerns help us to deepen our understanding beyond the superficial critique that is on offer? This naturally leads on to the question of continuity between the Old Testament God and that of the New. Are the two testaments at odds, or is there a clear consistency across the pages of the entire biblical canon? These questions and more will be addressed in the chapters that follow.

3

Meeting Dawkins head-on: texts in Genesis

In the rest of Part 1, I want to consider in more detail, and in a direct response to his criticisms, the main texts that Dawkins attacks in his book *The God Delusion*. I will also bring in the texts critiqued by Hitchens, although he tends to be less textually specific in his diatribe. I wish to contextualize these texts on two levels, the first in relation to the context(s) of their time within the Old Testament and the second in relation to a Christian reading of the texts, both past and present. These are some of the most difficult texts of the Old Testament, and so none of them is easy reading. But as Brueggemann advocates, we need to engage with difficult texts alongside more pleasing ones.[1] And let me assure you that there are some more palatable ones to choose from (as Alister McGrath made clear). I shall re-order the texts according to the biblical book they belong to rather than cherry-picking in a random fashion as the New Atheist authors tend to do.

Genesis

Adam and Eve: Genesis 1—3

It is towards the end of his section on the Old Testament that Dawkins has a field day with Adam and Eve, largely in relation to the concept of original sin (which, of course, post-dates the biblical text itself) and to the New Testament claims about Jesus. I will come on to that in a moment, but I wish to start by placing this story in its Old Testament context.

As discussed above, Dawkins points out that theologians make 'symbolic' claims when it comes to stories about the origins of the world and humanity. As I started to explain in Chapter 2, there is a fine line between myth and history when it comes to ancient stories. Genesis 1—11 as a whole is often regarded as a more 'mythological' prelude to the 'history' that starts with Abraham. Yet how far the rest of Genesis, beginning with chapter 12, is really 'history' is also debatable. The stories of Adam and Eve and the Garden of Eden, and of Noah and the Flood, are symbolic in that they form explanations of why the world is as it is. They are explanations in story form of why human life involves hard toil, why women suffer pain in childbirth, why there is estrangement between humans and the animal world and why relationship with God cannot be taken for granted. Whether these characters actually existed is not as significant as the truth that they represent in their interactions with one another, with God and, ultimately, with us. They may have had some distant existence, but that is not the main point of telling these stories.

It has long been noted in scholarship that there are two stories in Genesis 1—3.[2] Genesis 1—2.4a is a poetic, hymnic piece describing the creation of the world by God. It has the feel of a retrospective summary and explanation of known phenomena. It shows a primitive scientific understanding of the world, for example, with the creation of 'light' before sun and moon, and it gives a value to everything that is created as 'good'. It parallels a Babylonian eight-day creation account – when you look closely, you see that on days three and six two events take place rather than the usual one (Gen. 1.9–13, 24–31).

Meeting Dawkins head-on

At the climax of the seven days is the Sabbath, the day on which God rested (Gen. 2.2–3). The Sabbath is projected back on to the account of creation itself in order to prioritize it. It is clearly an account written with some hindsight, showing a developed view of God and his creative activity. It has an elevated view of God as creator of everything. Interestingly, this account features man and woman as created simultaneously and equally.

On the other hand, we have another, very different account of creation in Genesis 2.4b—3. Instead of the waters of the deep representing the chaos that has to be controlled by God, we find an earth that is dry until God waters it. We find God walking in the garden and talking with the human beings that he has made. We find Adam created first, and Eve afterwards – woman 'taken out of man' – and a hierarchy of man, animals and the wider creation is evident that does not feature in the other account. This second account is believed to be the older and more primitive. It was most likely framed later on by the Genesis 1 hymn, and in some ways the two accounts complement rather than immediately contradicting each other. However, the second account also represents a first attempt to explain certain phenomena in the world. It too has counterparts from the ancient Near East, especially in the use of themes of a paradisical garden and that of eternal life (represented here by the 'tree of life', Gen. 2.9; 32.4). Clearly the Israelite people were asking questions about their origins, and about the world in relation to their God, from which these stories, or myths, arose. They express truths about the creation and sustenance of life, about order and hierarchy in the world, about toil and suffering, about the relationship of human beings with each other and with God and about the relationship of God with the created world.

Reflection on creation might not have been the earliest element of the Old Testament chronologically speaking.

Even though these stories are positioned first, and placed in a primeval era, that does not mean that they are chronologically first in relation to how ideas developed within the period covered by the Old Testament. The likelihood is that the second account of creation was circulating early on and was written down possibly as early as the tenth century BCE, but that the first, with its deeper reflection and high view of God, could belong in the chronology anywhere from the sixth century BCE when the people of Israel went into exile. The well-documented influence of Babylonian material upon this account (given that they went into exile in Babylon) makes this likely too.

This difference in the time of writing of the two accounts exemplifies the concept of the development of ideas within the Old Testament that I spoke of in the last chapter and of the developing portrayal of God. The God who walks in the garden and does not at first know where Adam and Eve are, is a more primitive picture of God using human imagery, a picture that changed later on when God was portrayed in more universal terms. The limitation of the second account to a local garden and an immediate environment contrasts with the universal concern with the heavens and the firmament of the first account: the local becomes the universal. The placement of the Sabbath at the climax also reveals the importance of that concept for the later generation that added the first creation account.

While some do take the seven-day creation account literally, it is only a few fundamentalist-minded Christians who perpetuate the idea. Modern science has reinforced what has long been seen as a symbolic representation of 'days', probably indicating 'eras'. But the acknowledgement that the first account is symbolic, in that it is God's act of creation and continued sustenance of the world that is being described and praised here, does not detract from its truth – that all things have their origin in God.

In the second account we find only one man and woman in the world, accompanied by a talking snake, none of which is taken literally by most interpreters. Rather it is the story of the initial innocence of the pair, and the over-reaching attempt to acquire the 'knowledge of good and evil' belonging only to God that leads to their downfall. It is interesting that good and evil are written into both accounts – the first stresses the goodness of God's creation, and the second has at its heart the theme of humans' desire for more than they are given. The fruit given by the snake to Eve and by Eve to Adam may be symbolic too – traditionally depicted as an apple, it is unlikely to have been such in the world in which the story was born – hence Dawkins' 'scrumping' is not a choice word.[3] But that is a detail. Dawkins goes to town in talking about the symbolic fruit which led to knowledge of good and evil, which he says 'turned out to be knowledge that they were naked'.[4] Of course, he must see, as most do, that the realization of nakedness is just the beginning of a much fuller self-realization. It is symbolic of the couple's new awareness – they have lost their carefree ignorance and are now burdened with the 'knowledge of good and evil', in other words the realization that there are two sides – one good, one evil – to every choice and every decision. This is an origin story of the birth of sin, or at least of the birth of the awareness of sin. Yes, this is the 'mother and father of all sins' – not the awareness of one's nakedness, but the awareness of the existence of sin itself. Yes, this account is preoccupied with sin, because that is the way the story is being told. But it is not at this point 'original' sin – it is simply an acknowledgement of the worldview that good has its opposite in evil. The account that tells of what God made (Gen. 1—2.4a) tells only of 'good', but it does not say that evil did not exist. The second account makes it clear that evil does exist and that eating from the tree of knowledge opens up awareness of and temptation by it. The way of God, though, is still essentially the way of 'good'. God is not preoccupied with sin – sin (embodied in later ideas of a Satan or Devil figure) is the antithesis of God. Sin is what happens when humans fall away from God. This story shows that sin was not God's original intention for human beings: rather, separated from God's will for them, humans fell into the habit of sin.

It was natural for the writers of the New Testament, when reflecting on Jesus and the way he forgave sin, to refer back to the 'original sinner', Adam. Jesus did not die and so atone for 'a *symbolic sin* committed by a *non-existent* individual' (his italics), as Dawkins describes it.[5] For Christians, Adam represents Everyman and so Jesus died for humanity, in order to bring humanity back to God's goodness and realign what had gone wrong in the equation (see Rom. 5). This was a return to a paradisiacal state for believers in God's unselfish act of incarnation as a human being in order to experience the human condition and human sin and overcome it once and for all.

The Genesis accounts are of key importance in the Christian tradition, for they introduce the Creator-God and his design of 'good' for the world in all its diversity. Genesis 1 contains praise of the beauty and diversity of the world and Genesis 2—3 acknowledges God's creation of all animals, birds, fish and nature. Human beings are an essential and integrated part of their environment. It is only with the realization of sin that the harmony of their original existence is overturned and an antagonism between humans and animals, or between humans and the earth, emerges. Christ is seen to restore the original equilibrium, and so Jesus and Adam become type and antitype. This is

Noah and the Flood: Genesis 6—9

With the account of the Flood, we are still in the realm of myth or symbol and engaging with a worldview in which the world is described in the terminology of good and evil. Again there are ancient Near Eastern parallels, this time very detailed parallels in Sumerian and Babylonian myth,[7] which suggest that at the Exile, the Israelites were asking the question – what is our version of this flood story?[8] While the original idea for the story itself might have been based on a real experience of a great flood in the area, it entered the realm of myth from its earliest retellings. So the story probably belongs mainly to the same (exilic) period as the account in Genesis 1—2.4a, with a high view of God as all-powerful and in control of the cosmos, imposing order or chaos as God sees fit. Dawkins makes out that this account was simply 'derived from the Babylonian myth of Uta-Napishtim';[9] I would phrase it more precisely, saying that it is very different from that myth because it is given its own context and shaping from an Israelite worldview, but that there are clear parallels. There may have been an ancient belief in the reality of such a flood in the whole area of the ancient Near East, from which these alternative myths also sprang, but the biblical account of the Flood should essentially be seen as another 'explanation story'. The explanation this time is both of the enduring nature of the relationship of God with humanity and the animals and of the phenomenon of the rainbow.

While the destruction conveys a primitive picture of a God for whom human and animal life is cheap and dispensable, the story is at pains to point out in strictly 'good and evil' terms that these consequences were justified. This is perhaps our most difficult problem with this text. How can whole populations be cumulatively 'guilty'? (The same issue comes up later in Genesis with Abraham (Gen. 18) and in the book of Jonah.)

In order to take something positive from this text we need to look beyond the destruction to the aetiology of the rainbow. The rainbow is a sign given by God that wholesale destruction of the kind seen in the Flood is not God's ultimate purpose and will never occur again. The explanation then concerns natural disasters – and the need not simply to attribute them to 'an act of God', but actually to remember God's promise not to destroy his creation and to celebrate God's continued provision for humanity and the created world.

I do not deny that this story is appalling, with its apparent drowning of most of the human population and of the earth's animals in order to create something new, and I am not trying to justify the kind of strict morality conveyed by this text. Dawkins writes with some justification, 'God took a dim view of humans, so he (with the exception of one family) drowned the lot of them including children and also, for good measure, the rest of the (presumably blameless) animals as well.'[10] The concept of only one blameless individual and his family is also deeply problematic. Is anyone ever totally blameless (cf. one of the central points of discussion in the book of Job)? The episode is, in one sense, another Fall – it is in this case not about an individual falling out of favour with God but about large swathes of people falling away from God's intention of 'good' and God's subsequent attempt to go back to a kind of Garden of Eden on the ark, with humans and animals existing in harmony and a 'blameless' man, Noah, at the core of the episode. There is an element of moral construct about this story in that it presents an all-or-nothing approach to morality that loses any sense of nuance, giving it the nature of a 'morality tale' designed to frighten those who choose a sinful road. This kind of morality is not congenial to our modern ears, however appealing the story may look as retold in our children's Bibles. Indeed it is ironic that this is one of the most popular stories read out to children over the centuries and that many families own, or have owned, a model of the ark with Mr and Mrs Noah and the wooden animals in carefully carved pairs.

Dawkins also accuses Christians of giving cosmic significance to human sin: 'We humans give ourselves such airs, even aggrandizing our poky little "sins" to the level of cosmic significance!'[11] But this is not new – we have already seen, from the very start of Genesis, how good and evil are at the centre of the story of God's intention for the world and how human action led to the 'fallen state' that failed to fulfil the ideal. The animals are innocent bystanders, although the same concept of fallen state and an ideal is applied to them too. Maybe we do glorify the significance of our experience on this earth, good and bad, but such an emphasis is understandable within a worldview that regards good and evil, rewards and sins, as at the heart of human choice and behaviour. For Christians these choices are reflected in the divine ordering of the world, hence the cosmic dimension. We also go on giving cosmic significance to life on this planet in light of the fact that no other life has yet been found in the universe.

Dawkins attacks the idea – which is still widespread today – that natural disasters are bound up with human sin. However, it seems to me that this flood story is actually not only about human sin. God admittedly sends the Flood because of human sinfulness, but the story is more profoundly about God's desire to 'start afresh' with humanity and the world. The Flood represents an attempt to rectify a false start – and at the end of it all God makes a covenant, not only with humans but with the wider world, that such an event will not happen again and that God will accept a less than perfect order. It is God coming to terms with the reality of human sin and accepting a new state of affairs (as in the covenant in Genesis 9 where humans are allowed to eat animals in the new world after the Flood, having been vegetarians in the Garden of Eden) that is emphasized here. These choices within the divine/human relationship represent the terminology with which this ancient culture handled and sought to understand natural disasters such as this great flood. The so-called 'acts of God' are not God's ultimate purpose and desire for the world, as reinforced by the Christian understanding that sin is overcome once and for all by the sacrifice of Jesus on the cross.

To return to Dawkins' point about natural disasters and human sin. This was hardly a surprising conclusion to come to in the pre-scientific culture of biblical times. There was a clear need to explain natural disasters, which in a primitive worldview could only be 'acts of God' because those experiencing them lacked the knowledge to explain them scientifically. God was the only one with the power to do such things. Yet this story is saying that natural disaster is not God's purpose and desire – God's desire is for relationship with human beings, animals and the natural world in a way in which both sides can thrive.

To approach the discussion of the flood story from a rather different angle, Dawkins asks, as a more general point, how we pick and choose stories if we are not to take them literally. Of course picking and choosing is inevitable – people are still doing what their forebears also did and even the stories contained in the canon of Scripture are no doubt a choice from a wider selection. How do we make informed decisions about such choices? We are guided by a range of opinions, experiences and criteria. One such criterion is the rejection of the magical, which may lead us to problems with Genesis 1—11. For a key aspect of the primeval stories of Genesis 1—11 is that they are somewhat other-worldly – they have magical elements, such as the talking snake, and the tower that reaches right up to the heavens. Even the ark housing the animals 'two by two' is a fantasy given the habits of animals. I would argue then that the authors are telling us of the mythical status of these stories by the very nature of them. They make good stories for children, rather like the myth of Santa Claus, because they are tall stories. The important thing about them is the points that they make, theological, moral or otherwise, not their literality. They are 'origin myths', and they make a curious collection in this section of the Bible. They are given a cosmic and universal significance because that is the context of the shaping of the whole section by the exilic writers, who were asking questions about the creation and origin of their world in line with their ancient Near Eastern counterparts. These myths concerned not just the physical world, but the world of human/divine relationships with all their 'good and evil', light and shade. These myths were shared around the ancient Near Eastern world. In the absence of scientific knowledge, these peoples answered many questions on the mythological level. The fact that we have moved on from a primitive understanding of the world through scientific advances does not mean we should lose sight of the important messages such stories convey. While many have taken them literally over the centuries and many do today, these primeval myths do not have to be interpreted in this way, as I have tried to show.

Such stories are about the power of God, and while destruction does happen, I have argued that this is not ultimately what God intends for the world that he creates for 'good'. Yes, the moral order is written into the order of the world in this account, but that is how the writers of the Old Testament saw life, in relation to a set of opposites – good and evil, truth and lie, relationship or estrangement. Perhaps this does not translate easily into modern terms, although we can still choose to see the world in terms of opposing forces of good and evil if we wish to.

The language of opposing forces was also common in the world of the New Testament – illness, for instance, was often seen as an 'evil spirit' that Jesus cast out of people (see Mark 29.32–34). In our modern context we have to make some allowances for the worldview into which the Bible was born, both on the level of the original context in the Old Testament and on that of the New, which recontextualized the Old and developed its view of God in the light of the new revelation in Jesus Christ. The Flood features in the New Testament as part of an eschatological vision of the end of the old world and the hope of a new one ushered in by Christ (Matt. 24.37–39; Luke 17.27; 2 Peter 3.5–7). In Hebrews 11.7 Noah is seen as a paragon of righteousness in his obedience to God, but his obedience is still in the context of the mass destruction of life. We clearly cannot get away from the problems raised by the Flood story quite so easily as we might have liked.

Abraham and Lot: Genesis 19

Dawkins now moves on to Abraham. The Old Testament is full of individuals 'singled out' to become God's spokesmen and representatives. Dawkins is right to call Abraham's nephew, Lot, 'the Noah equivalent',[12] in that one family is saved in the destruction of Sodom and Gomorrah. We have moved, however, from primeval history in Genesis

1—11 to the beginning of the narrated history of Israel in Genesis 12.

There are many questions about the exact historical existence of the patriarchs and matriarchs of Israel. The material about them is piecemeal and incomplete and quite often stories are repeated in different contexts (as in the story of the wife passed off as the sister, discussed below). However, it is likely that Abraham had a historical existence in the remote past, and in that sense he is less 'symbolic' than Noah or Adam. It is with God's promise to Abraham – his new covenant with the patriarch and his people – that the chapter of God in relationship with Israel, his people, begins. This could be said to be the real start of Israel's story, especially with the primeval history material most probably dating to a time later than that in which Abraham lived.[13] But, like the origin stories of nations, the events described here happened a long time before they were written down in the form we now have them; stories about those events circulated orally and would have been adapted and changed. These may well have been essentially tribal stories largely concerned with the key events, places and personages in the life of the tribe. They are not factual history, even in the sense that some of the later 'historical' material of the Old Testament might be history. However, that does not mean they contain no kernels of historical truth.

What is more important, though, is why any story was told, repeated and committed to writing. Was the motivation primarily literary or theological? These are certainly gripping stories on a literary level – a storyteller's art comes through. However, the main point of telling the story seems to be theological – to tell us about God in relationship with his people and with certain key individuals, and to give the reader a sense of what kind of loyalty God demands. It is interesting that God's intermediaries – angels – appear in this, and other, early stories. God is often seen as acting through such intermediaries in the early days of the patriarchs and judges.[14]

I will use Dawkins' paraphrase of the Abraham and Lot story, albeit that it is related with some sarcasm, to put the reader in the picture:

> Two male angels were sent to Sodom to warn Lot to leave the city before the brimstone arrived. Lot hospitably welcomed the angels into his house, whereupon all the men of Sodom gathered around and demanded that Lot should hand the angels over so that they could (what else?) sodomize them: 'Where are the men which came in to thee this night? Bring them out unto us, that we may know them' (Gen 19: 5) . . . Lot's gallantry in refusing the demand suggests that God might have been onto something when he singled him out as the only good man in Sodom. But Lot's halo is tarnished by the terms of his refusal: 'I pray you, brethren, do not so wickedly. Behold now I have two daughters which have not known man; let me, I pray you, bring them out unto you, and do ye to them as is good in your eyes; only unto these men do nothing; for therefore came they under the shadow of my roof (Gen 19: 7–8) . . . As it happened, Lot's bargaining away of his daughters' virginity proved unnecessary, for the angels succeeded in repelling the marauders by miraculously striking them blind. They then warned Lot to decamp immediately with his family and his animals, because the city was about to be destroyed. The whole household escaped, with the exception of Lot's unfortunate wife, whom the Lord turned into a pillar of salt because she committed the offence – comparatively mild one might have thought – of looking over her shoulder at the fireworks display.[15]

Let us first try to contextualize this story. In order to understand it in its Old Testament context we have to consider the strict cultural rules governing hospitality to strangers (Deut. 10.17–19; 24.17–19; 26.5–11; Exod. 22.21; 23.9; Lev. 19.33–34),[16] also paralleled more widely in the ancient Near East. Only one chapter before this one – in Genesis 18.1–8 – Abraham offers hospitality to three strangers. Without knowing their identity, he offers them food and water, the washing of their feet, and rest. He slays a tender calf from his flock, provides milk and curds and instructs his wife to make bread.

This tradition of hospitality then has its roots in nomadic life. Fear of the stranger and the need for protection when travelling oneself are thought to have been the original motivations for the growth of such a tradition. One can see this hospitality at work in Lot's opening offers to the strangers, whom he seems to recognize from the start as of a higher status than himself:

> When Lot saw them, he rose to meet them, and bowed down with his face to the ground. He said, 'Please my lords, turn aside to your servant's house and spend the night and wash your feet; then you can rise early and go on your way.' They said, 'No, we will spend the night in the square.' But he urged them strongly; so they turned aside to him and entered his house; and he made them a feast, and baked unleavened bread, and they ate. (Genesis 19.2–3)

The tradition of hospitality is so strong that, further on in this passage, Lot offers his wife and daughter to strangers rather than expose his guests to ill treatment. He does not do so immediately – he does say 'I beg you, my brother, do not act so wickedly'. And while this raises all one's feminist hackles at the clear treatment of women as possessions or commodities, as well as one's ethical hackles that concern for the treatment of strangers is put above other ethical issues, it is an indication of the inferior status accorded women in this tribal culture, in which they were bought and sold and had only the roles of wife and childbearer, with no rights of their own. We are sadly all too familiar with the perpetuation of these kinds of principles and practices in some cultures around the world today.

Such is the background of this apparently unethical behaviour on Lot's part – thus it becomes understandable, but not, of course, to be condoned today in our very different culture and moral climate. The key point for Lot is that these 'angels' 'have come under the shelter of my roof' and so demand protection. Another aspect of his hospitality is that these are male angels, representatives of God, and so Lot is trying to protect 'divinity'. The demand of the men of Sodom sounds like a homosexual desire, but when the women are offered instead that motive becomes confused. In any case, the homosexual rape that was being proposed was rejected wholesale in Israel and surrounding cultures (although it was allowed in the context of humiliation of prisoners of war). In his rejection of the men Lot exposes himself to their jibes; they now threaten him and call him an 'alien' since he is not a native of Sodom. The outcome of the story, culminating in the miraculous 'blindness', is also evidence of the divinity of the guests and of God's power to effect his will, and it serves as a punishment for these lascivious men. The guests end up protecting Lot in a reciprocal gesture for his hospitality. They also end up protecting the women in the story – the angels (and by association, God) do not want the women to suffer on their behalf. There are many laws against rape in the Old Testament (e.g. Deut. 22.23–29), as it is something that God does not condone. A number of these stories are about God's power, and were told in a cultural world where that power was being questioned and there were plenty of rival gods on offer.

The context of the story also has to do with the good and evil that we have already encountered as benchmarks for provision and judgement. The story opens by establishing that Sodom is a wicked place whose inhabitants are deserving of punishment – and of course the behaviour of the men 'proves' this judgement. It is often forgotten that Abraham had tried hard to intercede for Sodom (Gen. 18.16–33), which was after all a foreign city, and had suggested to God that this kind of wholesale destruction was risky if even a few righteous people lived there. Abraham asks the famous question, 'Shall not the Judge of all the earth do what is just?' (Gen. 18.25), a direct challenge to God from his faithful servant.

But although Abraham appears to win the argument, he fails on this occasion because it is deemed that there are after all no righteous men in the city of Sodom. Like those who perished in the Flood, God has made a moral judgement on this place and has the power to effect his will. There is an essential interplay between power and justice – God may have the power to do what he likes, but God is bound by principles of justice, which are a key aspect of his relationship to humankind. This justice is based on the judgements of good and evil that we have seen at play in the primeval history. It may be deeply problematic to us that places can seemingly be marked out wholesale in this way (and that presumably land as well as animals, plants, etc. are affected), but this is the language of the Old Testament. At this stage in the development of ideas, judgement was a matter somewhat of black and white and applied wholesale to various groups of people; the idea of individual responsibility for sin developed only later in the Old Testament period. Lot's wider household is marked out to be saved (an example of God's mercy amid this somewhat destructive picture of God) and Lot goes to considerable effort to round up his troublesome sons-in-law. There is a literary flourish in the phrase 'But he seemed to his sons-in-law to be jesting' (Gen. 19.12b). Hardly a laughing matter in this situation!

There is also an element of plea-bargaining on Lot's part in the tale. He objects to fleeing to the hills, as is asked of him by the angels, and begs to go to a nearby 'little' city. There is a hint that this second city has also been marked out for punishment, but that Lot's fleeing there will save it. We have here an explanation of a place name – the city was hereafter called 'Zoar' (meaning 'little'). The Old Testament is full of such explanations of place names, which often get woven into wider narratives.[17]

There is, however, one individual who suffers in this story and it is Lot's wife. In the midst of the 'sulphur and fire from the LORD out of heaven' (Gen.19.24),[18] she looks back at the judgement and so associates herself with it. This is a terrible fate for a woman whose only sin seems to be to look back when she has been told to look forward. But another key element of the story is obedience to God's will. God has delivered this man and his household because he did not display the disobedience of others in the city. When deliverance comes, Lot's wife threatens that relationship of obedience.

It is highly unacceptable to us to think of a woman punished in this way, but one can understand the ancient context of the reasons for it, even when we rightly reject such reasons today. It is at this point that Abraham comes in and we see the wider context of the story – the saving of Abraham and his family, notably his nephew, Lot. Lot's wife is sadly a victim in the service of a wider goal. There is also another factor, that the story may well be an 'explanation' of why there is so much salt in and around the Dead Sea, or of a particular crystalline formation in the area – another origin story woven into a wider narrative, perhaps, and unlikely to be historically accurate in any case.

Later in the story the daughters of Lot get pregnant by their father. Dawkins comments, 'If this dysfunctional family was the best Sodom had to offer by way of morals, some might begin to feel a certain sympathy with God and his judicial brimstone.'[19] In fact the narrator of the story does not condone the actions described (indeed, later, in the story of Jacob, this patriarch is berated for not taking the rape of his daughter, Dinah, more seriously) – so no moral comment is made. We are simply presented with a bald, factual narrative. Nor is the family particularly a model one, as they are slow to fall into line and obey Lot's – and God's – command. They have divided loyalties, which ultimately leads to Lot's wife's punishment. It may well be that the story is more about the wider context of Abraham's obedience and fidelity to God than Lot's – who had the benefit of being Abraham's nephew.

Again it is apparently the women who detract from Lot's own obedient piety. This is a repeated story in the Old Testament (e.g. Tamar in Gen. 38), not that the repetition makes it any less difficult morally. This story is actually about the powerlessness of women, about the importance of childbirth as their only means to acquire status and position, and the desperate lengths they would go to in order to become pregnant. In a modern world where there is so much choice about the matter of childbearing, the idea is repugnant. And elsewhere in the Bible it is condemned that girls should conceive by their fathers (Lev. 18.7–8). The trickery of Lot's daughters is in getting their father drunk so that he is unaware of their actions, and there is an interesting parallel here with the drunkenness of Noah after the Flood in Genesis 9.20. In reality this is a story of desperation, and desperation is the very reason that the story was told – it was probably included in the tale because the situation was so unusual. The context is that Lot, by this stage, has withdrawn to a cave with his daughters and that they are leading an almost monastic life there, away from any other men. These women's options are limited and so they succumb to unnatural sexual relations to pursue their childbearing ends.

The wider context also helps us to find clues to the reason the Old Testament relates this strange tale; it is to explain the origins of other nations – Ammon and Moab, often the enemies of Israel. It could be then that this story is more 'origin story' than historical account – another explanation woven into a broader narrative, perhaps.

So Dawkins is right at least on one point, that nowadays we are unlikely to get our morals from this story. While we have our own conventions about hospitality, we would be unlikely to go to such lengths as Lot to protect our guests. The themes of God's power and requirement of obedience come through as essential to the understanding of this story, but we would be likely to have problems with unquestioning obedience and immediate punishment these days. Hence it is not a story frequently featured in Christian circles. It is not a regular lectionary item. It is regarded as culturally conditioned and difficult in many ways. 'Sodom and Gomorrah' became bywords in the Old Testament for sin and depravity, and that has continued into the Christian tradition and into modern parlance. And yet there is much more to this story than 'Sodom and Gomorrah', which are only mentioned in verse 24. This particular tale is sometimes regarded by scholars as separate from the main Abraham cycle, and only tenuously linked to Abraham himself. This is not to excuse it, but simply to try to understand its origins.[20]

Abraham

It would probably be widely agreed that Lot is not a good role model, but Abraham is generally regarded in a more positive light. He is after all the ancestor of Israel. That is not enough to make him a good role model in Dawkins' eyes though. Again he digs out the less sympathetic stories in the Abraham cycle, missing out the more positive portrayals (e.g. Gen. 12.1–9). Dawkins mentions first of all Genesis 12.10–20 and 20.1–18, two occasions when Abraham, concerned to evade a famine, travels abroad and supposedly passes off his wife as his sister in order to have her marry, in the first instance, the Pharaoh, and in the second Abimelech of Canaan, so as to increase his own favour at court. The inevitable indignation of the tricked ruler on finding out the ruse is repeated in both contexts. It is interesting that the same story occurs a third time in reference to Isaac in Genesis 26.6–11.

To Dawkins, such repetition of a story suggests 'textual unreliability'. Perhaps so, if one is taking these stories as literal history, but this is to misunderstand the nature of storytelling. A good yarn is often repeated many times in oral circles, and while the characters and the circumstances may change, the point of the story does not. It is to be classified as a folk tale, repeated for effect.[21] It may have parallels in the wider ancient Near East in Nuzi culture. For example, it has been suggested that the occasions on which the patriarchs pass off their wives as their sisters (Gen. 12; 20; 26) are to be interpreted in the light of a Nuzi custom of adopting a woman as one's sister, and that the childless Abraham's adoption of a slave, Eliezer, as his heir in Genesis 15 makes sense in the light of the Nuzi practice of childless couples adopting slaves. These observations do not necessarily mean that a story is without a historical kernel of some kind, but they do suggest that we should not build too much on what may well have been a stereotype and may have grown in the telling. The point of the story is surely 'getting one over' on a powerful ruler, which would have been lauded in the contexts in which the story was being told. Of course it is not respectful of the position of the woman involved, but then one has to realize its male-orientated nature – having a beautiful wife to show off and tricking the ruler at the same time seem a double benefit. True, such motivations might offend our morals today, but we have to see the story for what it is – not moral instruction but a good yarn, especially when circulated in male peer groups.

No one is saying that this puts Abraham in a favourable light, but we do need to understand the context of the time and situation. Clearly, faced with a choice between starvation and migration, Abraham and Sarah choose the latter path. Having a beautiful wife who could be taken from him, Abraham is fearful for his own safety, such were the possible threats at the time for foreigners in strange lands without the legal and social protection they would have at home. He is perhaps anxious not to cause offence by refusing her hand to a would-be husband, and so delays negotiations for her marriage for as long as possible under this pretence.[22] Of course, Abraham's action imperils the promise of progeny and descendants God made to him in Genesis 12.1–9, leading one to wonder why he would risk this, but he appears to deem it worth the gamble.

God seems to take the initiative in the story at this point and sends plagues on Egypt that lead to Sarah's dismissal. This is a 'flight from Egypt' story that closely resembles the later one of the exodus, and so again has the character of a 'type' story.[23] In the second version in chapter 20 it is a dream sent to the ruler from God that leads to the appropriate realization. This second tale has a strange twist, whereby Abimelech ends up being grateful to Abraham since he appeals to God to cure the illness blighting Abimelech's court. He even invites him to stay in the land of Canaan, the land already promised to Abraham by God. Abraham comes out of these stories less well in moral terms than the ruler concerned – the Pharoah is justifiably indignant, while Abraham seems to benefit financially both times.

The narrator makes no explicit moral judgement on Abraham here (nor does he say, as he did of Noah in Gen. 6.9, that he was good); he simply uses the story as part of a wider narrative about God's promises to Abraham, which are endangered but hold true due to the loyalty of Abraham's God. This is true of Genesis 20 too, where the story comes just before the birth of Isaac – the promise of progeny is jeopardized again, but then God provides (and Gen. 26, with its occurrence just before the birth of Jacob, Isaac's son, is the same). The narrator is careful to tell us that 'Abimelech had not approached' Sarah; thus there is no possibility that Abimelech could be the father of Isaac. The use of many echoes and parallels across the story cycles concerned with Abraham and Isaac are one way in which the narrator wants us to draw parallels between the two.

Genesis 22, featuring the near-sacrifice of Isaac, is the next text that Dawkins discusses. He categorizes it as 'child abuse' and writes, 'A modern moralist cannot help but wonder how a child could ever recover from such psychological trauma',[24] characterizing the piece as an exhibition of 'bullying' and 'obeying orders'.[25] I agree that this is a very difficult tale – whether it is allegory, myth or 'not historically true' does not detract from its difficulty. It is clearly not written from the child's angle, or with any interest in what the child felt or thought. In the culture of the time, however, children were very much subservient to their parents and to the authority that they represented, particularly that of the father (cf. Prov. 1.18; 3.12; 4.1, 3–4) and so this omission is not surprising. Dawkins is right that this story is about 'obeying orders' – it is God's test of Abraham's obedience. Dawkins writes, 'Apologists even seek to salvage some decency for the God character in this deplorable tale. Wasn't it good of God to spare Isaac's life at the last minute?'[26]

Biblical commentators too have often seen this as 'a monstrous test',[27] perhaps indicating a 'cruel streak' in God. It is certainly a difficult passage in many ways. In similar contexts, the idea of 'testing' appears quite often in the Old Testament – Job, for example, is subjected to a 'test' by God and Satan with the same question, as here of Abraham, of whether he 'feared God' (Job 1.9; cf. Deut. 8.2, 16). But child sacrifice is sharply condemned in the Old Testament as a practice often carried out by Israel's neighbours but not condoned in Israel or by Israel's God (Lev. 18.21). So the main point here is that God does not in fact require child sacrifice; God is only testing Abraham's obedience to see how far it will go, even to the point of sacrificing his only son (and the comparison with Jesus is clear here). Sacrificing animals was commonplace at the time, with the idea that the animal would atone for a person's sin, but child sacrifice as practised in the Canaanite high places was robustly censured. In this story a ram is sacrificed as Isaac's replacement, and in Old Testament times animal sacrifice was the regular pattern. It is the fact that God should ask such a thing of Abraham that is shocking to us, rather than what actually happens in the reprieve of an animal sacrifice.

The message here is one of relationship and of the obedience of servant to master. God has favoured Abraham with his special covenant and, despite deviations, that covenant is still intact. The birth of Isaac is a great blessing, according to the stories that intervene between Genesis 12 and this point. The thought of sacrificing him, the one true heir to the great promise of God, is unthinkable. Thus the passage is one of high drama. God wishes to test Abraham's obedience, and yet there is no way that God will allow Isaac to be killed. The drama comes because we as readers do not know whether

Abraham will object or obey. We don't know, and nor does he, about the last-minute reprieve – although Abraham hints at it when he tells his son, in response to Isaac's bewildered question 'Where is the lamb for the burnt offering?', that 'the LORD will provide' (v. 7). It is not that, in Dawkins' words, 'God was only joking after all' once the angel has intervened.[28] This is a serious test of the relationship, however challenging we might find the idea of obedience to God on this scale. We are never told what Abraham felt about being subjected to this trial (in contrast with Gen. 21, where we hear how distressed he was at Ishmael being sent away). In the wider narrative context, this story provides another aspect of the theme of 'promise' that began in Genesis 12 – it is about the promise being jeopardized again, just as the wife/sister story has endangered it. It still leaves us wondering, though, whether God has not behaved in an unnecessarily cruel way here in making Abraham choose between obedience to God and love for his son. Is this kind of test right? Is it fickle of God? And what about Isaac, the innocent victim, who could have lost his life at the hand of the one person he trusted, his own father?

It has been suggested by biblical scholars that this story is another 'origin story' as in Genesis 1—11, explaining the origin of the prohibition against child (or human) sacrifice. This is possible, and the story may have originated as a polemic of some kind, designed to horrify the reader. But that is not the form of the story in the context of the Abraham cycle and so we cannot explain it away that easily. It could also be designed to illuminate the origin of a place name, 'Moriah', where God could be 'seen' – later identified with Mount Moriah in Jerusalem, the site of the original Solomonic temple (2 Chron. 3.1) and today of the Holy Al Aqsa Mosque. There is also a point to be made about repetition between this story and the previous one in Genesis 21, where there is also an urgent message from heaven calling the sacrifice off. We are back in the land of recurrent and similar points being made in slightly different storytelling terms, and so this repetition, of course, detracts from its historicity. We are also back in the realm of 'good stories' – good not in a moral sense but in the sense of being dramatic and arresting for an audience. These are the kinds of stories that tend to be told and retold, and which often grow in the telling. There is a powerful narrative here that increases both our sense of suspense and disgust, until it climaxes in a dramatic rescue.

There is an even more generous set of promises from God after this test of obedience has been passed – the passing of the test becomes a guarantee 'because you have obeyed my voice' (Gen. 22.18). This is clearly the point of the story, because it begins with 'God tested Abraham'. God has put his trust in the future in this man Abraham, and the kernel of this story is a justification of that trust. Perhaps Abraham had shown a certain wavering of that trust in the wife/sister incident. Whatever the reason, the issue of trust in the relationship between God and Abraham is the primary context for this test. Obedience in the Old Testament is the essential prerequisite of blessing.

In a Christian context, the sacrifice made by God in the life and death of Jesus Christ was an evident parallel. The New Testament itself, in passages such as John 3.16, Romans 8.31–32 and 1 Peter 1.19–20, compares the death of Jesus to the sacrifice of Isaac. The character of Abraham as 'founding father' of Israel but also of the blessing to all nations is firmly established in Christian tradition. He is seen to have his weak points, but the central theological themes of promise, obedience, relationship, covenant are what are focused upon in Christian theological evaluations. The theme of sacrifice is a familiar one for Christians seeking to understand Christ's sacrifice on the cross, and so the story of the 'binding of Isaac', as it is often called, is well known and has been engaged with by Christian thinkers over the centuries.

In this chapter, then, I have tried to contextualize the stories from Genesis that Dawkins singles out for criticism. I have not tried to replace them with alternatives, which would be an easier route, but rather have faced them head-on, looking primarily to their Old Testament context but also indicating the way Christians have dealt with them. In the next chapter I will go on in the same vein to the legal texts of the Torah.

4

Homing in on Hitchens (and Dawkins): Exodus, Numbers and legal texts

The Ten Commandments

Christopher Hitchens uses the Ten Commandments as the centrepiece of his attack on the Old Testament. He writes, 'The foundation story of all three faiths concerns the purported meeting between Moses and god, at the summit of Mount Sinai. This in turn led to the handing down of the Decalogue or Ten Commandments.'[1] Turning to Exodus 20, he then points out that the first three commandments are not of an ordering or prohibiting kind and that the fourth concerns the religious observance of the Sabbath. It is not until commandment five that we find a more general command, although 'Honour your father and your mother' is in the context of 'so that your days may be long in the land that the LORD your God is giving you'. Six, seven, eight and nine are general prohibitions on murder, adultery, theft and false witness. The ban on covetousness is also given in a particular context, although the wider moral can be fairly easily extrapolated.

For Hitchens the context of these commandments of faith in Yahweh and in the cultural and religious context of the time, is evidence that religion is 'man-made'[2] and the commandments themselves 'a man-made product of the alleged time and place'.[3] No biblical scholar would deny this, nor that the material is written by humans (even if inspired by God). Hitchens decides that the crimes that are prohibited would need no special revelation at this point in time: 'No society ever discovered has failed to protect itself from self-evident crimes like those supposedly stipulated at Mount Sinai.'[4]

Hitchens finds a weak argument in the stipulation that one is supposed not even to contemplate in one's mind such heinous thoughts as murder: 'If god really wanted people to be free of such thoughts, he should have taken more care to invent a different species.'[5] He also makes the rather obvious point that nothing is mentioned regarding many other offences that might have been listed, and that other laws of that culture allowed practices (such as slavery) that we would find abhorrent today.

Dawkins has less to say on the Ten Commandments, but he points out that if we prioritized them as they are presented then 'we would rank the worship of the wrong gods, and the making of graven images, as first and second among sins'[6] and hence condone the practice of blowing up the ancient monuments of cultures that used to worship other gods. His logical move from one point to another is rather a leap – the Ten Commandments say nothing about the idols of the past or the destruction of past cultures, even though other parts of the Old Testament (e.g. Ezek. 30.13) do.

The Ten Commandments are perhaps best understood within their context as a kind of treaty – a drawing up of a contractual relationship between two parties. We have parallels in ancient Hittite culture.[7] The main parties offer some description of themselves, and there is usually a superior, overlord-type figure making the covenant with an inferior party who is in some way indebted to the overlord – perhaps a kind of master/servant relationship.

The Ten Commandments then are essentially a contract between God and Israel, mediated by Moses. Even if this contract was composed outside the context where it purports to stand – on Mount Sinai – and offers a later summary of a host of more particular laws, it was never intended to be extracted from the context of relationship. Hence the laws about the requirements of this particular God and the facts about his identity and desire for relationship – the exclusivity of which demands the prohibition on idols and other gods – are important from the start. If this is some kind of summary document, it is not that the crimes mentioned had not been known about before – rather, it is a summary that clarifies the particular and unique relationship between God and his people. And it is not that other crimes are unknown, as we know from other Old Testament law codes in Exodus and Leviticus. The Ten Commandments were not originally meant to be read as universal laws – as Hitchens points out, only four of them have that nature. Their authoritative tone and their appeal to moral behaviour within a particular relationship with God, though, has led to their broader appeal and application. Within a Christian context, they are seen to provide a summary of 'the law' about which Jesus spoke.

Easily enumerated on the five fingers of each hand, these commandments may well have originated orally before being written down in summary form in Exodus 20 and in Deuteronomy 5. In the context of the development of ideas across the Old Testament period, the commandments in Deuteronomy are often thought to be earlier in origin than those of Exodus, partly because the stress is placed in the Sabbath command on the flight from Egypt as a reason for the need to rest, rather than on creation, which has resonances of later exilic concerns. Hitchens picks up the fact that there are two accounts of the Ten Commandments but sees the set in Deuteronomy as a repetition or variant, without any sense of the historical development of the ideas and texts.

The Ten Commandments are ethical demands. Since they consist of general principles rather than detailed cases, they do not constitute a law code in the usual sense. They specify no punishments and imply only that those breaking the commandments will incur the wrath of Yahweh and the community. They are the words of Yahweh their God, which the Israelites accepted as their obligation when they entered into covenant with him. Acceptance of, and obedience to, the Ten Commandments mark Israel out as the people chosen by Yahweh as his own. The covenant relationship is not a provision of law, that is, it does not consist of commands to be heeded for fear of punishment. As the offering of the covenant was an act of grace on the part of Yahweh, so was the promulgation of the Ten Commandments. Israel freely accepted them and responded to them out of a sense of gratitude for what Yahweh had done for her.

The Ten Commandments call on the one hand for respect for a right relationship with God, and on the other for respect for the neighbour – the neighbour's life, property, good name and marriage bond. The first four commandments list duties to God, the following six concern conduct within the community. When viewed as a whole the Ten Commandments contain surprisingly little in their content that is uniquely Israelite. Unique elements are the worship of Yahweh rather than of any other deity and the conduct of that worship without the aid of idols. Any civilized society must have regulations to protect the life and property and good name of its members, and in that sense these commandments are not new and are 'self-evident' (as Hitchens states in critical tone). These particular commandments, however, were promulgated at the outset for

Israel alone and their application was limited to the Israelite community. In terms of style they are distinctive. The commandments are addressed to the individual within the Israelite community. All of them except those regarding the Sabbath and the honouring of father and mother are expressed in the negative.[8]

One question we might ask is, 'Did the Ten Commandments originate with Moses?' This is a different question from whether Moses wrote the whole Pentateuch, as pursued by Hitchens. Following Julius Wellhausen,[9] who thought, in the nineteenth century, that the Prophets introduced the idea of the relationship between God and Israel as a binding covenant, scholars have argued that the Ten Commandments are not from Moses but show the influence of the Hebrew prophets. They would have then originated after the beginning of the eighth century BCE. In its listing of crimes perpetrated by the Israelites – 'there is swearing, lying, killing, stealing and committing adultery; they break all bounds and murder follows murder' – Hosea 4.2 provides the first evidence for the existence of a decalogue. Jeremiah 7.9 is cited as evidence that it had been formed or was in the process of formation: 'Will you steal, murder, commit adultery, swear falsely, burn incense to Baal, and go after other gods that you have not known?'

By the mid-twentieth century, however, there was more scholarly confidence in attributing the decalogue to, or at least considering it as, an ancient pre-prophetic document.[10] It was pointed out that the decalogue does not really exhibit the concern for social problems found in the Prophets, while the general course of the development of Israelite religion was viewed in a different light from that of scholars such as Wellhausen. Prophets were seen as reformers, not innovators who wished to revive some of the ideals of an older age which went back in part to Moses.

Homing in on Hitchens (and Dawkins)

An ethical dialogue in a brief and succinct form could have originated with Moses but whether it did is lost in the mists of time. It is likely that if the Old Testament contains anywhere the 'ten words' of Yahweh spoken through Moses, they are in the ethical decalogue, but in what exact form is uncertain.[11] The Ten Commandments do not show, as some other supposed decalogues do, the influence of an agrarian background such as we would expect if it originated after the entrance into Canaan. There is nothing in them that is clearly cultic. Even the Sabbath was not originally a day for cultic observance but rather for rest from work (Exod. 20.8–11). However, it is possible that the Ten Commandments may have been read periodically in the cult and hence were shaped by a liturgical usage.[12] Alternatively they may even have originated in the customs and regulations of the families and tribes of pre-Mosaic times, as handed down by heads of families and clans, elders and wise men. The forces which gave the decalogue its present shape must have been rooted in the institutional life of Israel over a continuous period of time, not precisely datable. Changes could have occurred as a result of the decalogue's recitation in the liturgy, in preaching or in teaching, and these changes represent the different layers of tradition that are now combined. The function of the decalogue, or an earlier version of it, within the development of Israel's life may well have changed. It remains difficult, however, to trace the nature of all the forces at work and the exact history of its growth. Moses' part in the process may have been to select a basic set of commandments, put them in succinct form and relate them to the covenant. Later redactors would have been responsible for their present literary form.

Anthony Phillips in his book *Ancient Israel's Criminal Law: A New Approach to the Decalogue*[13] (1970) argued that the Ten Commandments represent just that – the criminal law of ancient Israel. The authority of God himself lay behind the demand implied in each commandment and so there was no need to specify the precise penalty for breaking the commandment. Phillips argued, however, that originally each of the issues covered by the commandments had carried a capital penalty. He thus subscribed to the view that there was originally a shorter decalogue.[14] The formulation of this list of ten commandments – the list being a teaching device to make them easier to remember – may therefore originally have taken place apart from Exodus or Deuteronomy and been designed for independent use, either orally or in written form or possibly both.

As the accounts stand, the Ten Commandments are placed at the beginning of other laws and so have traditionally been regarded as the presuppositions on which those laws were formulated. However, maybe we could see the dependence as working the other way. The Ten Commandments could be seen as dealing with matters which, for the most part, were proving difficult to negotiate through the normal processes of law – for example, Sabbath-breaking, which is difficult to legislate against. Perhaps then these commandments were designed to supplement and reinforce the law out of a recognition that it was often difficult and sometimes impossible to deal with matters of major religious and social importance solely through the processes of law. The burden of obedience had to be placed on each individual Israelite.

While the Ten Commandments may well contain elements of ancient clan ethics, it is possible that they were brought together, then, in order to strengthen and reinforce the religious and moral standards of ancient Israel in a period of social upheaval. This is argued by R. E. Clements in his Old Testament Guide to *Deuteronomy*.[15] He argues that those who formulated the list were bringing together matters that had been consistently and felt to be deeply important to the overall welfare of Israel. In this sense the Ten Commandments represent a part of the truly 'Mosaic' inheritance of Israel, since they concern matters that pertain to the basic religious commitment and social wellbeing of the nation. He regards the issues dealt with in the Ten Commandments as matters of deep concern to the Deuteronomists as a group, a fact highlighted by the way in which the homilies of Deuteronomy 4—11 elaborate further on the significance of the first two commandments, and so he concludes that the Ten Commandments are a product of this wider Deuteronomic movement in the seventh century BCE.

In a Christian context the Ten Commandments are probably one of the few texts that Christians know well, and they tend to represent what Jesus knew as the 'law' from the Old Testament. Their nature as a pithy summary facilitates their learning and use. They feature in the liturgy, notably in the order of service for Holy Communion in the Book of Common Prayer, and sometimes in church decoration (also in synagogue decoration). Jesus famously distilled the Ten Commandments down to two (Matt. 22.36–40), taking the first commandment and then promoting the love of neighbour as oneself (which could be seen as a wider principle based on the tenth commandment). In Luke 18.20 (and also Matt. 10.19), Jesus cites the Ten Commandments back at the rich man who has self-righteously proclaimed that he has 'kept all these since my youth', stating that this simple keeping of commandments is not enough. In Romans 13.9 Paul says that all the commandments are summed up by the principle 'Love your neighbour as yourself'. The general idea that keeping commandments – be it the ten or Jesus' summary – is a good thing is promoted in the New Testament. Rules are needed in any society, both for individual wellbeing and communal prosperity.

The golden calf debacle

Both Hitchens and Dawkins mention the incident of the golden calf, which follows that of the giving of the Ten Commandments, in Exodus 32—4. As Hitchens summarizes:

> Several whole chapters are given over to the minutest stipulations about the lavish, immense ceremonies of sacrifice and propitiation that the Lord expects of his newly adopted people, but this all ends in tears and with collapsing scenery to boot: Moses returns from his private session on the mountaintop to discover that the effect of a close encounter with god has worn off, at least on Aaron, and that the children of Israel have made an idol out of the jewelry and trinkets.[16]

Of course, Hitchens here is taking the chapter chronologically as read, without the insight that law codes may have attracted themselves to these narratives at a later date. But to turn to this difficult story: after smashing the tablets in anger, Moses first makes the people swallow the ground-down gold of the calf, mixed with water. But then, more dramatically, he orders those of the tribe of Levi to kill people indiscriminately, even brothers, friends and neighbours. Dawkins writes:

> This amounted to about three thousand, which, one might have hoped, would have been enough to assuage God's jealous sulk. But no, God wasn't finished yet. In the last verse of this terrifying chapter his parting shot was to send a plague upon what was left of the people 'because they made the calf, which Aaron made'.[17]

A few details have been omitted here in both retellings of the tale. The first is that, as seen in the Ten Commandments, the prohibition upon 'idols' is a major issue for God in relationship with his people. The first and second commandments are immediately broken in this story. The punishment sounds outrageous to us, but in the context this was once again about the power and authority of Israel's God in relation to his followers. The reason that the members of the tribe of Levi are picked out to deal with the others is that they are perceived to be particularly true to Yahweh. This story actually has as its aetiological point the question of the origin of the favour shown to the house of Levi as priests, as those in the closest relationship with their God. It is yet another origin story and it has a similar thematic overtone of 'obedient servant to the death' as that of Abraham and Isaac. The tribe of Levi were picked out for this purging of sinners precisely because they were the 'model' obedient ones. They may have murdered brothers or sons – something unbelievably painful to our modern ears – but this is seen by the text as a necessary purging in the wider service of God. While we still regard such deeds as horrific and unacceptable, this was the whole theological point: such obedience 'ordained' this tribe for special service to God.

Another theme is that Moses tries hard to atone for the people's disobedience – something that appears to happen twice, with different outcomes. The first time he requests and is given a respite for the people, but the second time he asks God to forgive and is prepared to sacrifice his own relationship with God for that atonement. But God does not grant Moses' request to be 'blotted out' of God's book. God has plans for Moses to lead the people out of Sinai to the promised land.

The plague, which follows this encounter, acts as a further punishment. Such repetition suggests doublets in the tradition, and it has long been noted that this passage is disjointed – Moses makes a first intercession after God has told him of the golden calf incident, but then seems to find out for himself afresh what the people have done and become angry. We are possibly dealing with different sources here. This excuses neither the difficulty of the story nor the violence of the slaying, but it does help us to understand more about the literary problems of the biblical text, which may well have had a complicated prehistory.

This incident is clearly the first test of obedience for the people and they fail it dramatically. In this sense it is yet another 'Fall', after Israel was 'recreated' in the earlier part of Exodus. God could have destroyed Israel at this point (32.10) but, thanks to Moses, God does not. The people do nothing to help the situation and express no repentance for their apostasy. Aaron is weak too. It is Moses who emerges as the hero of the piece. He appeals to God's promise and character – and to the better side of his own character too (34.6–7).

The story overlaps with one in 1 Kings 12, suggesting that variant streams of tradition are evident in the biblical material. The story in Kings is of King Jeroboam and his calves, and in both stories the calf is golden – this denotes that, later in the story, the people went over to the worship of Baal, commonly represented by a bull, in a paganized kingdom of Israel. Could some of this have been written back into the Exodus account?

The aftermath of the golden calf incident

We need to go further into Exodus 33 and 34 to understand the wider message of this narrative. The breaking of the covenant by the disobedience of chapter 32 is followed by a story about the presence of God in chapter 33 where Moses intercedes a more successfully, and learns more about the nature of God: 'I will be gracious to whom I will be gracious, and will show mercy on whom I will show mercy' (33.19). Moses is also comforted by the assurance of God's forgiveness in chapter 34, where we have a very different description of God as 'merciful and gracious, slow to anger and abounding in steadfast love and faithfulness' (Exod. 34.6). The nature of God in relationship is brought out here – as is God's willingness to have a change of heart.

This description of God as slow to anger is repeated in various parts of the Old Testament,[18] and so it clearly gained a favourable 'hearing' within the wider canon of Scripture. Exodus 34, though, is not without its problems: the idea of inherited sin (which is later attacked by the exilic prophets Jeremiah and Ezekiel) is introduced (34.7), and the renewed covenant seems to focus in negative vein on driving out other nations from the promised land and abolishing their false gods. Here we find a somewhat revised version of the Ten Commandments, one much more particular to the culture, ritual and specific land promises of the time. In its emphasis on worship – not surprising, perhaps, in the context of the threat posed by the worship of the golden calf – it is often known as the 'ritual decalogue'. It also reads to us today as culturally alien.

This second set of promises and prohibitions has to be understood in the context of the promise of land. While we find the idea of promising a land that belongs to others to a 'chosen' people unacceptable, that is the way that it is formulated here. Because of the particularity of this God for this tribe, and the notion that other peoples and their gods are 'the enemy', we find the listing of all who are to be driven out and the warning not to mix and mingle with them for fear of a watering down of the Yahwistic faith. The chief difference between this God and the gods of other peoples is the prohibition of idols, and so this prohibition is reiterated. Food laws and sacrificial laws also play a part in establishing a particular identity for this people in relationship with their particular God.[19] It is clear that all these 'blessings' are dependent upon obedience.

We are told at the end of chapter 34 that Moses's face 'shone' on his return from the mountain of God. This is an indication of his having been in the divine presence and being God's representative. From this point on, whenever Moses speaks with God his face shines, and at other times he veils his face.

God's anger

Both Hitchens and Dawkins point out the problematic nature of God's rage in these passages from Exodus – sexual jealousy at the people's flirting with rival gods or whoring with foreign gods; God's fury in driving out other peoples. We read of God's jealousy: 'the LORD, whose name is Jealous, is a jealous God' (Exod. 34.14). There is no attempt to hide this aspect of God's nature. Within this chapter of Exodus alone we have some startling contrasts in the portrayal of God. There is a contrast between an immediate anger that leads to wrathful commands and Moses' attempt to calm God down, and the ensuing description of God in 34.6 as 'slow to anger'. Clearly such a contradiction might be due to the use of different sources; the latter description might perhaps have been added to soften the impact of the passage. However, the anger we see is a fascinating and contradictory aspect of the character of God as portrayed here.

Moses makes an impassioned plea to God to change his mind before venting his anger over the golden calf. What is the point, he asks, of the great deliverance from Egypt if God is just going to 'consume them from the face of the earth' (Exod. 32.12)? Moses appeals to the past promises of descendants and land made to Abraham and others. He also throws in the argument that the Egyptians, if this should happen, will think that God, rather than punishing them in order to save God's own people, has simply submitted them to destruction for no reason. The inference here is that God has a reputation for fairness and thus for sustaining foreigners as well as Israelites, even those foreigners he counts among his enemies. God listens to Moses and, at this first point, changes his mind – his ultimately compassionate nature takes over from his more retributory side, even though on a strict scheme of reward and punishment, and in the light of the Ten Commandments, the people deserve to be punished. Like Abraham, Moses has successfully interceded with God. Echoing Exodus 34, in yet another passage in Numbers 14.13–20, Moses again intercedes for the people, reminding God that he is by reputation 'slow to anger'.

There are plenty more examples of God's anger, particularly when it comes to other gods and their worship by the Israelites. Dawkins cites Numbers 25, where Israelites were encouraged by Moabite women to sacrifice to the Canaanite god, Baal; he writes that 'God reacted with characteristic fury'.[20] This time the penalty was the beheading of the culprits.

Dawkins considers the punishment 'extraordinarily draconian' in relation to the crime. This may be so, but it has to be understood in context. The community in relationship with God had made certain promises. When the people reneged on those promises, they became outsiders within the community. It was the same with the Ten Commandments – the punishment for violation was death,[21] or at least exclusion from the community of faith. Since these narratives all concern the relationship between God and the people, and the obedience expected of the people (and of God), the message is that they are always falling short of an ideal. Yes, as Dawkins says, God is jealous of other gods, a fact that has a prominent place in the Old Testament. But one has to remember that these stories predate even a monotheistic view of God; at this period the community saw themselves essentially in a tribal relationship with their God and did not deny the rival claims and attractions of other gods. This strict line was taken in order to maintain fidelity to Yahweh, rather than to indicate that it was Yahweh's main characteristic. It is because God is in a close relationship that God is jealous of anyone who threatens that relationship. It is a primitive view of a nationalistic God who punishes other nations, a view that gradually changed over time in the period covered by the Old Testament and a view that we are right to reject in moral terms, even when we understand the original context.

Strict laws and the death penalty

Dawkins makes a list of some of the crimes punishable by death in the Old Testament, citing mainly Leviticus 20. This includes cursing your parents, committing adultery, having sex with members of your family who are not your wife, homosexuality, marrying a woman and her daughter at the same time, and bestiality. This is a mixture of transgressions – including some of the Ten Commandments, some purity and holiness laws and some concerning family structures and relationships. The death penalty, or at least exclusion, was liberally applied for any crime that lay outside the acceptable boundaries of the community.

One punishment, interestingly, that Israel does not go in for is maiming. In the laws of Hammurabi, a famous and ancient Babylonian law code, stealing involved the loss of a hand, a penalty that often applied only to slaves or poorer members of society, and not to the upper classes, who simply paid a fine.[22] Neither class difference nor hierarchy is involved in the Israelite laws – all, at least all males, are equal in the community. Women and children were treated as male property at this time – this was the Israelites' cultural norm and that of the nations around them.

Dawkins goes on to mention Numbers 15, which ordains the death penalty for a man who has gathered sticks on the Sabbath. He is stoned by the community, and Dawkins asks: 'Did this harmless gatherer of firewood have a wife and children to grieve for him? Did he whimper with fear as the first stones flew, and scream with pain as the fusillade crashed into his head?'[23] This is a good example of Dawkins' ability to lay the rhetoric on thickly when he wishes. Of course the story is morally repugnant to us, but then very few communities today (except the most orthodox Jews) maintain such strict Sabbath laws, and there would be no such extreme punishment today. The Sabbath was a time of rest, a time to honour God and refrain from work as God did after the work of creation. It also reminded Israel of the redemption from Egypt. It was even a sign of the covenant (Exod. 31.13, 17). No one was permitted to do any work on the Sabbath – an injunction protected even slaves from working. The death penalty for working on the Sabbath was a principle that was about upholding the relationship or covenant in the way agreed. There were to be no exceptions, and sadly the stick-gatherer fell culprit to this rule. Whether he knew the injunction or not, he was deemed to have been disobedient by the ruling powers.

Of course, a more enlightened moral code would make a case for leniency, as Jesus himself did. In a Christian context this is one of the strict laws that Jesus overturns, showing us the path to rejection of such a dogmatic morality. Such a law is declared to be disproportionate to the offence and unreflective of the true character of God. The command to rest and the blessing of it is clearly a good thing, but Jesus modifies the 'letter of the law' approach to it that some were taking (Mark 2.27). In some sense this command is also an explanation of the need for human beings to rest – it is a necessary part of the human condition that we are all too often ready to ignore.

In the context of some of the punishments meted out in the Old Testament, Hitchens mentions Numbers 31. On the occasion of a battle against the Midianites, Moses is angry that so many have been spared and asks that males and their wives be slaughtered, and that only female virgins be kept for the soldiers. This is part of the diatribe against foreign people and their gods. Of course this kind of behaviour in a battle situation was known all over the ancient world and was an element of the prevailing culture. Although most of us would condemn such activity nowadays, it still happens in some parts of the world. But understanding the context does not excuse the overactive use of the 'smite key'[24] on God's part, and the similar lack of any sympathy on that of Moses. There are, however, many other passages where Moses is keen to argue with God and defend the rights of his people. Hitchens mentions Numbers 12.3, where Moses is described as 'very meek', as laughable, in that elsewhere he regularly behaves in a 'bloody' manner. But such Old Testament characters are not monochrome; they are complex and varied. Moses is struggling between carrying out what he believes to be God's commands and trying to lead his people in a difficult situation.

Hitchens also mentions Deuteronomy 23.1 – 'No one whose testicles are crushed or whose penis is cut off shall be admitted to the assembly of the LORD' – as a 'demented pronouncement'. It does sound demented to our modern ears, and there is no condoning it. I seek merely to understand the context in which it was said in order to comprehend it, not to justify it. This law is, in fact, about purity and impurity, in that the wounded (in the broadest sense) are seen as too impure to be part of the worshipping community until they are whole again. The example cited is precisely about the exclusion of males who are not perfect specimens (as is specified in the matter of which animals are sufficiently close to perfection to be suitable for sacrifice). It may be that these men have deliberately destroyed their organs so as not to be able to perform sex or have offspring, an action that is most likely to have been carried out in the context of a pagan act in service of a foreign god, in the manner of the castration of a eunuch. So it may actually have as its context the attack on foreign religious practices.

Hitchens also mentions an order in Deuteronomy to have children stoned (Deut. 21.18–21), which ranks alongside other situations where people are stoned for violating the community law (e.g. Deut. 13.10; 17.5; 21.21). Once again this is due to the strict rules attached to being part of the obedient community in relationship with God. There are many benefits to the relationship, but also a code of discipline that at times is carried out to the letter.

This is unpalatable to us, and clashes with Christian ideas of a merciful God. We are used to having the right of appeal in such cases, but the 'black and white' morality at work here reflects the more primitive society of ancient Israel. We are not being asked to extrapolate the Israelites' morality to our day – in fact our very abhorrence of the morality evident here is an indication of the influence of more enlightened moral codes, not only that of Christianity but also secular ethics, on our modern viewpoint. Indeed the recognition of the norms of the culture concerned, and the understanding of the context of such practices, frees us from thinking that they are something to emulate.

Issues of historicity

Hitchens indicates that such gruesome things as those in the passages enumerated above 'probably did not happen and . . . we must be glad [they] did not',[25] basing this conclusion on the likelihood that Moses did not write the Pentateuch and that the whole account was composed later. But even if Moses had nothing to do with the Pentateuch this argument is not an effective one in countering the possible historicity of these books. Why would all these things be recorded, sometimes in great detail – battles, places, names and so on – if they were based on fabrication? Hitchens appears to be confused here about the way sources work; if the writer of Deuteronomy was writing later and did not have access to a first-hand historical record, the absence of such a record would not be evidence that something did not happen, or its significance diminished because it happened after Moses' death. Hitchens is taking account neither of any oral or written traditions that may have circulated at the time nor of the processes by which these tradents became written sources, often long after the event. The attribution of the writing process to Moses was simply a matter of giving authority to texts in the same way that the Psalms were attributed to David and all wisdom to Solomon. Given that there are later clues in the text, such as the description of Moses's own death (Deut. 34.7), there was no real attempt to hide the fact that these authors could not have written all that is attributed to them. But the fact that such accounts were probably not written by these great men does not detract from the possibility that they contain a kernel of historical veracity, even though, as we know, motivations for writing things down vary from strictly historical concerns to more artistic, literary or theological ones.

The fate of foreigners

Dawkins mentions Deuteronomy 20, the invasion of the promised land. He writes, 'Do not think, by the way, that the God character in the story nursed any doubts or scruples about the massacres and genocides that accompanied the seizing of the promised land.'[26] Again this is a moment for much bloodshed, and this is a deeply problematic text, in particular the following: 'You shall annihilate them – the Hittites and the Amorites, the Canaanites and the Perizzites, the Hivites and the Jebusites – just as the LORD your God has commanded' (Deut. 20.17). Of course we might take this with a certain pinch of 'triumphalist' salt. It is perhaps more of a wish than a reality. It is again about the distinctiveness of the Israelites and their God, and it smacks of a religious fervour that is extremely dangerous, as we know all too well today. The context within the Old Testament is the God of Israel and the needs of the Israelite people. Yahweh the Israelites' God was with them alone, and their eventual habitation of the land is seen as divine punishment of the Canaanites and others for preventing them being there, and for worshipping other gods.

Whether this view represents the reality of the time is another question. There is some evidence for a peaceful transition, with many Canaanites becoming Israelites.[27] We have to see some of the text's contents as rhetoric in favour of Yahweh, an attempt to stress God's power and the power of the nation God represents.

Concluding remarks

Deuteronomy has in it a strange mixture of good and bad. Some of the most inspiring texts of the Old Testament can be found within its pages, but also some of the bloodiest. There is no doubt that the worldview it expresses is somewhat black and white, but among the white there is compassion for widows and orphans, there are profound expressions of the relationship between God and Israel, assembled together and worshipping their God – for example, Deuteronomy 30.11–20, with its command to 'Choose life.' It depends which bits you pick and choose. Deuteronomy ends (ch. 34) with Moses forbidden to enter the promised land because of his own sin – an indication that God punishes his own, even one of his favoured leaders, as well as others outside the covenant relationship. The story is told with pathos: 'The Lord said to him [Moses], "This is the land of which I swore unto Abraham, to Isaac and to Jacob, saying, 'I will give it to your descendants.'"' But then comes the stark ending, 'I have let you see it with your eyes, but you shall not cross over there' (Deut. 34.4).

We get a sense of the rejection that Moses must have felt – that after a long and arduous journey from Egypt across the barren desert, he would not live to see the fruits of his labours, he would not live to experience the rest and abundance offered by settlement in the land. Moses was denied that opportunity, which was given to his successor Joshua. Despite having been a great leader, we are told that Moses disobeyed God so profoundly that his final moment of glory was denied. We read too of Moses' death in that place. He is described as an old man by this time, but 'his sight was unimpaired and his vigour had not abated' (Deut. 34.7b). God's mercy did not extend to allowing him to take that final step into the promised land. We read that the great man fell to his knees and died and that the children of Israel wept and mourned for 30 days at the loss of their great leader, a prophet like no other. This is a story told with pathos and it remains as powerful today as it ever was.

In a Christian context much of the legalism of the Old Testament seems out of place. Jesus is often regarded as having overturned the rather literal legal demands that characterized some of the Jewish authorities of his day, paving the way for a fresh understanding of God's compassion. The concerns of the New Testament do not extend to rival gods of a tribal deity, even though idol worship was not unknown (e.g. Acts 17.16), because by then monotheism had fully developed and it was all about one's individual relationship or not with God. Of all the legal texts, the Ten Commandments and parts of the book of Deuteronomy have probably had the most influence in Christian circles. Furthermore, Deuteronomy 6.4, 'The LORD is our God, the LORD alone' ('is one' in some versions) has a central place in Judaism.

In sum, the legal texts selected here by our New Atheists seem somewhat random and are discussed out of context. The legal passages of the Old Testament are extensive and detail the many good laws that were needed to keep society in order. We are all aware of the same need in our own day – we are glad that society protects us from those who break the law. Society would be in chaos without laws, and without punishments for breaking them. Legal texts were drawn up in a religious context in biblical times, within a relationship of human beings with God, and we have inherited that legacy for our more secular, formulations today. What we see in the Old Testament are the strict laws established in the context of this relationship. Many of them are completely culturally alien to us, outmoded and outdated, and there is no suggestion that we should extrapolate them wholesale to provide our moral code today. We have to take the wider principles from them, and even then we might decide to pick and choose depending on our worldview. Alister McGrath mentions a few 'good' laws, such as the laws stipulating hospitality to strangers in Deuteronomy 10.17–19 and the setting of limits on acts of revenge in Exodus 2. There are laws prohibiting slavery and declaring a jubilee for debt in Leviticus 25. There are laws forbidding child sacrifice (Lev. 18.1; 20.2) and the famous injunction to 'love thy neighbour as thyself', cited by Jesus, also features in Leviticus 19.

There are more texts to choose from, of course. We do have to pick and choose, and unless we hold a fundamentalist view of Scripture, that should not be a problem. A Christian perspective might guide such a choice, but it should not have the Marcionite effect of turning us away entirely from the many and varied laws of the Old Testament.

Across the period of the Old Testament the laws changed. The laws of the desert (the Book of the Covenant in Exodus 21—4) gave way to a more developed set of laws in Deuteronomy, and from that further development took place after the Exile, with a fresh emphasis on cultic holiness and purity in the priestly law in Leviticus and Numbers. The changing scene led to new laws and new variants on old ones – the situation was not static. The understanding of God also changed over time. The tribalistic law demonstrated in many of these stories gave way in later texts to a more nuanced appreciation of the relationship of God with humanity on a wider world stage. This God, Yahweh, still called for obedience and exclusive loyalty, even in changing situations, and even if God's concern for the inhabitants of the wider world started to come into view. This is a key point about the change and development of ideas and perceptions – human perception of divine revelation is not static, and commandments are culturally conditioned rather than absolute. Both human and divine perspectives and expectations change and develop over time, and the dynamics and demands of the relationship change too.

5

Countering Dawkins: texts in the 'histories'

Dawkins covers some of the early books of the so-called 'histories', notably of the Deuteronomistic history that runs from Joshua to 2 Kings.[1] It is interesting that virtually all his examples are from the early 'tribal' stories of Israel, where God is very much confined to a relationship with Israel and where concepts of God had not developed much beyond those of a local God fighting wars on behalf of his faithful people. In this chapter, then, I will consider Dawkins' treatment of stories in Joshua and Judges. The whole history of the monarchy does not feature in his concern, which is a very surprising omission given the importance of the monarchy to the history of Israel and the identity of its people (see Chapter 8).

Joshua

Dawkins characterizes the book of Joshua as 'a text remarkable for the bloodthirsty massacres it records and the xenophobic relish with which it does so'.[2] He cites in particular the famous story of Joshua and the falling down of the walls of Jericho, writing, 'Good old Joshua didn't rest until they utterly destroyed all that was in the city, both man and woman, young and old, and ox, and sheep, and ass, with the edge of the sword (Joshua 6:21).'[3] He anticipates the theologian's response that we cannot necessarily take this story as historical truth, a response usually based on an assessment of the archaeological problems that have beset the digging up of the site. But Dawkins turns the objection into a denial of the miraculous: 'Well, no – the story has it that the walls came tumbling down at the mere sound of men shouting and blowing horns, so indeed it didn't happen.'[4] This raises the question again of how we deal with any story that has miraculous elements within it. We can decide that it is myth rather than history, as with the story of the serpent in Genesis 3 or the flood of Genesis 6—9, and indeed the rest of Genesis 1—11. Or we can emphasize literary artistry in a story that grew in the telling. On stronger ground, archaeological exploration has not found walls in Jericho dating to the right period, suggesting either that the event happened at a different period or that it did not happen at all. Early excavators discovered a section of collapsed masonry in the 1930s and identified it with the biblical walls, but subsequent work revealed that the remains were later than the early Bronze Age, the time at which the purported event took place.[5]

At the time of the thirteenth century BCE, where the attack on Jericho fits chronologically, there appears to have been virtually no habitation there. Of course, the archaeological redating that has gone on in recent years (see Chapter 9) reduces the time gap slightly, but probably not enough to provide firm evidence of settlement let alone collapsed walls. This raises the wider question of the validity of archaeological evidence in 'proving' the Bible. Such evidence is clearly itself interpretative, so is this a good or desirable method?

Dawkins cites an experiment done by the Israeli George Tamarin,[6] where the Joshua and Jericho story was told to Israeli children who were asked to comment on its morality (they generally condoned it), and then to another group of Israeli children with the context changed to China (in which case they did not condone it). He concludes that religious upbringing is the factor causing the different outcome. Genocide in general is not condoned, but when your God and your religious tradition are involved, you tend to defend it. This is an interesting conclusion, and I imagine there is some truth in it. There is certainly more investment from within a faith tradition in seeking to comprehend, within the context of a rather different view of God, how such events might have happened and struggling to fit them into a modern moral framework. But that doesn't necessarily make religion into a bad influence. As a Christian I am an inheritor of the Old Testament, and so I need to make sense of it in that context. I also need to make sense of it in its own cultural context. We have come across this kind of slaughter in the situation of battle before, and there is no doubt that, had the roles been reversed, with Canaanites overpowering Israelites, the wholesale slaughter would have happened in the opposite direction – this was their cultural world. We cannot extrapolate from the story that this kind of behaviour is acceptable nowadays, and nor should we wish to. But we can understand it in terms of the special relationship between God and the Israelites (ultimately the same God as that of the New Testament), and the early stories about the conquest of the land of Israel. God was perceived to fight 'holy' wars on their behalf, and that often involved the destruction of enemy groups.

The story of Joshua and Jericho marks the beginning of the conquest of the land. We have already seen that the fact of taking over someone else's land, as it is presented in the Old Testament, is deeply problematic for us today, even though it forms the starting point of most modern conflicts, for example, that between Russia and Ukraine. The idea of a holy war[7] is present here, a notion universal in the ancient Near East where kings believed they were mandated by their gods to fight, defeat and conquer. The appearance of the angel at the start of the account indicates the nature of the conquest as divinely authorized military activity. So God asserts that the battle against the Canaanites is his own battle, with Joshua as the human leader. The ark of the covenant that is carried is also a symbol of holy war.[8]

The act of encircling the city, moreover, is primarily a religious one. The repetition of the number seven recalls the days of creation and the Sabbath (it also matches the seven days of Unleavened Bread following Passover in the later liturgical calendar). The emphasis here is not on historical veracity but on what these events tell us about Yahweh: 'The LORD said to Joshua: See I have handed Jericho over to you, along with its king and soldiers' (Josh. 6.2, cf. the gift of land in Deut. 4).

The account is repetitive, almost liturgical in style, and scholars believe it could have been recited and retold, maybe on religious occasions, as part of a litany of God's deeds on behalf of Israel. It is also a good piece of narrative artistry, with the necessary climax. The wholesale slaughter, including that of animals, is itself to be understood liturgically: the slaughter of the city's occupants was seen as an act of sacrifice to God, parallel to the idea of animal sacrifice. This was the 'first fruit' of the conquest, just as the first fruit or the first of the flock was traditionally sacrificed to God. Clearly there was an issue also of sin and its judgement – the Canaanites were perceived as sinners – but this was joined by ideas of holiness and purity. This does not make the events morally right, but it explains what is going on in the context and in the presentation of the whole story in liturgical terms, indicating that the account was forged considerably later than the events told.

One story that Dawkins ignores in the same chapter, Joshua 6, is that of Rahab, a Canaanite woman who offered hospitality to Israel. As a result she and her family were saved, indicating that God, on the side of the Israelites, was nevertheless not against saving certain foreigners who chose to help the cause. Rahab became part of the Israelite nation and had famous descendants – her genealogy even leads to Jesus in Matthew 1.5. Another passage towards the end of the chapter – but a less savoury one – is Joshua's curse on the city in v. 26. This is present to emphasize the complete dedication of the place to God, such that no one is ever to inhabit it again.

This story in Joshua is perhaps one of the most famous in the Old Testament – many Christians come across it in children's Bibles. The aspect that receives closest attention there is the falling of the walls brought about by the sound of the trumpets, the miraculous element that Dawkins highlights. This is what makes the story extraordinary and worth telling – it is a story about triumph against the odds, the kind of story we hear of especially in the context of war. That has been its appeal over the centuries and it has not functioned as a moral vindication of genocide.

Judges

There are two terrible tales in Judges that involve women. Phyllis Trible has identified them as 'texts of terror', both in general and in the context of a feminist hermeneutic.[9] The two texts are not well known – possibly because of their difficult nature, they tend to be excluded from lectionaries in Christian circles (see Chapter 10). Unsurprisingly, however, they are picked up by Dawkins.

Judges 11: Jephthah's daughter

The first text is Judges 11, the story of Jephthah's daughter. Jephthah, described as 'a mighty warrior' (11.1), who has been rejected by his brothers as the son of a prostitute mother, is welcomed home, after some years as a warring bandit, as the one most likely to be able to stave off the Ammonite threat. The 'success of the unlikely son' story is a regular one in the Old Testament (parallels between this story and that of David are clear). Jephthah negotiates becoming leader as a prerequisite of his return. He then makes the foolish promise that if he gains victory in the war against the Ammonites, he will sacrifice the first living being he sees on his return, specifically 'whoever comes out of the doors of my house to meet me' (11.31). That, tragically, turns out to be his daughter, his only child. Dawkins writes about this, 'Understandably Jephthah rent his clothes, but there was nothing he could do about it. God was obviously looking forward to the promised burnt offering, and in the circumstances the daughter very decently agreed to be sacrificed.'[10]

This is a story about obedience and the keeping of promises, even though the outcome may challenge our moral codes. It is also again about God being on the side of the victor but demanding something back from the relationship. The situation described is horrific to us as we naturally put ourselves in the position of the father and daughter. It has overtones of the Abraham and Isaac episode (where we again encounter the only child and the sacrifice) but without either the sacrificial ram that averts the horrendous deed or any divine intervention or approval or disapproval.

The irony is that in the earlier verses of Judges 11 Jephthah comes across as a capable leader who tries diplomatic talks with the enemy via emissaries, albeit in rather nationalistic terms, before resorting to war. He argues that Israel has, for a long time, possessed the disputed land and has no desire to fight over it now. It is only when the Ammonites refuse to heed his message that Jephthah makes his promise, which is said to be guided by the spirit of the Lord. The promise that Jephthah makes is in fact a solemn vow – a pledge that implies a self-curse if it is not upheld. This kind of vow in the context of preparation for battle is also attested in Judges 21.1–13 – it is seen as a fair exchange for victory, rather in the nature of a sacrificial offering (cf. the deeply problematic Deut. 13.16, where the spoil of whole towns, including inhabitants and livestock, are an offering to God). It has been suggested that Jephthah expected to have to practise human sacrifice as a result of his vow, but human sacrifice is not an Israelite practice – in contrast with Moab (2 Kings 3.26–27) – and is roundly condemned in Israelite circles. It is more likely that he was thinking or hoping that a domestic animal might be the first to greet him, but since the courtyard of the house was a typical workplace for women, he should perhaps have thought twice. He was being rash and foolish when he made his vow, and yet such vows were not uncommon.

His daughter (unnamed)[11] in fact comes out to greet him 'with timbrels and with dancing' (11.34), a feature of women's roles well attested to in the Old Testament (cf. Exod. 15.20).[12] Jephthah's response when he sees his daughter is to say, 'Alas, my daughter, you have become the cause of great trouble to me' (11.35), presumably referring to the impending loss not only of her but also of her descendants, this being regarded in the culture as the main benefit of having a daughter. He states that he cannot go back on his vow as it was made to God (contrast the situation with that of Saul and Jonathan in 1 Sam. 14.45, where a vow is broken). His daughter is, perhaps surprisingly in the prevailing culture, allowed a little initiative rather than solely being a pawn in a drama not of her making, although she is remarkably accepting of her fate. She negotiates a couple of months with her women friends to 'bewail my virginity' (11.37), which is granted, but ultimately the sacrifice is made.

A final note in the chapter links the lament over her virginity with a custom among the young women in Israel of lamenting this woman's fate for four days each year (Judg. 11.39–40), and also with a woman's rite of passage from virginity in her father's household to adult responsibilities of marriage and childbearing once she has a husband. It is thus revealed as the story behind a ritual – an explanation story, on a certain level, although one more closely related to a specific narrative. Unusually in this story, Jephthah's daughter is in fact his heir. In normal circumstances only men could inherit, unless there was no male heir (Josh. 17.3).

It is possible that the root of Jephthah's troubles lies with his parentage. His mother, we are told, was a harlot and his father was called 'Gilead' (meaning 'rugged'). He may not then have been brought up in the ways of Yahweh, and he may have therefore misunderstood the nature of the God of Israel. A suggestion that the god Chemosh (the national god of the Moabites, also linked here to Ammon) exists and has rights seems to imply a polytheistic context (Judg. 11.24). Jephthah is described as not God's but the people's choice, brought back by popular demand after being outlawed (11.5–6). Furthermore, his making of a deal before going into battle could be seen as out of line, an attempt to secure success before setting out, rather than trusting in Yahweh's deliverance (11.9).

The story, then, perhaps indicates a judgement on such ill-considered vow-making as part of a wider indictment of Jephthah. In this context the vow is to be seen as a self-indulgent 'insurance policy' that seeks to control God but backfires when his daughter appears. However, it is problematic that we are told that the spirit of God came upon him before he made his vow. Does that actually mean that God condoned it? Should we blame God directly for the outcome of the story? Or is this expression of the spirit of the Lord coming upon him more to do with preparation for battle, like Samson (Judg. 15.14)? Why, though, does God fail to intervene to prevent the sacrifice here in contrast to what he did in the story of Abraham and Isaac? There are a number of ways to interpret this story and many questions arise.

The concept of purity is also at issue: the harlot mother is counterpointed by the model of the virginal daughter. The daughter's acceptance of her fate is praised in the account and she is thereafter regularly remembered, which is seen as a sign of blessing. Indeed the regular remembrance of her might well be the reason this story was circulated – another explanation story of the origins of a particular custom.

My aim here has been not to condone a dreadful story but to seek to understand it, first in its culture and second in relation to the way the authors of the Old Testament tell it. As elsewhere, the weakness of the New Atheist attack is that the text is simply extrapolated for its lack of morality, without being understood in its own cultural context. That context does not condone texts morally, but it helps us to understand why the characters concerned behaved in this way and why we in turn need to reject such behaviour. The biblical world is a patriarchal one revolving around men, and yet, in the story of Jephthah's daughter, small touches communicate the pathos of the young woman's fate: her acceptance, her virginity and her passivity.

It is hardly surprising that this passage has not been prioritized in Christian circles, so culturally conditioned is it, and so unedifying, morally or otherwise. It is interesting that Jephthah appears in a list of Old Testament 'examples of faith' in Hebrews 11:

> Time would fail me to tell of Gideon, Barak, Samson, Jephthah, of David and Samuel and the Prophets – who through faith conquered kingdoms, administered justice, obtained promises, shut the mouths of lions, quenched raging fire, escaped the

edge of the sword, won strength out of weakness, became mighty in war, put foreign armies to flight.   (Heb. 11.32–34)

Christian commentators have been flummoxed as to why Jephthah is listed here when his vow had such disastrous consequences, and some have thought that this refers to his Ammonite victory rather than his vow. Nor is this text from Hebrews widely read. The passage from Judges, with its broader ramifications, offers us the challenge of encounter with a very difficult text. It is a challenge we need to accept from time to time, rather than sweeping such encounters under the proverbial carpet (see Chapter 10).[13]

Judges 19—20: The Levite's concubine

The next story, from Judges 19.16–30, is also horrific – and violent. Let us use Dawkins' summary (his citations are from the KJV):

> An unnamed Levite priest was travelling with his concubine in Gibeah. They spent the night in the house of a hospitable old man. Whilst they were eating their supper the men of the city came and beat on the door, demanding that the old man should hand over his male guest 'so that we may know him'.[14]

This may be a thinly disguised prelude to homosexual gang rape, but Dawkins doesn't mention this particular possibility. He continues:

> This access is denied by the old man since the other man is his guest. Instead he offers his own daughter and the other man's concubine with the words 'humble ye them, and do with them what seemeth good unto you; but unto this man do not so vile a thing.'

Dawkins pauses to point out the clear misogyny here, although it may be that by sending out the women the old man was hoping to get rid of unwanted male-to-male attention.

> So anyway the Levite handed her over to the mob who gang-raped his prostitute all night. When she lay prostrate on the doorstep next morning he abruptly told her that they must get going. But she didn't get up because she was in fact dead. Then comes the gruesome bit that he chopped her body into twelve pieces and sent pieces of her body to different Israelite tribes.

Dawkins then writes by way of commentary, 'Yes, you read correctly. Look it up in Judges 19:29. Let's charitably put it down to the ubiquitous weirdness of the Bible.'[15]

So let us look at the Old Testament context of this story, again not to redeem it in any way, but to understand it. I have already mentioned the strict rules on hospitality at the time, which meant that once a person found refuge in another's home that person's security was paramount. One might also mention the lowly status in this society of prostitutes and concubines, even though concubines often acted as second, more fertile wives (cf. Abraham and Hagar in Gen. 16). The old man, moreover, was a resident alien himself, marginal to the main Israelite tribes.

Many have seen the story as largely symbolic, the 12 pieces of the concubine's body representing the 12 tribes of Israel, scattered and in chaos, a prelude to a fresh era of united kingship in Israel that would calm erratic and violent behaviour such as that shown by the men of the town. Of course, even by the standards of the culture of the day this was unusual behaviour, and hence the story was related as noteworthy. In fact the same can be said of most of these stories. Why were they told (indeed, why is any story told)? They were the exceptions, the extreme examples, the unusual situations, the uncomfortable scenarios – that is why they were memorable.

The story in fact starts at the beginning of Judges 19 with the comment that 'In those days, there was no king in Israel' (19.1). This repeated phrase (which also occurs in Judg. 17.6; 18.1) is significant in relation to how the story has been composed in its wider context. If these stories were gathered together by later writers (they are thought to have been Deuteronomists from the seventh century) then they were looking back with the hindsight of history.[16] They inherited sources of material about the kingship which, for many, was seen as a high point in the development of Israel. They themselves, standing at a point in time when the kingship had essentially failed, were less positive. But there is still the sense that the time of 'pre-kingship' was less clear-cut. In a sense God had always been king, but that designation and its accompanying theology too developed over time.

The story begins with the Levite, who resides in a remote part of Ephraim, deciding to take a concubine from Bethlehem in Judah. We are immediately told in v. 2 that the concubine 'became angry with him', suggesting that she had reason to wish to leave, although this was probably interpreted by the Levite as unfaithfulness. She goes home to her parents and he has to woo her back. Sometimes the 'anger' of the concubine is taken as harlotry and so she is condemned for a punishable offence against her husband. This leads to reflection on why she was so readily admitted back to her parents' house and why seemingly forgiven by her husband at that earlier stage in the story. And yet that is perhaps to read too much into the story at this stage, where the Levite 'speak[s] tenderly to her and bring[s] her back' (v. 3). The exaggerated display of hospitality from the concubine's father heightens the irony of the whole story. He urges the couple to stay, and as a result they remain until the evening of a fifth day, but the Levite is determined to make a late departure.

The hospitality theme then continues when the Levite and his entourage can find nowhere to stay. It is ironic that the Levite will not stop in a non-Israelite town, thinking that his welcome will be less safe in such a place. Eventually a resident alien in Benjamite Gibeah from the hill country of Ephraim takes them in and offers warm hospitality, and they are said to be 'enjoying themselves' (v. 22) when their fortunes change.

The next scene, where the residents of the town of Gibeah try to violate the Levite, has strong parallels with the story of Lot and Sodom and Gomorrah (Gen. 19) that we considered in Chapter 2, such that it starts to take on the qualities of a 'type', a repeated tale. Here, however, the threat is from within and not outside – from another Israelite tribe rather than from the Sodomites. The old man defends his guest, just as Lot does his – the first request is for intercourse with the Levite. There is then the same threat of homosexual rape and 'womanization' of the victim in both stories.[17] The same offer of the women is made by the host. But this time the Levite, in contrast to his former allegiance to her, gives his concubine willingly to the crowd – he is described as 'seizing' her, presumably against her will. He also leaves her out all night while he is safe inside. Of course when the Levite finds his concubine 'on the threshold' (v. 27) and receives no reply to his call to 'Get up', she is dead, although the text does not tell us so explicitly. He loads her body on to a donkey and sets out for home. Nor are we given any hint of his emotions, but that does not necessarily mean that he had none. He later describes the events committed against him and his concubine as 'a vile outrage in Israel' (20.6).

This story, like many others, turns out to be an 'explanation' story. This time the subject is the beginning of war between the tribes of Israel. The Levite has to give an account to 'Israel' (all the tribes come except the Benjamites) of his actions and his subsequent division of the concubine's body into 12 pieces, as would be done with a sacrificed animal. The tale is also symbolic of the 12 tribes and an indication of their division.

When he has to justify himself, the Levite is economical with the truth, suggesting that his life was also threatened (which, if rape was intended, it probably was), and he leaves out of his account his seizure of the concubine. He justifies his actions, though, because of the outrage to his family perpetrated by the men of Gibeah. This leads to the destruction of the city of Gibeah and then to more inter-tribal warfare, culminating in the defeat of the Benjamites. There is a general decline in the unity of 'Israel', evidence of problems over clan or national loyalty, accompanied by a deterioration in the way women are treated. This woman shows some independence, which is possibly a reason for her harsh fate. Although she seeks refuge in her father's house, she has essentially left that house to be with the Levite; thus she is in a liminal place, fully committed to neither, which was unacceptable in the society of the time.[18] There is perhaps an explanation, then, but it does not justify the barbarity we perceive in this story when we read it today.

The fact that 'there was no king in Israel' is again cited at the end of chapter 20, this time as a reason for the deterioration of the unity of 'Israel', pointing us forward to the new period of the monarchy which begins in the next book, 1 Samuel. It is ironic however, that Saul, the first king in Israel, actually comes from Gibeah and is a Benjamite. There is also a parallel between this chapter and 1 Samuel 11.7, in which Saul chops up a yoke of oxen into 12 parts and delivers them to the tribes of Israel, to encourage their fidelity to Samuel and himself. The discrediting of the Saulide dynasty probably therefore influences this account in Judges 19—20, especially since it is written with the hindsight of the failure of that dynasty and the priority of the Davidic monarchy. It is possible that the whole account in Judges 19—20 was an artificial construct, a late imitation of the Lot story, written to condemn Gibeah and Benjamin, the home town and tribe of Saul.

The story goes downhill further in chapter 20 (which Dawkins does not mention) when the outraged Israelites (on hearing the above story from the Levite) decide to wipe out the Benjamites. They then realize that they have nearly exterminated one of their own tribes, so they try to make amends by attacking the men of Jabesh-Gilead and sparing only young women (virgins) to be given to Benjamite men. This is to fulfil an oath that these Israelites have made not to give their own daughters to the Benjamites. But they find that they are 200 virgins short and so seize some young women of Shiloh who are dancing in a festival, thus solving their immediate problem. Problems over vows raise their heads here, as in Judges 11. The incident is also a clear indication of the subjugation of women in this culture and their treatment exclusively as 'childbearers'. This is a very morally difficult story for us today and would have been another good example for Dawkins' purposes.

In Christian circles the story of the Levite's concubine is not generally read in church or featured in lectionaries. Nor is it usually preached upon.[19] Apart from its difficult moral issues, one possibly needs quite a bit of background in the Old Testament context really to understand it (although this is true for many of these stories). The background of anarchy rather than sound government is a theme that was taken up by early interpreters such as John Calvin at the Reformation.[20] The omission of the story in Christian reflection and liturgy does, however, raise the wider question of how we select texts and whether we are right, as we may well be in this particular instance, to ignore certain more difficult texts in the context of worship.

It is surprising that neither Dawkins nor Hitchens goes further in the histories of the two kingdoms to discover more 'unedifying' texts. There are plenty of them (1 Sam. 4—5; 2 Kings 23.21–30, to name but two), and plenty of edifying ones too. I am now going to move the focus away from the Torah and the histories because my stress, due to the emphasis placed upon them by Dawkins and Hitchens, has been almost entirely on those, and I wish to introduce the reader to other parts of the Old Testament. I will come back, though, to these sections towards the end of the book and hope to find some more appetizing passages within their pages. I realize that I am 'cherry-picking' texts in the same way as Dawkins and Hitchens – that is probably inevitable in any selective book – but I hope that my selection will at least help to give a more rounded picture of the Old Testament and its varied character.

Concluding remarks

Dawkins' main point throughout his chapter is that we shouldn't, and indeed ultimately do not, get our morals from Scripture. However, it is clear that his concept of 'Scripture' – and certainly of Old Testament Scripture – is very limited. A direct attack on difficult passages is an invidious approach. At least Hitchens' consideration of the Ten Commandments, or indeed Dawkins' of the Genesis creation story, has more reflective nuance. Ancient myths, such as the creation, are inscribed in our collective psyche and deserve more than a trite condemnation. Such myths and stories may be untrue historically, but they are often told with a serious point, teaching us about humanity in relationship with God, symbolic of greater truth.

I have made the point, in response to the issue of deriving morality from Scripture, that we cannot simply transcribe directly from the ancient cultural context of the Israelite nation to our own. If we choose only the morally suspect narratives, of course we are not going to get our morals from Scripture – but we could choose other parts of the Old Testament which might be morally applicable to our own lives, even if the cultural and chronological differences are still evident. Furthermore, if we seek to understand the context of these difficult texts then at least we have some chance of understanding why we do not derive our morals from them. Basically ideas moved on and developed over a long period of time within the period covered by the Old Testament, so that its nature moved away from tribal tales to kingship, to prophecy and to a sobering experience of Exile that made the Israelite people rethink and reflect. Certainly, by the time of the New Testament rather different aspects of God's character had emerged, many of which had already become known through the pages of the Old Testament, and the character of the Christian God is shaped by them. In a Christian context much Old Testament morality is recontextualized and often rendered redundant, although texts are still of value as story, as history or as a life lesson from the past. In one sense, we do get many of our morals from both Testaments, but not in a direct line – morality of this type, along with other types of engagement with texts, is mediated by centuries of tradition, reflection and consideration in changing contexts.

Part 2

ENGAGING WITH THE OLD TESTAMENT

Introduction

So where do we go from here? In Part 2 I wish to show the rich and multifaceted nature of the Old Testament by looking at some alternative passages from the canon, first from the Writings and then from the Prophets. Then in Chapter 8 I will look again at the Pentateuch and histories with a rather different lens from that of the New Atheists, before ending with two key chapters, the first (Chapter 9) on scepticism within the academic study of the Old Testament/Hebrew Bible that has had an impact on those wishing to teach and preach it and in the second (Chapter 10), some concluding reflections from a Christian standpoint, looking in particular at preaching.

In the next three chapters, then, I will attempt to place a study of some of the more liberating texts from the Old Testament in the context of an ancient canonical ordering of books. I will use the Jewish ordering of Torah, Prophets and Writings (Tanak), although in reverse order so as to highlight the Writings as a rather neglected group of texts. This will enable a fuller appreciation of the range and variety of texts and genres in the Old Testament. While I realize that I too am 'choosing' texts, I hope that it is clear from my discussion of many of the texts selected by Dawkins and Hitchens that I am not attempting to paint a one-sided positive picture simply to rectify their one-sided, negative emphasis. However, having dwelt on difficult texts in Part 1, I do wish to emphasize that there are many more edifying and nourishing texts to choose from in the Old Testament. The quest for morality is only one among many reasons why we might wish to engage with these texts. In addition, a fuller understanding of the Old Testament will help us to appreciate the way in which the 'old' is the essential precursor to the 'new' for Christians and enhance our understanding of the New Testament as well.

6

The Writings: a neglected corner of the Old Testament

In this chapter I want to take us to the later stages of the compilation of the canon of texts, into the section known as the Writings. A look at the canonical orderings in the different traditions tells us about the way these books have been interpreted in Jewish and Christian circles. In the Jewish ordering of the Hebrew Bible the Writings consist of the following: Psalms, Job, Proverbs, Ruth, Song of Songs, Ecclesiastes, Lamentations, Esther, Daniel, Ezra, Nehemiah and 1 and 2 Chronicles. So this section includes the 'later histories' (Chronicles, Ezra, Nehemiah), which in the Protestant canon are placed after Samuel–Kings so as to continue the history of the kingdoms, often with rather different accounts of that history. In Protestant Bibles, Ruth is after Joshua and Judges in what is perceived as a chronological order. Esther is also in historical order after Nehemiah; Lamentations is between Jeremiah and Ezekiel since it reflects the events of the Exile; and Daniel is after Ezekiel, being set in the period of the Exile, but in Babylon rather than Israel. In Jewish tradition there is also the subdivision within the Writings known as the Megilloth, including Esther, Lamentations, Song of Songs, Ruth and Ecclesiastes – the liturgical grouping of texts all used at key festivals.

The Writings are often seen as the final group of texts to come together within the canon. The canonization of the Torah came first (as indicated in Ezra 7.10 with mention of the study of the law), then the Prophets and then the Writings. Jewish circles prioritize Torah and Christian circles prioritize the Prophets; neither religion prioritizes the Writings. In Christian circles the Psalms are the exception to that rule, in that they are read and sung in daily services. They are actually cited 79 times in the New Testament, more often than even the book of Isaiah. Yet I would suggest that they should have higher priority than they have traditionally been given when it comes to understanding the development of ideas in the Old Testament itself. The Writings may be perceived as a strange place to start in the exploration of that development and of ideas about God, but they do provide an alternative starting point to the very nationalistic stories about Abraham and Moses that have tended to be the emphasis of the New Atheist attack.

Creation and the wisdom literature

The Old Testament begins with the creation of the world and the primeval myths of Genesis 1—11, discussed in Chapter 3. Many scholars see large chunks of this section of the Old Testament as exilic – formulated in reaction to the Babylonian versions of the creation of the world that the Israelite exiles met when in Babylon in the sixth century BCE.[1] However, certain parts of the account are earlier and have a different character, although dating these sections is difficult.[2] The earliest suggestion for their dating has been the early, united monarchy under David and Solomon (cf. Chapter 9), but with the presence of much oral material possibly dating to an earlier period than the written account. However, the written account could be as late as the Exile, again with earlier oral precursors. This material is often seen as presenting a different outlook or an alternative stream of ideas without the necessity of being too concerned, as scholars tend to be, about dating a passage precisely to a particular writing context.

A key point I wish to make here, though, is that there is another source of traditions about God as creator to be found within the Writings. This appears in the material known as 'wisdom literature' in Proverbs, Job and Ecclesiastes.[3] Again some of the more developed ideas about creation may be later, post-exilic developments within this literature, but there is a whole body of texts in Proverbs (10.1—22.16) that consists of sayings of a practical nature, possibly accumulated over many years, and reflecting a presupposition that God is the creator or orderer of everything. These are early and primary texts. They cover human experience of all kinds, which is whittled down to short, pithy sayings, sometimes related to the divine and sometimes not. This is a very different starting point from which to look at the Old Testament, one that very much begins with universal human experience and looks heavenward from there. It is not interested in the experience of a specific group, nor is it partisan in any way in its perception of human experience as universal. At times it shows signs of its own cultural norms, but many proverbs are, remarkably, as pertinent today as they were in the past. Their presentation is thus very modern.

Furthermore this series of pithy sayings also includes moral content. It is no list of laws, but it gives truisms based on human experience and in that sense is a key source of morality.[4] Some are simply observations, such as 'As a door turns on its hinges, so does a lazy person in bed' (Prov. 26.14), but many are exhortations: 'My child, fear the LORD and the king, and do not disobey either of them' (Prov. 24.21). Such advice can be based on bad experiences in the past, for example, 'Like a roaring lion or a charging bear is a wicked ruler over a poor people' (Prov. 28.15), or it can consist of recommendations for successful life choices: 'The beginning of wisdom is this: Get wisdom, and whatever else you get, get insight' (Prov. 4.7).[5]

Proverbs 16.1–11

Just as Dawkins and Hitchens have done, let us dive straight into a text. I take a sample from Proverbs 16, verses 1–11. This is a chapter where God ('the LORD') is surprisingly present in a 'manual for good behaviour' that is often said to characterize other sections of less God-orientated sayings. This then is a good place to see the nature of God in a rather different light than in some of the places that we have looked so far. The God of Proverbs is the creator, the orderer, the ultimate source of wisdom and knowledge, worthy of 'fear', rewarding fairly and punishing if necessary, commanding respect and guiding on the right path.

Proverbs 16.1 contrasts human planning with the more profound answer that comes from God: 'The plans of the mind belong to mortals, but the answer of the tongue is from the LORD.' The human mind tosses decisions to and fro and yet reliance on God for guidance is often the better way, says the proverb. Such 'right answers' are seen as God-given. Life is a series of contrasts for these writers, between good and evil, between the human and the divine – these are the parameters of their world. In verse 2, human beings may think highly of themselves, but it is God who makes ultimate decisions about their worthiness. In verse 3 the same message of reliance on God emerges – 'Commit your work to the LORD and your plans will be established.' Of course, so far we have heard little about the nature of the God in whom one is being called to trust.

Some of the proverbs smack of predestination in suggesting that God has people's lives already mapped out, as in verse 4 – 'The LORD has made everything for its purpose, even the wicked for the day of trouble.' God has a plan for the world, if not for every individual. Everything fits together in a series of opposites – even the wicked or arrogant, who may prosper in the short term, will get their comeuppance in the end. The sense of good and evil in the world and of God's central involvement in justice comes out here as it did in the Genesis account, where creation itself was seen as 'good', and evil entered by the back door with the serpent.

A sense of predestination might suggest that human beings should be passive, but it is clear from verse 6 that this is not the case – God is looking for active loyalty and faithfulness. The key phrase 'the fear of the LORD' features here (cf. Prov 1.7). This is not fear in the sense of fright; rather it is reverent praise of God with due respect and honour. So the nature of this God of Proverbs is emerging – a God who has an interest in good and evil and hence in human morality, but who is ultimately worthy of a trust and reverence that goes beyond human planning and morality.

This chapter of Proverbs recommends righteousness over sin, good deeds over bad. Verse 8 makes a contrast between having a small and a large income – better the former with righteousness, it says, than the latter in a situation fraught with difficulty. Verse 9 reiterates the point made in verse 1, that human beings may plan, but God is behind the scenes directing the action, as he directs the action across the story of the Old Testament. This could be seen as a rather simplistic view of God as the lover and promoter of righteousness. Such righteousness also prompts morality – in verse 8 it is clear that greed is misplaced in this delicate balance of righteous and wicked behaviour.

The Proverbs may well have been inspired, if not written, by an Israelite king – King Solomon (Prov. 1.1; 10.1 attribute them to him, cf. 1 Kings 4.32) and there are proverbs, as here (and in vv. 12–15), that describe the important position held by the king. This has the effect of linking this material with the history of Israel's kings (notably 1 Kings 1—11, the reign of Solomon), while also making broader points about the way the king uses his position and hence about his moral obligation to his nation. The king is God's representative on earth, responsible for justice and for maintaining social order. In verse 10 the king makes important, God-inspired decisions. He manifests what it is to live with God's guidance in one's life. In verse 11 the LORD loves honesty and all weights and measures are controlled by him, as by the king.

The God of Proverbs

The God of Proverbs then is straightforward. There is nothing here about God's warlike actions on the side of the people of Israel, nothing even about legal commandments, such as the Ten Commandments. In that sense Proverbs is very different from other parts of the Old Testament. It is a manual for life, primarily addressed to young people as they start out on life's way. This God is essentially the creator and sustainer of the world (as indicated in the description of creation in Prov. 8, see below) and the Proverbs concern themselves with the order in life to which any person wishing to gain wisdom can be attuned. The 'LORD' of Proverbs stands at the beginning and end of the learning process, hence the link with education and morality, the quest for knowledge and the acquisition of true wisdom. Wisdom is the virtue and privilege of kings and other leaders who have had educational advantages denied to others, and it is their responsibility to disseminate it to the wider populace.

If this section of Proverbs belongs in the period of the monarchy – which is possible, given the attribution to Solomon – and maybe has older oral roots in tribal culture, it is an indication that there was a worldview at work among the Israelite nation that contrasted with the portrayals of God we have seen in the Pentateuch, Joshua and Judges. Some of the essential traits of fairness and obedience ('fear') are there, although in a more gentle, measured way than in legal texts. The obvious omission from Proverbs is mention of the special election of Israel, although there are sometimes hints of other texts, such as Deuteronomy, in Proverbs 1—9 that suggest the material is not entirely divorced from other parts of the Old Testament canon.[6]

There is an indication of awareness of the act of creation in Proverbs 8, with its description of a female personification of Wisdom participating in the creative process. The list of creative acts (vv. 24–31) echoes the list in Genesis 1, imagining a time before the creation of the earth, before the depths and springs and shaping of the mountains. To God is ascribed the making of all these things – from earth and soil to the heavenly firmament and the boundaries of sea and earth, and ultimately the inhabited world and the human race. Wisdom is present as a literary and theological device to ensure the correct ordering and structuring of the world, but the poem also expresses the delight that Wisdom takes in the world that God has made.

This passage depicts an alternative account of the creation of the world by God, which is echoed in Psalm 104 (which also reflects the list in Genesis 1).[7] In the psalm, the luminaries, the elements, mountains and animals all praise the Lord and bear witness to his greatness. Again nothing is said about Israel's history, not even its prehistory (although v. 9 may hint at the Flood story in the mention of a boundary for the waters 'so that they might not again cover the earth'). It is a hymn of praise, not an account of any kind of punishment. It links the ordering of creation and its good intention with human values learnt through education, experience and living in society, and it brings them all together in God. It assumes that all creatures are equal in God's sight and asserts the dependence of creatures on the creator. It asserts the power of God in the creative act but also stresses the interrelatedness of all things – God sustains life just as the rivers provide water for animals and birds (vv. 11–12). Humans are part of that wider cycle of life and death.

In the light of modern scientific knowledge we may not wish to take this, or other creation hymns, literally. But the acknowledgement that the hand of God is ultimately in the process is the truth that is being conveyed here. The way these ancient peoples saw it was that God caused all to be and created out of chaos the kind of order that shapes everything in our world. This God was identified with the Israelite God Yahweh but was regarded, in this material, in a wider sense as the creator of everything for which a good purpose was intended.

The book of Job contains a similar paean of praise to God as creator and goes in depth into God's creation of animals, wild and domesticated. The all-seeing and all-knowing nature of God is stressed. God even brings 'rain on a land where no one lives, on the desert, which is empty of human life, to satisfy the waste and desolate land, and to make the ground put forth grass' (Job 38.26–27), suggesting that God's beneficence extends to animals and the land, and is not focused simply on humans. The book of Ecclesiastes too acknowledges an all-powerful God who is in control of all aspects of human life, hard as it is to understand it or always to view it positively. There are poems on God's control of 'the times' of events in human life – 'a time to be born and a time to die' (Eccles. 3.2) – and on the inevitability of old age and death. God's control of the cycle of life is emphasized here, a cycle reflected in nature as well as in individual lives (Eccles. 1.4–11) and in the inevitable passage of the generations, one after another. Ultimately this author concludes that 'all is vanity' in the light of the reality of death, but he also commends enjoyment as an essential part of appreciating the life that God has given to humanity.

The 'wisdom literature' then reveals a completely different starting point from the Pentateuch and historical books when it comes to God. It is arguably influenced by ancient Near Eastern genres of wisdom, and some have seen it as a 'foreign element' in Israelite thought. But I would argue rather that it is an alternative stream of thought that demands careful consideration when we come to characterize the Old Testament and its God and when we consider morality.[8] Much of the speculation contained in this literature is on the formation of character[9] – it offers an alternative model of morality to the legal texts and might have provided Dawkins with some interesting material in his quest for the biblical origins of morality. For wisdom literature, morality springs from two elements – first, the knowledge handed down from the past from generation to generation, a knowledge grounded in cumulative experience; and second, individual experience itself, which can contradict shared experience and lead to fresh insights. Job is a good example of someone whose experience of undeserved suffering, at complete odds with his expectations of reward and punishment, forced him to question his beliefs. The author of Ecclesiastes too is unafraid to challenge accepted norms.[10] This is how morality stays dynamic – it changes according to experience and the wisdom that experience brings.

Song of Songs

Another book that is traditionally attributed to Solomon but also stands outside Israel's national history is the Song of Songs, or Song of Solomon. Jewish tradition states that Solomon composed this work when he was young and in love, that he composed Proverbs in middle age and Ecclesiastes in old age. This would certainly fit in with the themes of these books. There are a number of exhortations in the Song of Songs, perhaps the most famous of which appears in 8.6–7:

> Set me as a seal upon your heart, as a seal upon your arm; for love is strong as death, passion fierce as the grave. Its flashes are flashes of fire, a raging flame. Many waters cannot quench love, neither can floods drown it. If one offered for love all the wealth of one's house, it would be utterly scorned.

The setting of a seal entails making a permanent mark in order to remind one of one's commitment – rather as, these days, people sometimes have tattoos with the names of their loved ones inscribed on their flesh. A seal is also a confirmation, as in the seal on a letter – keeping it confidential, completing the action – and it can also indicate ownership if worn around the neck as a necklace or as a ring on the finger (in a place of intimacy, cf. Gen. 38.18; 41.42; Jer. 22.24; Sir. 49.11). Here then the lover wants the love to be permanent and describes the nature of love as 'strong as death', thus aligning love with another of the powerful forces that all humankind eventually succumbs to. The image of a raging fire is also used to express the depth of emotion and the way being in love envelops the entire person – in fact the flashes of fire may perhaps refer metaphorically to the heat of passion that cannot be put out even by floodwaters. True love can never be quenched, nor can it be bought off in a base way by money.

This is perhaps a reference to the cultural custom of bride wealth, whereby money passed from the bride's family to the husband's family. There were sometimes negative aspects to this tradition, such as the bride being sold too readily and for a low price by her male family, but it was a largely positive practice designed to protect the bride. The phrase, though, could have a wider reference simply to the idea that money cannot buy true love. We might observe that in a very male culture, it is the woman in the Song who utters these words, and indeed more of the words of the Song than the male lover.[11] There is an equality about this book – despite the prevalent cultural conditioning – that is refreshing and striking.

The Song of Songs is a dialogue about the nature of love between a man and a woman who are in love. It is a celebration of love in both mental and physical terms, framed in poetry but also in a loose narrative structure. Over the centuries, of course, it has been interpreted allegorically and metaphorically – for many Christians it is about the relationship between Christ and the Church. And yet it contains no mention of God[12] and springs entirely from common human experience.

Psalms and Lamentations

Perhaps the most well-known 'Writing' is the book of Psalms. This book represents a microcosm of the Old Testament. I have said before that if we had only the Psalter we would have quite a good idea of what is contained in the Old Testament, because it reflects the diversity of interest of the entire canon.[13] It contains reference to the history, of course, much mention of God, and some difficult verses too (the last two verses of Ps. 137 are perhaps the most infamous). It also features many laments and thanksgivings, some psalms that relate to wisdom's morality, and others that reflect the law. It is a repository of the wider Israelite experience. Psalm 104 contains praise to God as creator (as do others, such as Ps. 74), linking up with the discussion of creation and the wisdom literature above.

Thanksgiving: Psalm 147

Let us begin on a positive note. The psalms in the final section of the Psalter are all about praise and glory and all that God does for people. Psalm 147, for example, begins on an upbeat 'Praise the LORD! How good it is to sing praises to our God' (v. 1), and it describes God as gracious. The psalm is largely about what God does for his city of Jerusalem, but Jerusalem is simply the magnet that attracts and shelters the afflicted and the outcast. The psalmist conveys God's kindness – 'he heals the brokenhearted, and binds up their wounds' – contrasting this with God's greatness, and thereby drawing out a tension familiar to us in varying pictures of God. He gives praise to God as creator and provider of all things, including rain for the earth and food for animals. Again he expresses the sentiments of 'those who fear him' and 'those who hope in his steadfast love'. These two ideas of 'fear' and 'steadfast love' keep recurring – this is what God expects from his followers, and God gives back fidelity and love in return. This is probably a late psalm in the way it brings together the themes of salvation, creation and the focus on Jerusalem, and yet it shows the kind of complex theological synthesis that was going on in the theological thought of the Old Testament as ideas about God developed and changed.

A taste of Psalm 119

Let us now take a section of a rather different psalm. Psalm 119 is the longest in the Psalter; its main focus is the law. I have chosen verses 105–112 only.[14] When I say that this psalm is concerned with law, I am referring not to concern with the letter of the law but rather the fact that it is about God and God's divinely given law, and human response to that law. This is not a narrow and constrictive law, nor does the psalm refer to a specific body of laws, such as the Ten Commandments. Rather the law is seen as freely given and all-embracing. God is lawgiver, and the law is the guidance on offer to human beings to help them through life. Like the idea in the wisdom tradition that God plans the steps of human beings behind the scenes, so this psalm has a wider view of law than one might expect if one simply read the laws of the Pentateuch. It is a view of God's grace in giving to humans a sense of morality. It is God's advice for human existence.

In verse 105 'your word' is the utterance of God. It is the same word that brought creation into being in Genesis 1, or which punishes rebellion (e.g. the punishment of Aaron in Numbers 20). It may be another way of referring to God's legal commandments, as in Old Testament law, but it probably also has the wider sense of the totality of God's purpose for his people. The psalmist here is speaking in reverential tones of the idea that God's word is a lamp and a light. The lamp illuminates the darkness and the light is more than physical – it is enlightenment that ensues. The language of feet and paths used here is reminiscent of the language of Proverbs, where wisdom guides the worthy person on the right path, while the path of the wicked is covered in thorns (Prov. 4).The psalmist takes the keeping of God's law – or ordinances – very seriously in verse 106. The suppliant swears an oath that cannot be withdrawn. There is no question that God's laws could be anything but righteous, even though the psalmist is in fact feeling afflicted.

The psalmist here is loyal to God, and he believes the law to be a moral guide to his life. This is clearly the source from which he gains his morality. He is in distress (v. 107), probably suffering from illness. He asks God for life, presumably meaning that he wants his life back from the weakened and distressed state that has come upon him. God is the sole source not only of the law, which encompasses all aspects of life, but of life itself. The psalmist has sworn an oath to God and expects God, the giver of 'life' to faithful servants, to keep faith with the psalmist in return. The use of 'word' echoes the opening verse – the psalmist longs for that enlightening word that always guided him in the past. In verse 108 there is a hint of a sacrificial oath in the use of the expression 'offerings of praise', although of course these could be purely verbal offerings. There is a distinct note of praise here – the psalmist trusts in God's presence, even when severely afflicted.

This psalmist is not complacent but is always learning. He asks God to 'teach me your ordinances'. He knows God's law but he is unaware of the extent of it in its fullness and revelation. He believes in God's goodness and in the goodness of God's law, which, even in dire straits, will not be forgotten. The temptations of the wicked are all around – the language of snares recalls traps for animals (cf. Prov. 1.17–18). Temptations come in many forms, but the loyal God-fearer will not stray (cf. Prov. 21.6). Danger and determination characterize these verses.

For this psalmist there is too much at stake to think of straying far. He rejoices in God's precepts and his decrees, both synonyms for his law. They are, like God's word, his greatest joy. The psalmist cannot imagine life without them and he will do anything to hold on to that happiness. He is determined to obey God's statutes – his heart is the expression of his will. This is about endurance and loyalty and commitment for the long term.

This psalm has the feeling of being a later composition than many, reflecting on a tradition of law that had evidently become quite dominant, possibly in the later Old Testament period when the lack of king and Temple led to a new stress on Temple and law. It has a personal aspect, like many psalms, that draws us into the faith experience of the individual. This is perhaps the reason for the popularity of the psalm – communal or individual, it is reflective, like wisdom literature, of individual human experience, the joys and the woes. This psalm clearly has elements of lament, and we can find many of those in the Psalter. Let us briefly look at an example.

Psalm 77: a lament

Psalm 77 is a particularly extreme example of a lament from the depths of affliction and despair. When the psalmist thinks of God 'I moan; I meditate, and my spirit faints' (v. 3). The psalmist feels cast off by God because there is a remembrance of happier days. This psalm is interesting in that it sets out various expectations of what God is usually like, or ought to be like – of what the suppliant expects from God. The psalmist expects God to treat him favourably, to show steadfast love and to give promises that will be kept. God is normally gracious, compassionate, full of wonders and mighty deeds; guiding in a holy way, working wonders, and displaying might and a strong arm in deliverance of 'the descendants of Jacob and Joseph' (v. 15). God is also the creator who made the waters of the deep 'tremble' and caused thunder and lightning, as well as leading his chosen people 'like a flock by the hand of Moses and Aaron'. In the context of lament, and with the purpose of calling for a return to former happiness, the psalmist is asking why these things have gone, why these characteristics of God are hidden.

The psalm displays an interesting mix of genres – there is reference to some of the ancestors of Israel, so giving a grounding in the distinctive history of Israel, and to God's creative and salvific acts. Yet the context is very personal and trusting. As in Psalm 119, the psalmist will not be cowed by affliction. Scholars have often drawn comparisons between this psalm and the book of Job, in the way that Job also describes the great affliction he is suffering, and yet never wavers in his trust in God and in the kind of God he expects to find (and knew before). There is a depth of emotion in the Old Testament laments that is at once startling and yet strangely reflective of real human life, with all its hardships and tragedies.

Lamentations

Another book of the Writings also concerns 'lament', and that is the book of Lamentations, traditionally ascribed to Jeremiah and so placed after his book in the Protestant canon. Lamentations is set at a particular period and in a particular place – the time of Exile, specifically during a year-long siege in Jerusalem. It was a time of particular hardship for the people, and the book contains only a little that is hopeful. There are some very stark and difficult images in it, with starvation during the siege culminating in the people eating their own dead offspring. These are images of desperation, all too familiar to us from our television screens today as we hear the news from around the world.

The more hopeful section is to be found in chapter 3. The thought of all the hardship is slightly mitigated by the sentiment that 'The steadfast love of the LORD never ceases, his mercies never come to an end; they are new every morning; great is your faithfulness. "The LORD is my portion", says my soul, "therefore I will hope in him"' (3.22–24). This expresses the idea of an overarching faithful and lasting love as the ultimate character of God, whose tendency is towards mercy that springs from fidelity to his people and to his individual servants. When the poet starts to think about the true nature of God, this positive note emerges. The idea of portion is that of one's lot in life (cf. Eccles. 9.9). One's lot here is the relationship with God, which in itself is seen as the ultimate ground for hope. The seeming absence of God is bewailed throughout much of this piece; and yet, like the psalms of lament, it expresses the people's expectation of more and a hope of renewal. The relationship was already in place – why then this seeming abandonment?

Lamentations does not end on a high note, but goes back to a low one – it is realistic about the hardships of life, especially during war. Its overall tone is one of torment leading almost to despair, were it not for a few fleeting glimpses that there is more to life than simply abandonment.

Ruth and Esther

Emphasis on the 'steadfast love' of God as seen in Psalm 147 (above) occurs in another writing, the book of Ruth. Although this is set in a more specific historical timeframe – that of the Judges – it is a very individual 'family' tale with an agricultural context. The theme of a Moabitess (Ruth) gradually winning acceptance into an Israelite community is an unusual one, especially in contrast with the hostility against Moab shown elsewhere (e.g. Num. 21.29), and this piece of writing reveals a more open universality than seen in such passages. That this woman should turn out to be none other than the great-grandmother of King David is even more surprising!

Ruth is a narrative text, short and concise (like a novella). Female loyalty is an important theme, as indicated by the relationship between Ruth and her mother-in-law, Naomi – Ruth stays with Naomi even when urged to leave her and the two advise and support each other throughout the book. The theological themes are varied, but one key theme is the 'steadfast love' that the characters show both towards each other and God. Early on in the book when Ruth meets Boaz, her kinsman, he comments on the 'steadfast love' that she has shown to her mother-in-law and this gives him reason to be generous to her. Boaz says, 'May the LORD reward you for your deeds, and may you have a full reward [i.e. wages in full] from the LORD, the God of Israel, under whose wings you have come for refuge!' (Ruth 2.12).

There is an appeal here to the idea that rewards come to those who do good deeds (as in the wisdom literature) and to the concept of good character, but this is taken further with the idea of a 'full reward' given by God that goes beyond a strict principle of retribution and recompense. The image of God's 'wings of refuge'[15] is found elsewhere, in Psalm 91.4, and will reappear in Ruth 3.9 in reference to the protective cloak that Boaz lays over Ruth on the threshing floor. It is illustrative here of a God who protects each individual in the same way that a man may protect a woman. Boaz through his action turns out to be the agent of God's blessing, since Ruth finds security with him. There is little reference to God in this book – it is about a human story, and a women's story at that – but God's presence, if not obvious, is implied in statements such as this one. It is when the characters show 'steadfast love' that they are at their best, and are reflective of God's purposes for them.

Another women's story in the Writings is that of Esther – a brave woman who saves the Jewish nation. She has real pluck and courage (as shown in her speech in 4.14–16). She and Ruth are very different characters: Ruth is quite submissive, although she too shows some quiet determination to achieve results. The book of Esther is a more nationalistic piece and so also forms part of the 'historical' jigsaw puzzle. Interestingly there is no mention of God at all in this book, simply of the machinations of power politics of a later period when foreign rulers reigned over the Jews.

The climax of the book of Esther comes at a moment of celebration when the nation is delivered and there is much rejoicing. The month of Adar becomes

> the month that had been turned for them from sorrow into gladness and from mourning into a holiday; that they should make them days of feasting and gladness, days for sending gifts of food to one another and presents to the poor. (Esth. 9.22)

There are key reversals here – sorrow is turned into gladness and mourning into a holiday. It is noteworthy that in their rejoicing the people look outside their own needs to those of the poor. It is also important that the place in everyday life of feasting, rejoicing and rest is acknowledged. The event of deliverance is thought to mark the origin of the Jewish festival of Purim and the book is read on this occasion.

This later period is also reflected in Chronicles, Ezra and Nehemiah, which form Writings in the Jewish canon. Chronicles is a later rewrite of earlier stories in the history, seen through the new lens of life in the post-exilic Temple with the importance of worship and legal observance now established. Ezra and Nehemiah are both governors of the area of Israel under the auspices of foreign powers in the period after the Exile and continue the history of the nation. I will consider these in Chapter 8 under 'historical books', as in my view they align better with Samuel and Kings than with the other Writings.

Daniel and his vision of 'one like a son of man'

Finally, the book of Daniel is another late inclusion in the Writings, reflecting not only prophetic tendencies but 'end-time' visions and hopes. The first half of the book is set in Babylon at the time of the Exile and consists of narratives about the antics of Daniel. We are all familiar with his time spent in the lion's den from our children's Bibles; his visions, though, are of a more prophetic nature and are often cited by Christians in connection with claims made about Jesus in the New Testament. In fact, after the Psalms, this is perhaps the best known Writing for Christians. One of Daniel's visions is recounted in chapter 7, where he sees 'the ancient of days' and 'one like a son of man'. Let us pause for a moment with this strange but important text.

Chapter 7 stands at the heart of the book of Daniel. It has close links with both stories and visions and so forms a bridge between the two halves of the book.[16] Its vision of the end of the world's empires and the establishment of God's kingdom, however, is linked more closely with the further visions that follow.

At the beginning of the chapter Daniel has a vision of four beasts, culminating in the appearance of a terrible creature with ten horns, 'different from all the beasts that were before it' (v. 7). In verse 8 the creature is given an eleventh horn and verses 9–10 feature a description of the heavenly throne, which continues in verses 13–14. This is interrupted by an account of the slaying of the fourth beast, while the other beasts only have their dominion taken away; their lives are 'prolonged for a season and a time'.

Daniel approaches one of the heavenly beings in his vision and hears the interpretation of the vision. First, he is told in verses 17–18 simply that the four beasts are four kings and that the holy ones or saints of the Most High shall possess the eternal kingdom. But then he asks again, first about the fourth beast and then about the eleventh horn, and here his recapitulation of the vision introduces new elements. The fourth beast now has claws of bronze (v. 19) while the horn 'made war with the saints and was prevailing over them' (v. 21). It was judged and its kingdom passed to the 'holy ones of the Most High'. The interpretation that follows speaks of the fourth beast as a terrible kingdom, but concentrates on the horn, and specifically on the features just introduced – its warring against the 'holy ones' and its 'changing times and the law'.

The meaning of the chapter as it stands seems to be that the age of the oppressive empires is about to be terminated by the sovereign act of God who, when his kingdom is brought in, will delegate sovereignty to the faithful. This information is conveyed to Daniel in the form of a vision which is then interpreted by an angel.

Daniel 7 uses symbolism in varied ways. Its symbols have been viewed as a code: the lion refers to Babylon; the leopard to Persia or Greece; and the small horn to Antiochus or some other historical or future person. Suggestions have been made that a creation myth underlies the conflict between God and the nations.[17] Thus the theme of the chapter may well be the new creation, when God's kingdom is set up and the kingdoms symbolized by the beasts (with overtones of the primal monster overcome at creation) are either destroyed or deprived of their sovereignty. This is followed by an enthronement scene of the 'one like a son of man' over the lower creation, with overtones of the sovereignty of man over the animals as found in Genesis 1. The author compares this to the enthronement of the human king, as in Psalm 89; and he finds parallels with royal psalms in the theme of kings striving in rebellion against Yahweh and his anointed, and Yahweh rebuking them and affirming his anointed king's destiny to crush them, as in Psalm 110.

This passage clearly has a cosmic dimension; the world stage becomes the sphere of divine activity, thus recalling other divine actions such as the creative act and the anointing of Israelite kings. The main concern of Daniel 7, then, is with what God is about to do in history. Faced by what he believes to be the culminating wickedness of the powers of this world, the author gives expression to his triumphant conviction that God is about to intervene and replace the rule of tyranny with that of the saints of the Most High, which will be the embodiment of the purpose and sovereignty of God. The 'one like a son of man' in verse 13 would in this context more readily refer to the authority given to Israel over the nations. The author's climactic point would be that the tyrant nation symbolized by the fourth beast is so terrible that it can be subdued only by total destruction.

With verse 13, therefore, we reach the climax of the passage. The scene is located on earth, but with reference to the clouds of heaven on which the son of man comes. The earthly and divine worlds are closely interlinked and the figure seems to be coming from heaven to earth. Here we have the appearance of 'one like a son of man' – or 'one like a human being', as the NRSV inclusively translates. The figure's resemblance to humanity rather than an animal suggests authority and closeness to divinity, and the picture is one of power and kingship. The vision is of a man-like being escorted by the clouds of heaven and introduced into the presence of the Ancient of Days. The author clearly intends to contrast the one like a son of man with the beasts issued from the abyss. The kingdoms represented by beasts will pass away, but what will replace them is both human and supernatural. There may be overtones of enthronement here, either of a human king or of a god. There is to be a reversal of fortune brought about by God, and the one like a son of man is to be the vehicle.

Who is this character? Suggestions have been that he is simply a human being, maybe a kind of primal man; that he is a leader, human or divine, with royal authority; that he is either a representative or a symbol of the nation of Israel; and finally that he is a purely divine being, a symbol of the celestial, called up by God for a specific purpose.[18] In Jewish and Christian tradition the humanlike figure has been understood to be the hoped-for future king of Israel who would fulfil the hopes of a Davidic redeemer as expressed in Old Testament prophecy – the Messiah.

Needless to say, this passage is very important to Christian understanding of the role and significance of Jesus, and particularly of Jesus as the awaited Messiah. The fact that Jesus used the nomenclature of 'son of man' in reference to himself might indicate that he was making a link with this intermediary heavenly figure, who in many ways represents his own role. Revelation (1.13; 14.14) picks up this language in referring to the end-time when 'the son of man' will return once more. The language is highly symbolic and in many ways obscure, but this passage exemplifies those in the Old Testament which Christians have seen as predictive of the events of the New, and as essential for any understanding of the significance of Jesus and his message (see Chapter 10).

7

The Prophets: a more convincing source of morality?

Prophecy covers a huge stretch of the historical period recorded in the Old Testament, starting before the monarchic era and finishing as late as the second century BCE, arguably changing along the way into the kind of futuristic visionary material that we have seen in the book of Daniel. The narrative texts contain important prophetic figures – 1 and 2 Kings, for example, feature Elijah and Elisha – but I am concerned in this chapter with the prophets who have books assigned to their names. The prophets are key individuals in any timeline and they all make claims to be historical figures, even though where books are attributed to specific prophets a careful distinction needs to be made between prophet and book. Many prophecies contain third-person narrative about the prophet and many include material from different periods – prophets did not write their own books; rather, words and prophecies attributed to them were preserved by those who composed the books. This fact requires us to turn our attention to the editorial redactions of the prophetic books, and such a concern with the difference between earlier and later material has tended to dominate scholarly study of these books. It is only in more recent times that scholars have begun to consider the nature of each prophecy as an accreted but unified 'final form'.

The Prophets

Canonically, the prophetic books in the Hebrew Bible are placed after the Torah. In the Protestant Old Testament they are placed after the Writings. The individual books remain in the same order; the 'book of the twelve' minor prophets stays together, preceded by the three longer prophecies of Isaiah, Jeremiah and Ezekiel. The ordering therefore is not chronological.

It is widely accepted that the book of Isaiah came together in three main parts. Chapters 1—39 constitute First Isaiah, a prophet living in the eighth century BCE, although not all the material in the book dates from that period. This is followed by Second (or Deutero) Isaiah (Isa. 40—55), living during the Exile. It is likely that the Second Isaiah was the editor of the first. Then there is a third swathe of material likely to have come from an even later period, after the Exile; some scholars call this Third (or Trito) Isaiah, while others think the material is not actually derived from a separate prophet.

How do we decide on these divisions? This is where the idea of development over time comes in – with the assistance of small historical pointers, we can see the development from the changing theological concerns expressed. Second Isaiah, for example, contains reference to the Persian king Cyrus (Isa. 44.28; 45), who overcame the Babylonians at the Exile and made it possible for the people of Israel to return to their own land. This is reflected by the joy and thanksgiving expressed in the book, which is in massive contrast to the long sections of judgement found in First Isaiah. However, the recent tendency of scholars is to try to find the connections between the different parts of Isaiah and to foster a greater appreciation for the book as a whole.[1]

Of course it must be remembered that prophecy is a wider cultural and social phenomenon than just an Israelite one, and significant parallels can be found from the ancient Near East.[2] There is also a distinction to be made, as I mentioned above, between the prophets as historical figures (or otherwise, as some would hold)[3] and the books which bear their name. The two are not identical, in that even if prophets wrote some of their own material, much would have been shaped and reshaped by later authors and editors, who had their own purposes in presenting the material afresh to their own age. This is a process that only stopped with the closing of the canon. In that sense the books are rich theological resources, far exceeding the bounds of their original intention.

Social justice and right relationships in Amos and Hosea

Unlike some parts of the Old Testament, the Prophets are an important source of morality, in their own time and today; their 'bias' towards the poor is well known and has been taken up by many a preacher or teacher over the centuries. Although it might seem obvious to extrapolate present-day morality from these texts, one needs to take care not to do so directly without understanding the context. It is too easy to pick out the 'good bits' from which moral guidance can comfortably be drawn and to overinterpret those parts to the neglect of others. As with the difficult texts, so too with the easier ones.

Amos was a prophet who fought for social justice in his time (the eighth century BCE). He castigated those who looked only to their own gain and self-aggrandisement, calling the opulent women of the day the 'fat cows of Bashan' (Amos 4.1). He did not mince his words!

A good example of Amos's prophetic fervour is Amos 5.6–7, 10–15. This passage is about choices. The people of Israel are offered a choice – to seek God or face judgement. Seeking God is not simply a religious commitment, it is a moral one too – that was the emphasis that Amos, preaching to the northern kingdom of Israel, wanted to make to the people. It is a simple 'either/or' choice. At the time the society was corrupt – the rich were getting richer at the expense of the poor and people had lost sight of their moral as well as their religious commitments. In verses 6–7 the refrain of 'seek the Lord and live' is heard again, expressing a hope that repentance might be possible and judgement averted.

The particular threat here is the judgement of fire against the 'house of Joseph'. The focus is the shrine of Bethel, which has particular connections with the tribe descended from Joseph, the same shrine founded by Abraham when he rested there on his journey from Haran to Israel (see Chapter 8). These outlying shrines easily became places where idolatry and worship of Baal, a god of thunder, was perpetrated. It was hard for the central priestly administration in Jerusalem to keep an eye on them all and so the worship they accommodated quickly fell into malpractice. So the judgement is a matter both of cultic impropriety and the corresponding ethical code that should go with correct observance. Justice and righteousness, the two key virtues stressed over and over again in the Prophets, are being compromised, just as the ownership of the shrine itself is compromised.

The inhabitants of Israel do not take kindly to the prophet's chastisement, and through him, that of God. Those who dare to speak out in reproof receive criticism and the person who dares to speak the truth is shunned. The reason is that those perpetuating misdeeds do not wish to examine their consciences. The social sins committed are listed – the wealthy and powerful trample on the poor, and this cannot continue. They have built grand houses to live in, but the coming judgement is such that they will not be able to live in them. They have planted vineyards hoping for the fruit of the vine to give them wine, but they will not see that day. God is going to judge.

The issue of morality looms large here. What is the motivation for doing right? Israel are said to have transgressed all decent behaviour – a kind of universal law, even though specific transgressions of the law have taken place too. God notices the sins committed because nothing escapes God's all-seeing eye. The righteous are afflicted by the unrighteous. Bribery is rife and the needy are ignored. The whole atmosphere is one of distrust and evildoing. It is the kind of time when those who are right-thinking have to lie low as they are in danger of being sought out and punished. This sounds very familiar in the modern context, where often good people live in fear of their lives for no other reason than that they are the few who hold on to what they believe to be right.

The passage ends on the positive note of 'seek good'. The reward for good behaviour is nothing less than life itself. The exhortation is to opt for life and receive the support of God. Seeking good means hating evil and actively working against it. Once the society has a moral underpinning where justice is paramount, then the whole will become ordered and people can live their lives in peace. There may only be a small number of the tribe of Joseph left to receive God's blessing by the end of the process, but they will be a faithful remnant and will receive what God has promised.

God's concern for his people Israel is evident in the prophetic writings, but in fact there is also an increasing concern for other nations. The last chapter of Amos, although it is primarily about the restoration of Israel, speaks of 'all the nations who are called by my name',[4] and this theme is taken up in Second Isaiah with sentiments such as, 'I will give you as a light to the nations, that my salvation may reach to the end of the earth' (Isa. 49.6) and 'turn to me and be saved all the ends of the earth' (Isa. 45.22). This is an unfolding theme as far as Israel is concerned and demonstrates the point made earlier about the development of ideas. In early times the people were not even sure whether there was just one God, or simply one God – Yahweh – for them. But gradually they realized that their God was the one and only God, creator of the world and a God for all peoples and nations. Hand in hand with this emergent monotheism was universalism, a gradual realization that God had purposes for all nations, even if Israel was his 'first love'. By the time of the later prophets, such as Zechariah, there is a scheme of world history in mind, coupled with a cosmic and other-worldly view of God that would have been unthinkable to the earliest prophets and writers of the Old Testament.

Another idea that developed over time was that of covenant. We have already seen how the Ten Commandments establish the covenant relationship, laying down a set of stipulations as to how the people are expected to behave within their relationship with God. However, this idea is explored further in the Prophets, notably in the eighth-century prophet Hosea with his idea of the relationship between God and humans as a marriage. Hosea is told to take a prostitute as his wife, and it is with her that he has children. He is told to 'Go, love a woman who has a lover and is an adulteress, just as the LORD loves the people of Israel, though they turn to other gods and love raisin cakes' (Hos. 3.1). This is likened to God's relationship with Israel – Israel was lost and wayward, like a prostitute, but God rescued her and made her a beautiful bride (cf. Ezek. 16). One of Hosea's main concerns is with the tendency of the people to go after other gods, or to pollute the Yahweh cult with practices that are associated with other gods, particularly with Baal of the Canaanite pantheon. So he says, looking forward to a future time of good relationship, 'On that day, says the LORD, you will call me "My husband" and no longer will you call me "My Baal"' (Hos. 2.16).

Hosea goes on to speak of making a covenant with Israel, not this time in the language of the law but in that of creation:

> I will make for you a covenant on that day with the wild animals, the birds of the air, and the creeping things of the ground; and I will abolish the bow, the sword, and the war from the land; and I will make you lie down in safety. (2.18)

This shows how closely integrated are ideas about God's creative power and the distinctive covenant with Israel, a further indication of the broader remit of God's concern. It is not a narrow relationship with one people; these people are a paradigm for relationship that has a wider concern to include animals, birds, even creepy-crawlies! Hosea then expresses God's hope that 'I will take you for my wife for ever ... in righteousness and in justice, in steadfast love and in mercy' (v. 19). These are high ideals and show the true nature of God's love in relationship.

Judgement and pathos in Jeremiah and Ezekiel

Of course much of the prophetic material contains notes of judgement, and that is often what people remember. The sad fact is that the Israelites did not adhere to the covenant relationship in the way that God wanted – they were always going off the straight and narrow and forging their own paths, especially when it came to the attractions of the worship of other gods. God's only option was to announce punishment in order to try ultimately to bring Israel back. The book of the prophet Jeremiah contains much that is judgement – he uses images of war and pillaging armies. But throughout his prophecy there is a real sense of the pathos of God, who does not really want to be carrying out this punishment – he wants a real relationship, as set out in Hosea. The prophet himself takes on much of the burden of the punishment. He says, as the mouthpiece of God,

> My joy is gone, grief is upon me, my heart is sick. Hark, the cry of my poor people from far and wide in the land . . . For the hurt of my poor people I am hurt, I mourn and dismay has taken hold of me. (Jer. 8.18–19, 21)

He continues, 'Oh that my head were a spring of water, and my eyes a fountain of tears, so that I might weep day and night for the slain of my poor people!' (9.1). This is the hurt of the wounded husband who loves his wife but has seen her go to another man and treat him badly. God's hurt is felt here by the prophet and he conveys it most powerfully. God has to punish this wrongdoing, despite his love, because it is the only way to bring the nation back to him.

Part of the imagery employed concerns the land – the effect of rampaging armies, sieges and war also makes itself felt on the land itself. We have already encountered promises about the land and discussed how problematic they are for our modern ideas of land rights.[5] The Prophets were very aware of the importance of the promised land for Israel and appalled at the people's lack of concern for it. Now that they possessed what they had so desired, they took it for granted. This is a particular theme in the prophet Ezekiel, who has a famous vision of dry bones in a desolate land (Ezek. 37). He envisions God bringing humans and land back to life after the near-fatal neglect that is the effect of turning away from God. His vision is one of renewal, of new life, of a revived relationship after judgement.

Ezekiel also moves prophecy on to a new plane: he has visions and psychosomatic experiences that enable him to translocate and see events happening in another place. He is a strange character as a prophet and some of his imagery, especially female imagery relating to the idea of the harlot Israel, can be unpalatable.[6] He too, though, has visions of hope, such as the dry bones prophecy. He sees his own role as that of 'watchman' – watching on God's behalf, observing events unfold as the judgement of Exile becomes a reality. He is able to interpret his visions, and so when it comes to the reclothing of the dry bones with flesh and the breathing of life into those bodies again, he comments:

> Then he [God] said to me, 'Mortal, these bones are the whole house of Israel. They say "Our bones are dried up, and our hope is lost; we are cut off completely." Therefore prophesy, and say to them, Thus says the LORD GOD; I am going to open your graves, and bring you up from your graves, O my people; and I will bring you back to the land of Israel. And you shall know that I am the LORD . . . I will put my spirit within you and you shall live, and I will place you on your own soil; then you shall know that I, the LORD, have spoken and will act, says the LORD.' (Ezek. 37.11–14)

This is a highly surprising passage. It suggests that God has power over life and death and can restore life if he wills. The idea is radical for the Old Testament, which as a rule does not contain ideas of resurrection or life after death. It again conveys the point that God really wants to be in a good relationship with Israel and beyond, and he will do everything he can to achieve that aim, even conquering death.

Jonah's fish

There are many minor prophets, and there is no space to discuss many of them here – one more example will have to suffice. Another children's Bible favourite is Jonah, that strange tale of a reluctant prophet who runs away from God when asked to proclaim God's word. Running away is not the usual reaction of a faithful prophet![7] The book of Jonah

The Prophets

illustrates clearly that the message of a redeeming God is becoming universal, in that Jonah is sent to the Ninevites to call them to repentance, whereupon, surprisingly (and unlike Israel), they all repent. This leads God to keep his word and save them from their planned punishment: 'When God saw what they did, how they turned from their evil ways, God changed his mind about the calamity that he had said he would bring upon them; and he did not do it' (Jonah 3.10). We might ask why God changed his mind in this situation but not in others, such as the calamity of the Flood.

Perhaps the most famous aspect of Jonah that we know from wonderful illustrations in our children's Bibles is the incident when Jonah is swallowed up by a big fish (usually depicted as a whale), has time to utter a psalm and then is spewed out again. Here, as in the early chapters of Genesis, we are back in the realm of myth. This raises the further question of how far we are to take narratives about the doings of prophets literally and how far some are intended to be symbolic. For example, did Jeremiah really walk around in nothing but a loincloth? Was he shut up in a cistern for his message? And did Ezekiel literally perform all the strange actions attributed to him, such as lying on his side for a year and parting and cutting his hair? There is probably a good deal of licence, both narrative and poetic, in the shaping of these stories; they are stories that grew in the telling.

Perhaps the main narrative point of Jonah's 'symbolic' interaction with the fish is that it gives him some 'time out' to reflect. He is thrown into the sea at his own command when a storm gets out of control and the sailors panic. The incident leads the men to faith – 'Then the men feared the LORD even more, and they offered a sacrifice to the LORD and made vows' (Jonah 1.16) – and it causes a crisis of faith for Jonah, causing him to lament his plight and ask for deliverance: 'As my life was ebbing away, I remembered the LORD; and my prayer came to you, into your holy temple' (2.7). It is a colourful corner of the Old Testament and has a profound message: peoples, individuals and nations are offered the chance to repent and to come to God afresh.

First Isaiah (Isa. 1—39)

Since much of the message of First Isaiah is one of judgement, it might be surprising to us that Isaiah is so popular among Christians. At the time of the prophet in the eighth century BCE, there was a massive threat from the Assyrian armies who threatened to overcome the nation Israel. In that context Isaiah speaks the language of war, with God as the one designating the judgement as punishment for sin. Israel has not lived up to the stipulations of the covenant relationship. Society is in a shambles morally: miscarriages of justice occur, while some individuals are treated poorly by others. For Isaiah, social hierarchy was a given – society would be chaotic if people forgot their place and tried to overreach themselves. For him, the rich had a duty to protect the poor and the poor a duty to respect their betters. At the heart of his message is trust in God (Isa. 30.15). He speaks of stillness, and of being open to receive God's word in the face of a good deal of 'rushing around' and warmongering.

Isaiah's God, as described in the account of his call, is an awesome presence. Isaiah has a vision of God in the Temple, God on a throne with only the edge of his robe seen by the prophet, God accompanied by angels. This is for him a frightening experience – a theophany of God that makes the threshold shake and is perceived through the smoke of incense.[8] Isaiah also advocates humility, both in the face of this awesome God and also in the context of war. Better to wait and see what God has planned for the nation, he says, than to rush around making short-term alliances or worshipping empty idols. Isaiah was in favour of taking a long-term perspective. Trusting in God was about being in a relationship for the duration, whatever ups and downs that might bring.

Much of First Isaiah is presented in the words of God, using the first person (I) of prophetic utterance. A few sections, however, notably chapters 20 and 36—39, are third-person narratives, relating historical events of the time. There is some overlap of 36—39 with the book of Kings in which Isaiah is also mentioned, an overlap that suggests a common (Deuteronomistic) editorial hand. Another section of First Isaiah – chapters 24—27 – is also of an individual nature; often known as the 'little apocalypse', it is thought to have been added later, as the sentiments do not fit well with Isaiah's own.

We need to be cautious of carving up First Isaiah too much, given that at a later time the prophecy was conceived as a whole. Awareness of layers of authorial redaction, however, can help us to understand the nature of biblical books and their often complex construction over many years. Indeed First Isaiah has the nature of a compendium, where material is added and updated as the context changes, and this process continues as the book of Isaiah reaches its final form over a long period of years.

Isaiah 1.1–20

Isaiah 1.1–20 as the opening to the entire book of Isaiah raises some interesting points and introduces us to many key aspects of the message of First Isaiah as the focal prophet. Isaiah 1.1–2a is arguably an introduction to the book of Isaiah in its final edited form – it is a vision of God speaking to the prophet and to humanity, ostensibly in a single context but with broader thematic links that go beyond it: 'The vision of Isaiah son of Amoz, which he saw concerning Judah and Jerusalem in the days of Uzziah, Jotham, Ahaz and Hezekieh, kings of Judah. Hear, O heavens, and listen, O earth; for the LORD has spoken...'[9] First Isaiah is put into his historical context according to the formula of using the names of kings (as found throughout the Deuteronomistic history, although in this case only the kings of Judah), and then calls for all to listen – not just humans but also the created world (the earth) and beyond (the heavens).[10] We might compare this introduction with that of the Song of Moses in Deuteronomy (Deut. 31.28; 32.1 – see Chapter 8) where heaven and earth are called on as witnesses in the same way, suggesting that this is a standard introduction of some kind.[11] We are told both of the authority of the prophet in giving a vision and of the divine authority of his words. Strictly speaking, a vision means a divine revelation received by a human but originating outside him; here the word has a wider remit that includes all the prophet's activity, signs and messages alike. This tension between the prophetic voice and God's voice characterizes all prophetic utterances. The immediate historical context grounds the message in its time, but the vision moves beyond an immediate context to a bigger drama directed by God, a drama that will be continued in the later parts of the book of Isaiah by fresh prophetic voices.

Then, from 1.2b to verse 6, the tone of First Isaiah is set. The mood is one of judgement. In verse 2b we get the sense of God as a father who has reared his children with all the tender care of a parent (cf. Ezek. 16). Israel are God's children, his chosen people, and yet they have rebelled against him. In verse 3 a brief parable is used – 'the ox knows its owner and the donkey its master's crib', but Israel no longer knows God.[12] The actions of the people speak louder than words (v. 4). They are already estranged from 'the Holy One of Israel', a common designation of Isaiah's for God.

The holiness of God and his desire for purity in worship is another theme of Isaiah. The following verses (5–8) indicate that some punishment has already taken place.[13] There is talk of 'further beatings' and mention of 'bruises and sores and bleeding wounds' that have not been healed. Critics of the Old Testament would perhaps see this as evidence of a violent God inflicting physical ill upon his own people, but the point here is that it is regarded in context as a chastisement for sins committed. It is all about the covenant relationship and the need for a corrupt people to offer proper respect to God, who wants neither to chastise nor to feel distant. The reality falls far short of the ideal.

This message is also in the context of war. There is talk of the land being desolate and the cities burnt. It is foreign armies who have done this – although they are perceived by the prophet as a deliberate punishment from God, with God using other nations to effect his purposes. In verse 8 only Zion – here another name for Jerusalem, referring explicitly to the holy hill – remains as a small area that has not been overcome. The people are indeed rejoicing because the judgement has not affected their holiest of sites and so there has been some deliverance (v. 9) – but their rejoicing, says First Isaiah, is misplaced. They need to learn from this. The message is to make clear that God's own people have sinned and have become distant from God. They have incurred a punishment that has come right to their door. There is a fresh call, then, to a new repentance and acknowledgement of their sin.

The people of Israel are then called to 'Hear the word of the LORD' (v. 10). The language of Sodom and Gomorrah is parodied, echoing verse 9 – these are bywords for sinfulness. This is what the rulers of Israel have become – as sinful as these nations! Isaiah 1.10–17 speaks of corrupt worship – people are going through the motions of sacrifice without the right heart to accompany the gestures. The prophet speaks out against such rituals, saying that they have 'become a burden' to God. The priestly rituals are under attack – what good is ritual without the right heart to accompany it? God has stopped listening (v. 15).

God calls the people to purify themselves outside and in and to 'cease to do evil, learn to do good, seek justice, rescue the oppressed, defend the orphan, plead for the widow' (1.16–17). The prophet's call is for social justice, and this points the way to deliverance. In 1.18–20 an ultimatum is provided, offering two alternatives. First, there is the possibility of redemption through repentance: 'though your sins are like scarlet, they shall be like snow' (v. 18). God wants to restore the right relationship, he wants to forgive, he does not want to inflict more punishment: 'if you are willing and obedient, you shall eat the good of the land' (v. 19). Land and wellbeing are closely associated. And yet, the second option is punishment: 'if you refuse and rebel, you shall be devoured by the sword' (v. 20). This is a God of power, a God who is not afraid to judge and punish. This is a mighty and holy God who wants a relationship of peace, of mutual trust and respect with his people, but an essential part of that might is that God is not afraid to punish where it is needed. Once again, the reality is often in conflict with the ideal.

Second Isaiah (Isa. 40—55)

In second Isaiah there are notes of thanksgiving and salvation and, at times, a fresh universalism that seems to embrace all nations. Within the first few verses of the prophecy of Second Isaiah, the tone changes from judgement to hope: 'Speak tenderly to Jerusalem, and cry to her that she has served her term, that her penalty is paid, that she has received from the LORD's hand double for all her sins' (Isa. 40.2). The message here is that Israel has not only suffered enough, but has suffered more than she deserved.

That is a new and radical thought. Judgement is usually measured and meted out accordingly; here we find the idea of a kind of suffering that goes beyond such measuring. It opens the door to the idea of an individual servant who might suffer more than others and on behalf of others, even of the whole nation (as explored in the servant song passages).[14]

In Isaiah 40 we have an introduction to and commissioning of the prophet, not in the nature of the introduction to First Isaiah and the whole book, but in more veiled terms. We are told that a voice cries out 'in the wilderness, prepare the way of the LORD'.[15] The message here is that God is coming, this time to deliver. The language of nature is used: make a highway in the desert, lift up every valley, bring low mountains and hills. God can overturn nature itself in his actions: 'the uneven ground shall become level, and the rough places a plain' (Isa. 40.4). The normal and the usual become changed and transformed. It is all ascribed to the 'mouth of the LORD', the same formula used of the judgement in Isaiah 1.20. The message is one of hope – the people are reminded of their impermanence (40.6) but in contrast with the eternal word of God. This time Zion will become the place from which 'good tidings' (v. 9) will be broadcast.

The context here is the return of the people from exile to Jerusalem, and the imagery portrays God at the head of the procession. There are images of a mighty God (v. 10), of a rewarding God (v. 10b) and of a nurturing God, likened to a shepherd herding his flock and even carrying the lambs in his arms. This kind of imagery is why Second

Isaiah has been very popular with Christians from early times to this day.

Isaiah 44.1–6

Let us turn to another specific passage. Isaiah 44.1–6 begins with an oracle of salvation. The assurance of salvation is given to Israel in terms linking the people and the land completely together: 'Do not fear . . . I will pour water on the thirsty land and streams on the dry ground' (vv. 2–3). A new era of salvation is announced for the descendants of the generation of the Exile; after a summary of the past, the prophet speaks of Israel's future, which God will intervene to secure. Natural imagery is used: 'they shall spring up like a green tamarisk, like willows by flowing streams' (v. 4). These are two interweaving images of increase. One is a metaphor of trees, both springing up and nourished by water because they are growing beside streams; it foretells the increase of the descendants of the exiles in the fruitful land. The other prophesies an increase in the numbers of worshippers of Yahweh, like the burgeoning number of different types of trees, due to the accession of non-Israelites – individuals of other nations who can turn to Israel's God and join in their worship. The passage continues with the gods of other nations 'on trial', in response to which God is concerned to show their utter nothingness. God has acted in history on behalf of his people and God is also the powerful Creator-God: 'I am the first and I am the last; besides me there is no god' (v. 6).

The vision is of great hope, expressed in lofty poetic language: 'For thus says the LORD, who created the heavens (he is God!) who formed the earth and made it (he established it . . .) I am the LORD . . . I the LORD speak the truth, I declare what is right' (Isa. 45.18–19). The character of God emerges

The Prophets

here as righteous, loving justice and truth, fair and with a desire to be worshipped from far and wide: 'To me every knee shall bow, every tongue shall swear' (Isa. 45.23b).

I have tried to show in this chapter a little of the diversity of the prophetic word. There is both judgement and promise within the pages of the prophetic books and an ambivalent picture of God: on the one hand as judge and punisher, on the other as desirous of a relationship of obedience, respect and love. Many images – parent, shepherd, Holy One – are used of God. The overwhelming impression is of fairness – yes, God smites, but he does not do so without cause, without provocation or without any thought for his people. There is a moral aspect to this understanding – perhaps these are the kinds of texts that Dawkins should have been looking for if he was seeking morality. God is concerned for the poor and the oppressed, for the widow and the orphan; God wants to promote a just society, punishing greedy rulers and protecting the innocent and the oppressed. This is a message of morality for us today, in that it easily translates into our contemporary world and priorities. The picture of God is also more accessible to us. God experiences loss, pathos, anger – all emotions with which we, as human beings, are familiar. God, like us, thrives on hope for the future and wishes to wipe away every tear (Rev. 21.4, echoing Isa. 25.8).

Let us turn back now to the Pentateuch and historical books to complete our overview of the Old Testament canon and see if we might find a few more inspiring passages than we encountered in the early chapters of this book.

8

Back to the Pentateuch and historical books: the power of story

While in previous chapters I have contextualized and explained some of the most difficult passages in the Old Testament, I feel now that I need to go back to the Pentateuch and the historical books to show that this is not the last word on such a rich group of texts. An alternative selection can give a very different picture from the one painted by our two New Atheists. As well as dipping into some rather different texts, we need to understand the broader context of key themes and the development of ideas across these books. This will help us to understand the broader context of Israel's narrative.

In the Pentateuch and historical books I would argue that the overriding genre is that of story. While the Old Testament gives us a grand narrative from primeval times through to the years of foreign domination after the Israelite Exile, there are also many hundreds of smaller, self-contained stories, the pieces that combine to make the whole. These can be read, and very often are, as individual tales (which often contain their own 'point'), or as part of wider cycles about a particular character or period of history, or they can be placed within that broader chronological sweep and cross-comparisons between them can be made. This is another element of the diversity and scope of the Old Testament. In this section, then, I hope to show

Myth and history in Genesis

I have already discussed the nature of Genesis 1—11 as a collection of myth and origin stories. Another episode we might have chosen is that of the Tower of Babel in Genesis 11.1–9. This is not an easy story once we begin to explore it. Once again it is a myth (possibly loosely based on the historical existence of high towers (ziggurats) in Babylonian culture) designed to illustrate a fact of life – that there are many different languages around the world.

This text tries to explain the phenomenon of language. It is in a sense also a second 'fall' narrative – it is about human pride overreaching itself and being called to account. Just as Adam and Eve ate from the tree of knowledge of good and evil thinking that they would become 'like God' (Gen. 3.4), so the inhabitants of Babel construct a tower reaching to the heavens to try to 'make a name' for themselves. God's verdict in both cases is that this act is beyond his purpose for humankind; in this second story God says 'this is only the beginning of what they will do; nothing that they propose to do will now be impossible for them' (Gen. 11.6). And so the consequence is the 'confusion of their language', so that instead of speaking one language, they speak many and cannot understand one other. They are then scattered widely and all thought of building the tower is forgotten.

The story is not then to be taken literally – it is a kind of parable. One might object that it seems to diminish human achievement and curiosity; we like to think as a race that 'nothing we do is impossible' for us. The story, though, is making the theological point that God has a purpose and a plan and that human arrogance in trying to anticipate that plan or take charge of matters is not acceptable to God. Furthermore, we might have a problem with the fact that the very positive aspects of the kind of diversity that we see in the existence of many languages are here diminished by the idea that such diversity was actually a punishment from God. This is not an easy text for our modern values.

In the context of the primeval history, though, the primary message across these paradigm stories is one of God's provision, and of human pride in challenging the call to trust and obey. It could be said that this is simply an aspect of being human – pride tends to dominate over humility, while acceptance and obedience are qualities that are difficult to master. This story, like the others in this section, is about relationship and, even from the earliest times, there was an uneasy jostling for position between God and humanity.

In theological terms, the opening chapters of Genesis take us straight to the doctrine of creation, a key theme within the Old Testament.[1] This theme is linked to the equally important theme of covenant in Genesis 9, where a covenant is made between God and Noah after the Flood.[2] This is God's promise that the created world and all who inhabit it will never again be blighted in this way by a flood. It involves new stipulations regarding the relationship between humans and animals, specifically regarding the treatment of animals and the eating of meat prepared in a certain way. It also mentions the idea of the sanctity of human life (contra Hitchens, this is in fact the first time a prohibition against murder appears in the Old Testament). The covenant here is not simply with Noah and his sons, it is with the human race, with animals too, and with the earth itself (which has led to some interesting ecological readings).[3] This is a departure from the earlier portrayal of the first human beings as vegetarians, of the paradisal harmony between human and animal worlds that is lost after the Fall. In Genesis 9 there is a feeling of compromise – a necessary one, perhaps, to define new boundaries to the relationship between God and humans. The rainbow is a sign of God's promise.

Although this Genesis 9 narrative was probably written by priestly writers in the exilic period, the covenant with Noah is presented as being made at a key moment in the unfolding of the 'young' relationship between God and humanity. Perhaps unsurprisingly after the purge of the Flood, the emphasis also falls on the importance of progeny and the continuation of the human race, and this is a theme that will be taken up more specifically in Israel's story, beginning in Genesis 12.

We then arrive at Genesis 12 with Abraham, 'where it all started'.[4] The idea of a covenant is now narrowed down to a particular individual in a particular time. While we might regard Noah as a symbolic character,[5] this is where the history of Israel claims to begin. There may be much about the account of Abraham that we wish to take with a historical pinch of salt. But there is a fundamental difference in the presentation here. The Old Testament perceives such characters to be historical and makes reference back to the ancestors, 'Abraham, Isaac and Jacob', time after time.

This ancestral presentation is the historical timeline presented by the Old Testament. We can choose not to take it at face value (cf. Chapter 6): there were probably many stories around that eventually came together in the synthesis in which we have them today; there may well have been different tribal stories, different cycles of stories around the same ancestor, and oral tradents that gradually came together into longer tales. We can catch glimpses of these processes, for example, by noting the very different character of Jacob in different tales, as usurper in one and patient labourer in another.[6] But we have no certainty about the antecedents of the text. The only solid ground we have is the text itself, and the text presents these tribal ancestor stories to us in a very different way from the myth that preceded them.

Genesis 28.10–19

I want to consider a particular text in Genesis that is rather different from the ones previously examined. Genesis 28.10–19 relates Jacob's dream of a ladder reaching from the ground to heaven, with the angels of God going up and down upon it. Jacob remembers the dream on waking up and knows that in this dream God has spoken to him. On waking, he acts on the dream and sets up a sanctuary in a desolate place to denote that God has been present there. This sanctuary of Bethel was to become one of the key sites for early Israel in the north of the country for many hundreds of years. In some ways this is another explanation story – it is designed to explain the appearance of the shrine of Bethel.

In this narrative Jacob, son of Isaac, is alone, having left home for the first time. On his journey he is unable to find a bed for the night, perhaps because of the remoteness of the place. He makes the best of the situation by using rocks for a pillow and, so tired is he after the journey, he falls asleep. In his dream he sees the heavenly realm opened up before him, with angels riding the ladder and God at its head. When God speaks to Jacob he introduces himself as one and the same God who appeared to Abraham and Isaac.

This is an expression of continuity, as we often find in the patriarchal narratives, intended to establish that this is the same God, Yahweh, acting for various tribes and individuals in a consistent way that will build up into a cohesive and coherent history of God's concern for his people. The function of the angels is hard to know – they are possibly watchers of humans, patrolling the earth (an idea found in

Gen. 48.15–16; Job 1–2), or even guardians or protectors of certain individuals (cf. Ps. 91.11–12). It is certain that they are also participating in the adoration of God, and part of the wonder of the heavenly realm.

The climax of the passage is the promise of land and descendants to Jacob/Israel, the same made to Abraham and Isaac. The promise includes the idea that all nations will ultimately find blessing through this small sample of Israelites. An additional pledge is made to Jacob here, that 'I am with you' to protect you. The same promise is made subsequently to other key leaders such as Moses (Exod. 3.12), Joshua (Josh. 1.5) and Gideon (Judg. 6.16),[7] and was given to the outcast Cain in Genesis 4. Likewise, God undertakes to protect his people in Numbers 6.24 in the famous priestly blessing 'The LORD bless you and keep you'. Jacob is also told that he will return to his homeland, a promise that is kept, although it takes twenty years to realize.

A key element of the story of the Israelites is not simply God's promises to human beings but their response, in relationship. Here Jacob has had a direct encounter with God for the first time. He chastises himself for not having realized sooner the holiness of this spot, but soon recognizes the truth and significance of what he has seen. He wonders, in the light of seeing the ladder, whether this is indeed some kind of gateway to heaven. He uses the same stones that afforded him comfort as a makeshift pillow to build an altar, choosing the largest stones for the purpose and consecrating the place with oil.

The naming of the place is an important point of recognition of God's presence in it. Bethel, meaning 'with God', replaces the old name of the place, Luz. Naming of sanctuaries in this way is frequent in the early history of Israel, and is essentially part of the process of gradually assimilating the land of another nation into Israel. Whether the integration of Canaanites and Israelites was ultimately a peaceful one, as some scholars believe, or whether it was a more hostile affair, as the Old Testament seems to witness, is a point for discussion (see Chapter 6).

Genesis 29.15–28

One issue in the Old Testament on which I have not touched so far is polygamy. In the culture of the time this was entirely acceptable, although keeping more than one wife was an expensive business and so was not embarked upon lightly. The reason multiple marriages were desirable was usually the need for offspring. It is not that love did not enter into the equation – there is evidence that it did, in this story as elsewhere – but there was a practical side to it too, in that a father had the duty of making sure his daughters were married to good suitors. There were clan loyalties to attend to, along with the exchange of money and gifts.

In this story Jacob, on discovering his relative Laban, falls in love with Rachel, Laban's younger daughter, having met her at the well when she is fetching water. He seeks her hand in marriage and asks Laban if he might work for him as his 'pay' for marrying her, thus binding himself in allegiance to Laban (cf. Exod. 22.15). Jacob is unable to ask his family for any bride money (cf. Deut. 22.29) and so has to offer his cumulative wages instead.

What Jacob fails to notice is that Laban never actually mentions Rachel in his reply to his marriage requests – Laban carefully refers to 'her' without specifying a name: 'It is better that I give her to you' he says, 'than that I should give her to any other man' (v. 19). Jacob thinks he is referring to Rachel but it is clear from what ensues that Laban has Leah, his eldest daughter, in mind for marriage. Thus Laban deceives Jacob into working for him, not for six years (the usual period of slave-debt – see Exod. 21.1–16; Deut. 15.12–18) but seven, for a bride that he has no intention of giving him. Or, more charitably, we might think that Laban is keeping his options open by giving a guarded reply and maybe hopes that a husband for Leah will emerge in the seven-year interim.

In any case, instead of Rachel, Jacob ends up on his wedding night with Leah, the older and less attractive sister. Leah has been brought to him under cover of darkness 'in the evening', and veiled as was the custom, so that Jacob does not realize the trickery until morning. Jacob's surprise shows in his disbelieving question, 'What is this that you have done to me?' (v. 25, cf. God's words to Eve in Gen. 3.13). He did not expect such treatment from his uncle after his loyal and hard work.

The question of Laban's motive arises here. Has he acted in this way because, as he himself states, giving away 'the younger before the firstborn' is not done, or is it because he wants to exploit Jacob, and get him to work for him for even longer? The jury is out on this question. The outcome is that Jacob is also given Rachel, but is bound to working for Laban for another seven years to secure her bride-price. In a sense it is lucky that in their world both wives can be accommodated; if Jacob had only one chance of a wife, as in modern times, then he would have been landed with Leah alone.

We are told throughout that, although Leah had nice eyes, Rachel was the attractive one, 'graceful and beautiful' (v. 17). Such is Jacob's keenness to be married to her that the seven years 'seemed to him but a few days because of the love he had for her' (v. 20). As soon as the time is up, he has to remind Laban of his promise: 'Give me my wife' (v. 21), he says, 'that I may go into her'. A blissful consummation is nigh. This is a good example of the Old Testament's lively narrative style – this story tells of trickery and deception, but also of true love and patience. There is an interesting comment too here on the way time becomes distorted for us – Jacob's love and ardour for Rachel makes time run fast, but time drags when one is parted from the object of one's desire or forced to work against one's will.

Against the wider backdrop of the story of Jacob, we might think that in this section he gets his 'comeuppance'. There is a certain poetic justice in the outcome, in that it was Jacob who previously tricked his father Isaac (Gen. 27.29–35) and stole his elder brother Esau's birthright (Gen. 25.27–34; 27). The deceiver has become the deceived. There is perhaps some divine justice at work here. Ironically, it turns out later that Leah is by far the more fertile of the two sisters, and so the promise made to Jacob of many descendants is largely fulfilled through her rather than her more attractive sister.

Joseph and his 'amazing Technicolor dreamcoat'[8]

Before leaving Genesis I wish briefly to mention the story of Joseph, which takes up a large chunk of the book (chs 37—50). This is very much a moral tale or 'example story', and perhaps provides a more nourishing text for consideration of ethical and relationship issues than many of the texts to which Dawkins and Hitchens draw our attention. It is, however, a narrative with many twists and turns, and it would be reductionist simply to read it for ethical instruction.

I am aware that, despite my best efforts, my retelling of the story here immediately loses the narrative detail that characterizes this piece – I encourage the reader to go away and read it at first hand (as with the other texts I have mentioned). In outline, however, it runs as follows: Joseph may have been a favourite of his father (and hence the recipient of an elaborate multicoloured coat) – he was intelligent and handsome – but that was not his fault. Life can be difficult for the handsome, clever offspring of a family. Jealousy grips his brothers and leads them to sell him to the Midianites, and to deceive their father into thinking that Joseph has died. Sold as a slave in Egypt, Joseph at first works in the house of Potiphar and demonstrates his loyal, hard-working character, to such an extent that he is promoted to overseer. It is Potiphar's wife who is Joseph's undoing – she attempts to seduce him and, when Joseph will not succumb, frames him and has Potiphar cast him into prison. When his prison companions have mysterious dreams he is able to interpret them, and so his reputation grows as a man who has a special connection to his God. This is very much a 'comeuppance' story, in that Joseph manages to rise from the most lowly position as a slave to the highest one, as the right-hand man of Pharaoh. It is another version of the 'rags to riches' tale that is a favourite type in the Old Testament (cf. that of David in 1 Sam. 16—17) for, despite the problems with Potiphar's wife, Joseph's God-given ability to interpret dreams leads him to become the one man that Pharaoh cannot do without (cf. Daniel in the court of the Babylonian king Nebuchadnezzar in Dan. 2).

One of the Old Testament's liveliest narratives, and another children's Bible favourite with the coat featuring prominently, comes to a satisfying conclusion with the brothers tricked in return by Joseph, who only later reveals his identity. This is a story, too, about forgiveness: the past is eventually laid to rest and Joseph can embrace his brothers (and his father) once more.

Exodus and liberation

Perhaps the most famous story of the Old Testament is that of the exodus – that great tale of liberation that has functioned as a paradigm for subsequent generations.[9] The tale is related in the books of Exodus and Deuteronomy and followed up in Joshua, the book centred on Moses' successor, who brought the entry of the land to completion. The figure of Moses looms large in the exodus – the Old Testament tells of his life from his discovery in a basket of reeds, his later challenge to Pharaoh and the liberation of his people from slavery, to his lawgiving and leadership during the wilderness wandering and his final denial of entry to the promised land – and I refer the reader to my discussion of the cycle elsewhere.[10]

The exodus tradition is not straightforward – God is very much on the side of the Israelites, and many Egyptians suffer in the process both in the plagues and in the drowning in the Red Sea. The story is presented in a triumphalist way that might offend modern sensibilities. It also contains miraculous elements such as the Red Sea crossing that perhaps needs to be interpreted symbolically or metaphorically. It is an example of the Old Testament view of God as acting simply for one nation, a primitive portrayal of God that changes over the Old Testament period but is not without its problems. And of course the promised land is no doubt 'a land flowing with milk and honey', but it is still someone else's land, and we would find that, too, deeply problematic.

Deuteronomy 32.1–4

One snippet of the Old Testament that I heard in church recently is this text from Deuteronomy. It is a prime example of hearing something out of context and not necessarily appreciating the wider picture (see Chapter 10). It takes the genre of a 'song', in this case a song from Moses performed in the hearing of the whole assembly of Israel, as revealed by the verse (Deut. 31.30) that precedes this passage. Of course it may not have actually emanated from Moses himself but might represent another strand of the tradition placed in his mouth, but either way this is its position in the text now. In some of its sentiments it might be mistaken for a psalm of praise and thanksgiving: 'I will proclaim the name of the LORD; ascribe greatness to our God! the Rock, his work is perfect and all his ways are just. A faithful God, without deceit, just and upright is he' (vv. 3–5). Another part of it sounds like teaching material, such as you might find in the wisdom tradition, 'Hear the words of my mouth. May my teaching drop like the rain, my speech condense like the dew; like gentle rain on grass, like showers on new growth' (vv. 1–2). And yet we find this passage in the book of Deuteronomy, in the context of the 'life of Moses'. This is a good example of the mixing of genres within certain texts that makes it hard to pigeonhole them into particular types.

In order to understand the passage we need to know the wider context – that it is a moment of reflection by Moses towards the end of his life, when he has been told (in ch. 31) that Joshua will be his successor after he has written up the law (Deuteronomy's particular emphasis) for posterity. This song then is part of Moses' legacy to his people. It is his praise of God and his teaching to the next generation of the ways of God and of God's relationship to his people, past, present and future. It culminates in Moses blessing all the tribes of Israel (ch. 33) and giving news of the granting of the promised land, in which the people will be able to settle, to put down roots, to multiply, to bring up their children in safety and till a fruitful land. The only sad and surprising news is that he, Moses, will not live to see it (cf. Chapter 4 of this book). This is a story told with pathos, exemplary of the power of biblical narrative at its best.

The story of Samson

As they were Dawkins' focus, I have already spent quite some time with Joshua and Judges, so I am going to mention only one other 'judge' here. This is Samson (Judg. 13—16).

There are problems with this story too – Samson is a rather self-interested person, a womanizer who treats women badly on the whole. He is a 'strong man' who acts before thinking and commits an act of appalling animal cruelty, tying together foxes' tails and setting them alight. He is chosen by God and given special status, but he abuses his favouritism and allows himself to be manipulated.

But for all this, he is an interesting figure and deserves to be better known. He is a man of great loyalty, particularly to his parents, who feature in a number of scenes, and to his wider tribe. Perhaps the most famous story about Samson is that of the cutting of his hair, set in the wider context of the ongoing battle between the Israelites and the Philistines. Samson is manipulated by Delilah, a seductress sent by the Philistines, into losing the source of his strength, so that he is easily caught.

Many of the stories in Judges are about 'one-upmanship' on one side or another – normally with a bias towards the Israelite side. The power of the account of Samson is emphasised by its techniques of repetition. In the sequence relating Delilah and the cutting of the hair she asks Samson repeatedly where the secret of his strength lies and how she might overcome it. At first Samson says, 'If they bind me with seven fresh bowstrings that are not dried out, then I shall become weak, and be like anyone else' (Judg. 16.7). So she arranges to do so and binds him up, although of course he snaps the bowstrings with ease, 'So the secret of his strength was not known.' The scene where Samson says that binding with ropes is the secret is then repeated; again Delilah organizes it, but 'he snapped the ropes off his arms like a thread' (16.12).

Finally he tells her something nearer the truth, that if his hair is bound into the loom and woven into the material, then he will be overpowered. But 'he awoke from his sleep, and pulled away the pin, the loom, and the web' (16.14). She accuses him of mockery and finally he tells her the truth – cut his hair and his strength will be gone. Delilah, we are told, realizes that this time what he has said is indeed the truth. Her repeated calls have worn Samson's resolve down, and so finally when the Philistines come he is trapped: 'So the Philistines seized him and gouged out his eyes.'

This is not a pretty ending, but the storyteller cleverly closes his tale on a small note of hope. As Samson sits bound in shackles and grinding the prison mill, 'the hair of his head began to grow again after it had been shaved' (Judg. 16.22). This is to anticipate the end of the story, when Samson's strength returns and he wipes out 3,000 Philistines at a stroke, dying himself in the process. Once again we are in the land of a violent Old Testament, the violence entailed on both sides in a war. But the story is told because God's and Israel's champion defies the odds and achieves success over an old enemy – that is, until next time ...

The historical books

It is very surprising that Dawkins did not engage with Samuel–Kings in his book, given that it constitutes the second half of the 'history', after the period of the judges, and is a climactic moment in the life of Israel. There are certainly unedifying texts to choose from in this section too (e.g. the smiting of Uzzah in 1 Sam. 4—5).[11] Here we have the history of the monarchy, starting with Saul and continuing with David and his line. Let us dive straight into a text to see what is going on at this stage in the unfolding Israelite tale.

1 Samuel 8.4–20; 11.14–15

Perhaps the most famous of the judges of Israel is the last, Samuel. This story tells of the moment when Israel's leaders, until then great individuals who often combined the roles of leader (judge) and prophet, became rulers with all the accoutrements of kingship. This was a 'revolution' for Israel, and it is presented by the author of 1 Samuel in an interesting if rather contradictory way. The desire for a king is seen as the choice of the people rather than that of God or Samuel. There is a real ambivalence here in the call for a monarchy.

The text tells us that the aged Samuel's sons are not suitable successors to their father, and that the elders of Israel know as much. They present the fact bluntly to Samuel, accompanying it with the demand for a king, the reason being given that Israel wishes to be 'like other nations'. Samuel, unsurprisingly, expresses immediate displeasure at the idea of a king, as it usurps his power and that of his offspring. The theological stance of the text is such, however, that Samuel, as God's spokesman, asks the Lord his opinion of this request.

God's reply in this context is somewhat unexpected. A straight answer is not forthcoming. God tells Samuel to listen to the voice of the people, but says that their request is in fact a rejection of God himself. God has been king in Israel until this point, and a human king would threaten that relationship. God seems to draw a direct parallel between the people's rejection of Samuel and their rejection of God. God is in effect telling Samuel not to take it personally. The heady days of the exodus from Egypt are brought to mind, but with the twist that God is now saying that from those times until now the people of Israel have let God down by worshipping other gods. The call for a king is in effect likened to idolatry. God is on Samuel's side here, but is offering sensible advice: that while Samuel should listen to the people – the power of the 'mob' being substantial and often ignored at one's peril – he should also warn them in advance so that if the kingship goes awry, he will avoid blame. Samuel is urged to list (as he does in vv. 12–15) all the things that might go wrong with a kingship. This list is thought to be based on the actual later experience of kingship, possibly on the problems of Solomon's reign, and so represents the (Deuteronomic) 'voice of hindsight'.

Kings need large forces of men to carry out both warfare and administration. Samuel warns that the people will find their sons and daughters commandeered for all kinds of tasks. Again, the people will find that their offspring do not follow in the footsteps they had planned for them, just as Samuel's sons have not done. Even the family slaves will be taken and put to work; the animals too. Indeed, a tithing system will mean that both people and goods will become the property of the king. Samuel suggests to the people that in the future they may regret this desire for a king and cry out for their freedom. It will be too late, though, by then, and in contrast to the past, God will not be listening. There is a threat here that the people are manoeuvring themselves on to the wrong path.

The voice of hindsight (thought by many scholars to be the work of a redactor), though, falls on deaf ears. When revolution and change are in the air, the last thing people want to hear is the voice of caution. The desire for change has an inexorable momentum of its own. The people refuse to listen to Samuel and express their determination to have a king. Another reason is now given – a king would fight their battles. Of course, this was already done by the judges, but in a more piecemeal, local way. A nation led by a king would embark on grand military exploits. One can see why the idea was appealing.

So both God and Samuel appear to 'back down'. The people have won the day – they have been listened to, they have been warned, but ultimately their persistence pays off.

1 Samuel 11.14–16 states that a king will now be anointed at Gilgal. That king will be Saul, with whom the story continues.

Saul and David

I have dealt elsewhere with the Saul cycle,[12] so here I wish to focus on David. Like Moses, the Old Testament gives us his entire life story, from his young days as a shepherd boy, the youngest son in a large family, to his slaying of Goliath with a mere pebble and his coming to the notice of both God and the king. The Saul cycle tells of the dynamic between Saul and David – a relationship of great friendship and love and yet undermined by a sense of rivalry, jealousy and flawed character on the part of Saul. David emerges the victor of that tale, but of course we have to take into account the role of the narrator in the telling of the story, a narrator trying to promote the interests of the Davidic line. Let us once more dive into a part of the narrative.

2 Samuel 6.1–5, 12–19

This is the story of David dancing before the ark of the covenant as it comes to its new abode in Jerusalem. His dancing is joyful and uninhibited, accompanied by music that sounds a note of praise. It is a day of rejoicing – David has just become king, and now is the moment to cement the union of palace and Temple with the bringing up to Jerusalem of the holiest object of the Israelite people – the ark, the case housing the tablets of the Ten Commandments, and hence the presence of God.

We are told that the 'chosen' men of Israel numbered 30,000, which may reflect poetic licence on the part of the narrator, who wishes to stress the significance of the event. Whatever the precise number, it was a significant occasion in the life of the nation. The ark had traditionally been taken around from place to place, as its power and presence was needed to help fight battles and establish power. Now, however, it was receiving a permanent resting place in Jerusalem; a new cart was even built for the occasion. The ark was an object of great potency and had to be treated with reverence, as one would treat God; before the development of the idea of a temple as the most appropriate place to worship God and be in the divine presence, it was God's abode. The building of a temple would be further down the line – the life work of David's son and successor, Solomon.

The ark rests for a while in the house of Abinadab 'on the hill', before arriving in the household of Obed-edom. It brings special blessing to all who keep it, but it also strikes down those who abuse it. Now it is on its way to Jerusalem, to the city of David, and the new king is in charge of its placement next to his palace, in a household of the highest honour. We are told that, as a gesture of obeisance and purification, David performed a sacrifice in front of the ark. He danced again, thinly clad, and there was much noise and rejoicing.

At this point in the story we are introduced to Michal, the daughter of Saul. She has reason to be bitter after her father's demise, although when we first meet her she loves David and shows loyalty to him over her father. When she looks out of her window to see the merrymaking David, she quietly despises him. Her love has turned to hate. She is described as first and foremost the daughter of Saul, which indicates that her relationship with David is ambivalent. Normally a woman would take on the name of her husband and be described first and foremost as his wife. However, although 1 Samuel 18.27 states that the pair are married, to which David also refers (2 Sam. 3.14), Michal has, after the passage of some absence from David, been given to another man as wife (1 Sam. 25.44). David asks for her back (2 Sam. 3), and he probably has a prior legal claim to her, although we are not told of the success of such a claim. Michal leaves her second husband, and we are told that his weeping figure can be seen following her as she goes on her way (2 Sam. 3.16), so it seems that he at least did love her – which cannot be said for David, who seems to use her as a political pawn. Michal will later criticize David's half-naked revelry to his face and suffer the punishment of barrenness for opposing the king.

The moment now comes when the ark arrives in the tent that has been set up in Jerusalem. This is not a permanent temple as yet, but it is a gesture towards permanence. More sacrifices are made and David blesses the people in God's name, sharing with them a covenant meal of plentiful food. The kingship seems now to be newly affirmed in David, and God is happy with divine representation on earth through this new dynasty. The negative thoughts about the kingship are gone and the Davidic line is set up.

The Old Testament's portrayal of David

The Old Testament is very positive about David as a warrior, as God's favourite, as a king and ultimately as a cultic leader – and of course one wonders whether he really was such a great hero, or whether he has been painted in a more favourable light than reality allowed.[13] Whatever the truth of the matter, this is the portrayal that we now have, and it is from this base that many of the great hopes about the Davidic dynasty grew, finally linking up with Jesus and the desire of the writers of the New Testament to connect Jesus to David's line (see Chapter 10). This is perhaps ironic in the light of the David and Bathsheba story, to which I will now turn.

David's weakness: 2 Samuel 11.1–15

Like Samson, David has a weakness for women. In the famous story in 2 Samuel 11 of his adultery with Bathsheba, the wife of Uriah, the person who suffers is Uriah, a faithful army warrior who is fighting David's wars for him at the very moment that David is eyeing up his wife.

War is being waged by David's commanders but unusually David has stayed at home in Jerusalem. In an idle moment, from his position on the palace roof, he catches sight of a woman bathing. In a hot climate, more of these activities would have taken place outdoors, so this would not be an unusual occurrence. We are simply told that the woman is 'very beautiful'. In this scene, David forgets his responsibilities and simply becomes a man ardent for a woman. He knows, though, that his position as king will help him to 'get her' and have his way with her with ease. Little does he know at this point in the story that his casual immorality will cost him dear.

We learn that Bathsheba has not long had her period and so is 'purifying herself' by washing. This makes David's act even more inappropriate – not only is this another man's wife, as he is told, but she is impure after a period, a time when women were not to be touched. This aside also tells us that she could not be already expecting a child. Of course, the inevitable happens and she becomes pregnant by David.

Now comes the climactic moment: David comes face to face with 'the husband', Uriah the Hittite. Will David own up and do the right thing? It seems not – and here the story takes an unusual turn. Joab, David's right-hand man and chief of his army, is instructed to bring Uriah to him. After a little small talk about the progress of the war (a wonderful dramatic 'pause'), David instructs Uriah to go home and wash his feet, following the order with a present. What is David's motivation for this gesture? Is he hoping that Uriah will lie with Bathsheba so that any possible pregnancy can be passed off as his? That David was conniving for Uriah to go home and have intercourse with Bathsheba seems the most likely answer; the reference to washing the feet may refer to a ritual that would undo the oath made at the start of the campaign (1 Sam. 21.4–5) to abstain from sexual relations. But Uriah is a worthy type – he will not renounce his promise while on active duty.

So David is already being portrayed in a negative light, on account first of the adultery and second of his plotting. Now it all goes from bad to worse: David's only solution to the problem is to plot the death of Uriah. In order to ensure that his adultery remains hidden, David goes to extreme lengths, effectively becoming a murderer. He commands Joab to put Uriah at the forefront of the fighting and leave him without military support so that he dies. No one will then suspect anything and David can go on to marry Bathsheba and have a child with her. Problem solved, but at what moral cost?

This story clearly illustrates how one mistake can lead on to another with sometimes devastating consequences. A casual slip in morality results in an unwanted pregnancy, to the cuckolding of a husband and ultimately to treachery and the loss of the perpetrator's moral character. It shows us that even 'great men' have their failings and that one immoral act often leads to others. This passage could well be classified in Dawkins' category of difficult texts, from which taking home a moral point might be problematic. Here we have one of the greatest Israelite heroes behaving frankly abominably. Where is God in all this?

God is remarkably absent from the tale. In general God seems to condone David's behaviour in that David has raised up his kingly line over all others. And yet this tale shows that there is ambivalence in that choice, just as there was ambivalence with the choice of Moses. These characters are not monochrome and neither is God's relationship with them.

Chronicles, Ezra and Nehemiah

Perhaps it is little wonder that the books of Chronicles omit the tale told above of David and Bathsheba – their author's aim was to portray David in an idealistic light as the great warrior and temple-builder. But which account is the more honest? Which account do we as Bible readers prefer? Do we prefer to know about David even in his less moral moments, such as the encounter with Bathsheba, another man's wife? Or do we prefer to remember him without these failings as the great king and template for the Messiah that he later became? I have discussed elsewhere the portrayal of David by the Chronicler,[14] which offers a fascinating insight into the way the same 'story' is told a second time from a different perspective. This shows us that the storyteller has an agenda – how a story is written, how a narrative is presented, what is emphasized and what is not is absolutely key to the message or messages that any reader will take home from it. This, combined with the reader's bias itself, is the way the process of 'reading' unfolds.

There is, too, the related question of history. I said earlier that it is with Abraham in Genesis 12 that the 'history' of Israel really begins. And yet that history is so infused with story and other traditions that there is a question about the historicity of all these accounts. While I do not believe that they are built on falsehood, poetic licence has no doubt been taken. The authors of the Old Testament have gone to some trouble to provide us with a chronology, largely in the way that genealogies are included to contextualize people with regard to the tribal relationships of Israel. The Chronicler is particularly fond of genealogies which help him to make connections between the tribes of old and of his own time. People as well as events are linked in a grand master plan. One can of course compare the information in the Old Testament with annals from the ancient world that relate the same events, and when this has been done considerable overlap has been found (see Chapter 6). However, other nations wrote up their 'histories' with the same kind of bias – no account of any historical event is ever bias-free.

Ezra is another key figure in the history of Israel. These later historical books are set in the period after the Exile, when Israel had returned to her land, although still under foreign rulers. Two strands of thought were appearing: the first, as represented by Jonah (see Chapter 7) and Ruth (Chapter 6) was a more universal strain that began to see God in monotheistic terms as the one God of the whole world, with a concern for all peoples and their ultimate salvation; the second was a more particular and nationalistic strain of thought – the feeling among the beleaguered Israelites (now usually referred to as Jews) that they needed to consolidate, to tighten their family and national identities, to mark themselves off as different from others by their rules and customs such as circumcision, Sabbath-keeping and ritual food laws. They were a people returning from exile into a country that was no longer theirs, and yet with a mandate from a generous ruler who would allow them to worship their own God and keep their own laws. They needed to build a temple, for which money was provided – a desire that came to fruition only after many delays and frustrations.

It is into this world that Ezra and Nehemiah came. Ezra is the one with the mandate from the king of Persia to work out the details of a fresh start for the Jews now that they are back in the land. He is the first 'scribe' to consolidate the law – and much of the law may have been finalized at this time or just before in the priestly material of the Pentateuch. Ezra presented the written scroll to the people with great rejoicing and much proclamation. This law authorized edicts regarding the cohesion of the people, united as they were in their distinctive worship in the Temple of their God. One aspect of the law was generosity to the poor and needy, as enshrined in Exodus (in particular in the book of the covenant in Exod. 20—24) and Deuteronomy, and taken up in this period by the prophet Zephaniah (Zeph. 2.3). Both Ezra and Nehemiah worked in Jerusalem in the fifth century BCE. Nehemiah was a governor of the city and helped to consolidate Ezra's work. His particular remit was the rebuilding of the walls of Jerusalem, which itself provoked friction and opposition. This account is not all positive for modern sensibilities – there was a problem at the time with mixed marriages (whether racial or religious), and so people were told to unmarry their 'foreign wives' and remarry within their own cultural group. An unattractive form of xenophobia was evident at this period – understandable perhaps in the light of the need to consolidate and protect the Jews' own people and in the light of laws regarding purity and separateness, but surprising in the light of the more universal understanding of God that was beginning to emerge.

Concluding remarks

It has been very hard to try to characterize the Old Testament in three chapters, even to decide on example passages, because there is such a huge choice and diversity of genre. Narrative tends to be dominant over other genres because it is the most accessible, and it certainly features prominently in the section of the canon considered here. But of course there are many other important genres – law codes, prophetic oracles, proverbs, ethical injunctions, theological statements – and it has not been possible to cover them all.

The Old Testament provides a rich picture of the relationship between God and humans, a relationship that develops over time. That development, though, appears complicated because the stories were written up later than the time in which they were first told (although they may have existed in oral circles from earlier times), and because the various sources within the books and the wider clusters of material that we have probably also came together over a long period of time (see Chapter 2). This means that the development of the faith of Israel cannot be related straight from the pages of the Old Testament but has to be reconstructed from what we know of the sources and their placement. A recent trend is to date this reconstruction to a much later period than was previously thought, or even to suggest that it was largely invented, as I will discuss in the next chapter. Even if we place a late date on the development of ideas, there is still evidence that they did develop, or at least coexist, and so understandings of God, of God's nature and plans for the world also changed. It was an unfolding picture, and it was into this world of ideas that the New Testament was born.

The self-presentation of the Old Testament is haphazard rather than systematic. It is not unified, it is not a systematic theology, although many have sought for a system within it. But the image of a jigsaw puzzle is a helpful one. There are many individual pieces but the whole picture does exist somewhere, although reconstructing it is a hard task.

9

Questioning the history of Israel: scepticism within the academy

In this chapter I wish to address the issue of how the Old Testament is perceived and approached in scholarly circles, and the impact such a perception makes beyond those circles upon the preachers and teachers in the Church. The Old Testament is not getting a 'bad name' only through the attacks of the New Atheists. It is already under attack from 'within', from those researching, teaching and educating from its pages as well as from those ignoring it in church circles. In this chapter I wish to indicate the changes in academia that have taken place in the last few decades in approaching this canon of books. In many ways this is a positive development which has opened up a critical and unbiased debate on a subject that was previously dominated by the scholarship of different faith traditions. Its negative side, though, is that anything and everything is up for criticism. There are no taboos and there is even an active agenda for the dismantling of faith perspectives from an analysis of the scriptural texts themselves.

In the next chapter I will look at the attitudes of preachers and promoters of the Old Testament within the Church and at the marginalization of the Old Testament in those circles too. Academia and the Church have long had a solid and important relationship and yet we have in many ways lost that crucial link – blame lies on both sides, with the academy moving ever further away from explicit confessional stances and the Church nervous of presenting scholarly views and findings to the wider public within a context of declining numbers and a wider loss of confidence.

Hitchens in relation to biblical scholarship

I will start with Christopher Hitchens, as he gives us a window on to the kinds of discussions that have been going on in biblical studies in recent years. Hitchens dabbles in modern scholarship in archaeology and biblical studies; he mentions the dating of texts and artefacts in relation to the point that many of the events of the Old Testament are likely to have been 'made up' considerably later. He is referring here specifically to the exodus and stories about Moses – he concedes that archaeology has shown there was a 'kingdom of David', 'albeit rather a modest one'.[1] He ridicules the attempts of those in the late nineteenth and early twentieth centuries to 'prove' the Bible with archaeology and commends recent archaeologists who have allowed the archaeological evidence (or often the lack of it) to speak for itself. Calling this work more 'objective', he describes it as 'asserting evidence over self-interest':[2] 'There was no flight from Egypt, no wandering in the desert ... and no dramatic conquest of the Promised Land. It was all quite simply and very ineptly, made up at a much later date.'[3]

One cannot help wondering whether Hitchens is promoting recent archaeologists such as Finkelstein and Silberman (see below) who have argued for later dating simply because he wishes to agree with them (although he does charge them with being misguided in their view that the Hebrew Bible[4] is 'beautiful'). He bad-mouths older archaeologists such as General Gordon[5] and W. F. Albright[6] with whom he does not agree. Indeed, he misrepresents their views, and this needs to be investigated. He is also, without explicitly saying so, combining the findings of archaeology with those in biblical studies of the so-called 'minimalist' school, those scholars who, from analysis of the biblical text itself, have argued that there is evidence not simply for the 'writing up' of early material at a much later period but rather for the 'making up' of a past ideology to justify a present reality (see below).

Hitchens goes on to make the point that to any thinking person it is quite clear that the 'revelation' at Sinai and 'the rest of the Pentateuch' was 'an ill-carpentered fiction, bolted into place well after the nonevents that it fails to describe convincingly or even plausibly'.[7] It is not quite clear to me why he attacks the Sinai events specifically. Perhaps it has something to do with his use of the idea that Moses could not have written the Pentateuch as evidence to undermine the historicity of the account. This is to show a lack of understanding of the way biblical studies has moved in the last century or more – even in the late nineteenth century, the idea that Moses wrote the Pentateuch was well out of fashion. It is, however, to raise the issue of sources in the Pentateuch and beyond and ideas about authors, writers and redactors that have long been the 'bread and butter' of biblical scholarship. The emphasis on final form and final redactors has led reductionist scholars to posit that we have in front of us a text which may or may not contain ancient material, and which is more likely to be a later construct than an early witness. In fact it is not simply a construct, it is an ideological one that distorts history in the light of ideology and in the service of literary fiction.

As an aside, Hitchens says at one point that 'No Egyptian chronicle mentions this episode [the conquest of the promised land] either, even in passing',[8] which raises the issue of the evidence of comparative nations in relation to the Bible. This has traditionally been another important 'tool' for biblical exegesis and for the placing of biblical events in the context of the broader ancient Near Eastern world. This too has been an area of shifting ground, with some wishing to use such comparison to support an early dating of biblical material and some asserting the opposite, as I shall discuss below.

Another related discussion point is that of the canon of Scripture. Clearly not all the books ever written in the biblical period were retained in the canon, and we have evidence of debate both among the rabbis and in early Christian circles about what should be left in and what taken out. As we saw, Marcion's version of the canon was selected according to his own preferences. In that sense we too have a 'chosen' selection of what constitutes the Bible. And indeed we all tend to select our own 'canons' as we seek to understand these ancient writings. Reflecting on the canon leads to two results – first, an interest in 'canonical' readings, the belief that any story or event or idea needs to be related to other similar ones across the canon (a method that might redeem or at least recontextualize some of the difficult stories I have outlined in previous chapters); and second, the raising of questions about what might be learnt about the wider cultural context by studying those texts that were left out of the canon (and of course there is more than one canon, as we saw in Chapter 2). This is of particular interest in New Testament studies at the present time, with non-canonical texts such as the gnostic gospels of central concern.

Finally, Hitchens criticizes the Old Testament's parochialism, saying that 'the context is oppressively confined and local. None of these provincials, or their deity, seems to have any idea of a world beyond the desert, the flocks and herds, and the imperatives of nomadic subsistence.'[9] This is truer of the 'earlier' material than of the later, more theologically developed material, but, as I said earlier, an interest in the 'local' is hardly a crime. The local reflects the Israelite context. Of course, many of those who wrote up the stories were doing so from a context, a point in time and a worldview that was limited. As others added material and reflected on earlier ideas, the local became more national and international. There was development over time. Emphasis on this 'overarching story' or theology of the whole has been the traditional interest of scholars over the years, particularly in Christian circles. However, there is an increasing tendency in some quarters of biblical scholarship to study 'one text at a time' (as advocated by Brueggemann)[10] – an interest in the piecemeal, in the local.

Another interesting move in biblical studies in recent times, indeed, has been greater appreciation of the local, at least in terms of interpreters rather than authors. Interpretations of texts are often 'local', carried out on a piecemeal basis for those in specific situations with specific needs. Biblical scholarship itself may today be international in scope, but there is still a good deal of individual interpretation taking place in small communities and groups. We are increasingly aware of cultural relativity when it comes to biblical interpretation; the 'local', then, has both positive and negative aspects to it.

The changing face of biblical studies

The last few decades have seen a massive shift in biblical studies and its related disciplines, including biblical archaeology. I expect that this has all but passed the Church by. In biblical studies, however, the shift has been on the scale of a volcanic eruption. It all has to do with the nature of evidence. Scholarship of the past spoke of tradents, of sources, of authors and redactors, and of trying to reconstruct some kind of objective history of Israel and theological account of the development of ideas over a long period of time. Although there was much about the biblical text that was questioned, its essential value as a witness to events that were loosely historical and were certainly of literary and theological worth was assumed.

It is the reliability of the biblical text as a source of evidence that has largely been undermined in this new era of biblical study. This has in turn been influenced by postmodernism and by the idea that we are all readers of texts, that we shape texts in our own image and that the quest for objective history is futile. Viewing the Bible as a set of literary texts has also led to an emphasis on the literary over the historical. The possibility that texts have been shaped well after the events that they purport to relate and that only the text in its final form, as we inherit it in our Bibles, is 'reliable' has become a dominant assumption.

The debate in biblical archaeology

In relation to biblical archaeology, the older scholarly tendency was to begin with the biblical text and work outwards to archaeological, cultural and wider sociological and anthropological concerns. Biblical dating is done in conjunction with dating of events known from the wider ancient Near Eastern world, for example, the dating and chronology of pharaohs and events written up in Egyptian archival material. A new scepticism about the reliability of the biblical text, though, has led to an opposite approach, of valuing the other kinds of evidence just mentioned – i.e. the annals of the ancient Near East – over the biblical evidence itself.[11] This methodological problem has a direct influence on how we approach the archaeology. Along more traditional lines, Gabriel Barkay, a leading Israeli archaeologist, writes: 'For the Iron Age ... the Bible constitutes a principal historical source ... the approach of the archaeologist must be to integrate archaeological finds with the written sources, of which the Bible is the most important.'[12] But opponents argue that this correlation of archaeology with biblical traditions is wrong because the latter are essentially late constructions. This same critique is not made of the ancient Near Eastern sources, however, and so they are then perceived as more reliable than the Bible.

There is a further factor, though – what if one dares to redate the archaeology itself? This is what has been done by the 'post-Zionist' archaeologist Israel Finkelstein,[13] who since the 1990s has adopted the 'low chronology' that I will outline here. Biblical scholars generally date the emergence of Israel in Canaan to around the beginning of the twelfth century BCE, a dating known as 'high chronology'. 'Low chronology', on the other hand, involves dating most of the events and finds of the Iron Age about a century later than was previously common among archaeologists. Taking the lack of archaeological finds from the tenth century (the traditional dating of the period of the early Israelite monarchy) in particular as evidence of the shrinkage of the overall period, it is to argue that conventional dating of the archaeological finds has been too strongly influenced by the chronology reconstructed from the texts of the Bible. It is an attempt then to look at the archaeology without this bias.

So, for example, an Egyptian stele mentioning the invasion of Israel by Pharaoh Shoshenq (also known as Shishak) has depended for its dating on the biblical text of 1 Kings 14.25–28, which puts this invasion 'in the fifth year of Rehoboam'; this can be calculated according to the overall biblical chronological scheme as 925 BCE. The Egyptian stele mentions 150 towns and villages which the Pharaoh claimed to have captured during a campaign in Palestine; the Bible states that Shishak came against Jerusalem and took away all the gold from the Temple and the royal palace. For many years this correlation has provided a central benchmark for dating not only that particular event but much wider historical and archaeological data from the period.

It was similarly assumed that destruction layers at Megiddo related to this same point in history – the tenth century (so pioneering Israeli archaeologist Yigael Yadin equated the event with destructions at Hazor, Megiddo, Gezer and Beersheba)[14] – but Finkelstein in redating the destruction layers themselves and 'losing' altogether a century of the biblical timeline has cast doubt on that benchmark. So, if one takes away the assumption that the biblical dating can be trusted, the door is opened to a radically different approach. Influenced by this dating debate, even Barkay writes, '[it] has not been proven that any sites were destroyed by Shishak in 925 BCE and the attribution of destruction layers to the end of the tenth century at many sites is mere conjecture'.[15] This redating then opens up the possibility that the destruction seen at the sites in question relates to a later period than this particular Shishak invasion, perhaps to the ninth century instead. This may suggest either that the chronological dating of events in the Bible is wrong, that the events described in the Bible simply did not happen, or that they happened during a later period than traditionally supposed.

There is a further question as to how far archaeological evidence in turn can be used to 'back up' the Bible in historical terms. The literary nature of the text means, on one level, that the material is not generally of the nature of 'historical proof', and on another that archaeological evidence is often open to various interpretations and is often sporadic and piecemeal. Even written texts such as inscriptions, which seem to offer more solid evidence, are open to the same dating questions and to issues of authenticity and bias. This is not to deny that extremely important finds have been made, but I tend to agree with John Bright when he wrote in his *A History of Israel* (1959) that archaeology leaves us with a 'balance of probabilities' when it comes to the Bible, no more and no less.[16]

Another recent trend has been to open the subject up to wider sociological and anthropological studies and to get away from material finds alone. Keith Whitelam,[17] for example, comes from a sociological perspective looking at patterns of settlement, population and so on. It is from this perspective that the idea has arisen that there was no exodus as related in the Bible, indeed that it is 'a fiction'[18] and that the Israelites were a subgroup of Canaanites who gradually became dominant over other groups. This is to challenge the biblical account of one of the central 'historical' events – arguably the defining event of the Israelite nation – choosing to sideline or ignore the textual evidence from the Bible itself. The sociological approach is a useful angle on the material, but often seems broad and conjectural, lacking the detail of either archaeological inscription or biblical text. It is often forgotten that not only is there an extended account of the exodus in the book of that name but also it is a paradigm that is mentioned throughout the canon of Scripture. Can it be so easily cast aside?

Redating and reconstructing the Davidic monarchy

The kind of approach that distrusts the biblical evidence and redates the archaeological layers has pulled the proverbial rug out from under the feet of biblical interpreters. It has revealed many uncertainties and also led to some healthy questioning of previously established certainties. But this does not mean that Finkelstein is right about the dating, or that we are to become too sceptical about the value of the Bible for either confirming or refuting archaeological finds. Recent presentations of the biblical evidence, such as that of Francesca Stavrakopoulou in the television series *The Bible's Buried Secrets*,[19] have followed the Finkelstein line, for example, in relation to the historical existence of King David, dating his 'reign' to the ninth century BCE rather than the tenth and thus shifting the dating of the biblical chronology by a century, thereby questioning the historicity of the entire account of the united monarchy (i.e. the period when the two states of Israel and Judah were one) under David and Solomon.

Finkelstein has joined forces with Silberman in *The Bible Unearthed: Archaeology's New Vision of Ancient Israel and the Origin of its Stories* (2001),[20] a recent presentation of the material relating to the united monarchy – or rather an argument for its non-existence. They take their starting point from the reign of the Israelite King Omri (885–874 BCE), for whose reign we do have archaeological evidence in the form of a mention of the 'house of Omri' on the Moabite Stone (also known as the Mesha Stele). At this time there was peace, sufficient to begin major building works (such as were attributed to the reign of Solomon under former dating schemes). It is in the reign of Omri that, they state, the grand claims made by the Israelite monarchy begin. Because there is a lack of archaeological evidence for the reigns of David and Solomon, the idea here is that what actually happened was not as the Bible relates. Rather there was a fledgling state in the north (the kingdom of Israel) which was established under King Jeroboam but fully developed only during the reign of Omri. With his capital in Samaria, Omri founded the first proper state in the kingdom of Israel; indeed the Bible tells us that Omri 'bought the hill of Samaria from Shemer for two talents of silver; he fortified the hill and called the city that he built Samaria, after the name of Shemer, the owner of the hill' (1 Kings 16.24). Note that the Bible is wheeled out in support of a new reconstruction even though its evidence is ignored for the older models.

Finkelstein and Silberman write of their reconstruction:

> The Omrides are remembered as among the most despised characters of biblical history. Yet the new archaeological vision of the kingdom of Israel offers an entirely different perspective on their reigns. Indeed, had the biblical authors and editors been historians in the modern sense, they might have said that Ahab was a mighty king who first brought the kingdom of Israel to prominence on the world stage and that his marriage to the daughter of the Phoenician king Ethbaal was a brilliant stroke of international diplomacy. They might have said that the Omrides built magnificent cities to serve as administrative centers of their expanding kingdom. They might have said that Ahab and Omri, his father before him, succeeded in building one of the most powerful armies in the region...[21]

Here Finkelstein and Silberman are saying, tongue in cheek perhaps, of the Omride dynasty all the things that scholars before them said of David and then Solomon, his successor. Finkelstein is dating the whole development of the Israelite state to a century later, keeping to the biblical chronology for the later period but dismissing the whole biblical edifice of the united monarchy, which he puts down to creative writing by the Deuteronomists who wanted to portray the house of Omri in a negative light. Why? Because they are influenced by the theology of the seventh century BCE, which saw this period as a time of apostasy and sin perpetrated by successive kings, who were confronted by God's prophets Elijah and Elisha. Finkelstein and Silberman dismiss the biblical stories of David and Solomon and the negative portrayal of the Omrides as a 'historical novel', and put in its place their own new understanding of the Omrides as the first, powerful, military rulers of an Israelite state.

Before I leave the archaeologists, I must raise a further question – how far do we trust the archaeology? Is the lack of current evidence (and of course that might change) a reason for swallowing up a whole century? Does the lack of archaeological evidence for monumental architecture in Jerusalem in the tenth century, for example, completely discredit the historicity of the period? And what about the reliability of those who are writing up the archaeology? Kenneth Kitchen is on the completely opposite side of the scholarly divide from Finkelstein and his book is full of criticisms of such scholars. He writes:

> The whole correlation of the archaeological record for the eleventh to early eighth centuries is based upon Finkelstein's arbitrary, idiosyncratic and isolated attempt to lower the dates of the tenth century by up to a century if need be to rid himself of the united monarchy as a major phenomenon ... the redating will not work. All it does is show how precarious are the attempts by any of us to correlate the nontextual material remains with the written history available.[22]

Well, it is good to hear both sides of the debate! It is clearly a heated one.

The minimalist position

We are starting to get a taste, in the work of Finkelstein and Silberman, of the minimalist position that has played a large part in the volcanic overturning of older ideas in biblical studies in the last few decades. This movement was

Questioning the history of Israel

originally dubbed 'The Copenhagen School' and was led by four scholars – Philip Davies, Nils Peter Lemche, Thomas L. Thompson and the late Robert P. Carroll.[23] Although they differ on the details, their basic theory is that the literature of the Old Testament was composed late – no earlier than the Persian period (fifth century BCE) and possibly even later, in the Hellenistic period (third century BCE) – and was essentially ideology or propaganda. It was composed by a group of scribes commissioned to write a national story (not a history) by the elite ruling class of that late period. For Davies[24] this entire group was one that came from elsewhere in the Persian empire to occupy Judah, and which had no historical connections to Judah. A back-story was therefore needed, to convince the inhabitants of this land that they belonged here and that they had ancestry and a story in this place. Thus this is not history but ideology, written by scribes in schools sponsored by the ruling elite with their base in the Temple.

This approach means that both the earlier and later (pre- and post-exilic) phases of the history of Israel are an elaborate literary fiction. It puts the emphasis entirely on the final form of the literature and does not allow for the existence of older material within its pages. The Old Testament is no longer on this scheme the deposit of centuries of writers and authors in a developing timeline over the centuries of history; rather it is a one-dimensional, once-for-all script from a much later age. Davies allows that the archaeology may reveal historical traces of 'Israel' dating from the ninth and late eighth centuries, but that it was only a separate state for a very short while before being taken over by the Assyrians. Judah did not exist, for Davies, as a separate state. There was therefore no time of David and Solomon; that, like the idea of 'biblical Israel', is entirely fabricated.

Davies sees a sharp break between what might have been the case historically and what was actually written in the

Bible. Even if older oral material was incorporated, its original context is entirely lost to us due to its new context in this biblical 'write-up'.[25]

It might surprise readers that this view has been so influential, in that it does not take long to expose as the fiction it so clearly is. We have no evidence that there was such a scribal group in either of the posited periods, while the nature of the text, with all its inconsistencies, duplications, repetitions and odd details, not to mention its changing theological ideas over time, completely militates against such a monochrome view. This is, too, a very large body of material – is it credible that it could all have been invented? If one was inventing something, would it really be so disordered and chaotic, so varied in genre and mixed in viewpoint? The idea of idealistic propaganda belongs better in former communist Russia or China than in ancient Israel. It is equally unbelievable that a group of people with no connections to a place would move in and create such an elaboration. We all know that people are interested in their own past, their ancestry and ancient places – it would be some brainwashing process to get them to believe in the past of a completely different place and nation, even if it were presented as if it were their story and they were the descendants of those who had once lived there.

Davies probably represents the extremity of the minimalist position. When asked to explain prophecy, which appears to rail against social injustice in the eighth century BCE and after, as the product of this later official propaganda, his response is to see these scribes as deliberately mastering a known genre for educational purposes, taking all of the societal bite out of it by seeing it not as a critique of its own period but as poetry deliberately adopting a past context. He ignores key ancient Near Eastern parallels – if those are much older, and form reliable evidence (as we know, all texts are written with bias), why not include their evidence, and for that matter why not the biblical material too? Once again it comes down to a new disbelief in the testimony of the Old Testament itself.

Thomas L. Thompson's view is slightly less radical[26] – while he believes that ancient Israel never existed, he is prepared to allow the possibility of a Judean state and he finds in the Bible two overarching storylines – that of the golden age of the united monarchy from old Israel that had gradually been lost over centuries while a succession of unworthy kings ruled the divided kingdoms, and that of exile and return from new Israel that dominated the late scribal composition. However, Thompson still maintains that it is citizens from elsewhere in the area who were being persuaded that they were being 'returned' to the land of their ancestors. It is still propaganda, at best an 'origin myth' made up of largely fictional events and characters.

While we might dismiss the minimalist position fairly easily, its influence casts a long shadow, and biblical studies today is very changed. Many current biblical scholars, though they are not minimalists by name,[27] still tend to date texts to a late period and to see the chronology of the development of texts as a much shorter one, culminating in much production in the Persian period, a period we actually know little about.

An example comes from the pen of Lester Grabbe in his book *Ancient Israel: What Do We Know and How Do We Know It* (2007). Grabbe largely accepts Finkelstein's reconstruction of the dating, but he believes that Saul, and then David and Solomon in the united monarchy, definitely existed. The reason for this is that he puts weight on a mention in the Deuteronomistic history of 'the annals of the Kings' as a source used by the authors then but no longer extant. He argues that, while some accounts of the monarchy do have a fictional flavour, there is a clear attempt to refer to factual sources such as these. Considering the widespread evidence for such chronicles in the ancient Near East, notably in Mesopotamia, Grabbe considers it unlikely that the author here was inventing fictitious sources. He writes, 'Some of the other sources may sometimes have contained reliable historical data, but most of the data in the text confirmed by external data as reliable could have come from such a chronicle.'[28] There is an interesting shift of method here, which is the valuing of external sources more highly than the biblical text itself, as I mentioned above. It is often by appeal to parallels in other cultures that clearly come from older periods that verification of biblical data can be made. But why be so cautious over the biblical evidence itself? Is this a reaction against the over-reliance upon it of earlier scholars?

There is a lot of interest in current scholarship in the Persian period as a time when certain texts might have been composed (or at least established in a final form). This replaces a tendency a few decades ago to see the exilic period as the most formative one in relation to the production of texts, which in turn replaced the earlier efforts of scholars to go back much further, dating some texts to the monarchy with oral antecedents even beyond that.

There are trends in biblical studies as in many other disciplines, and I cannot help feeling that majority opinion will shift again in the next few decades. My own view is that we are now concentrating excessively on the late production of texts, with a nod to earlier antecedents, and are undervaluing the earlier stages of thought and production of both oral and written texts.[29]

For the minimalists, then, it is about the later production of texts in their final form being the most definitive stage. At the extreme they are completely manufactured, on a less radical view they are gathered together as a finished product in this later age. The minimalists interact with the archaeological evidence too, to emphasize the difficulty of 'proof' and the likelihood that much of the Old Testament is simply not historically provable on this level, and so is probably a fiction of a later age. Everything has to be corroborated archaeologically, and so in the absence of archaeological evidence (and the reinterpretation of what there is) it is easy to dismiss most of the biblical text. On this scheme the biblical text becomes the poor relation to all other forms of evidence. We need to ask: Does the biblical account afford reliable evidence? How far do we trust it? Does the lack of hard evidence mean that there is really nothing there?

Before I turn from the academy to the Church and to those who might wish to preach on these texts, a question needs to be asked. What motivates this new downgrading of the evidence of the biblical text? Is it because scholars no longer come from a confessional stance where the biblical text is seen as the evidence upon which faith is based and nurtured? Is there – as with Dawkins and Hitchens – an atheist or, at least, an agnostic agenda underneath the layers of reconfigured archaeology, questioning and scepticism? Biblical scholarship has always said that it is looking for objectivity that does not depend upon a confessional stance, but with the move towards 'reader-response', where it is recognized that we all have agendas, maybe we are exposing older certainties as expressions of faith as much as they are attempts to reconstruct Israelite history? The minimalist view also claims to be objective, but is it really? Can anyone come to any text without bias? This is to open up the debate between subjectivity and objectivity that has been generated in a postmodern age.

10

A Christian perspective on the Old Testament

> Of all our friends in faith, the Old Testament is easily the quirkiest. This friend is from another culture and speaks with a thick Hebrew accent. There's also quite a generation gap – one that spans over two thousand years. As soon as the Old Testament begins to speak, our minds fill with questions. Yet we need this oddball of a companion precisely because the Old Testament shatters our expectations and forces us to think about things in new and creative ways.
> (Matthew Schlimm, *This Strange and Sacred Scripture*)[1]

I begin this chapter with Schlimm's idea of the Old Testament as a friend, albeit a rather contradictory and difficult one. It is a helpful and attractive image. Schlimm makes the point that this is a friend who is brutally honest, is unafraid to tackle difficult topics, is a 'male chauvinist', a 'legalistic prude', is confused and contradictory at times, is intense about anger and grief and so on.[2] Its authority is such that, like a very close friend, we should sit up and listen when it challenges us, and we should care about what it thinks. Schlimm encourages us to bring this quirky friend more closely into our lives.

We saw in Chapter 1 that Marcion had no great affection for the Old Testament, indeed that one of his life's missions became its rejection and the rejection of its 'lesser' God. For the New Atheists too, not only the Old Testament but faith as a whole has no place in their lives, and their attack is a mission to persuade people to ditch the whole 'faith' package. As Christians we are encouraged to engage with the Old Testament – it does after all make up four-fifths of our Bible – and yet this sense of its being our friend is not one that is generally promoted by many preachers and teachers of its pages. Indeed the tendency to ignore it or be apathetic towards it is almost a form of decanonization, even though not so official a form as Marcion wanted it to be.

A progressively revealed deity

One of Marcion's main reasons for excluding the Old Testament was its view of God. The New Atheists too suggest that in its pages God is angry or vengeful most of the time. One often hears a simplistic comparison drawn between the God of 'love' of the New Testament and the 'God who smites' of the Old. I hope I have already shown that this is not only a mischaracterization of the Old Testament – there is much about the love of God and his enduring patience in its pages – but also a mischaracterization of the New, in that Jesus gets angry at times with good reason. Let us not forget that a famous liturgical phrase such as 'The LORD bless you and keep you', often used in conjunction with the giving of the blessing of grace at the end of a Christian service, is from the Old Testament (Num. 6.24); equally let us not forget Jesus' anger at the presence of the moneychangers in the Temple (Matt. 21.12; Mark 11.15; John 2.14). We risk sanitizing both Testaments in an effort to make ourselves feel more comfortable than we really should.

The Bible is about challenging us, about confronting us with a hard picture of reality, about human life with all its cunning, its trickery, its cruelty, its complexity as well as its positive aspects of love, relationships, sharing and hoping.

The Old Testament presents a more complex picture of God – a rich and varied one that changes over time – than the New, but it is no less real and informative. It is simply slightly less predictable than we might like, as we wrestle with contradictory ideas about God's anger and his desire to punish sin on the one hand, and on the other God's pain and pathos as he sees the suffering of humankind.

I have stressed the point that there is a progressive revelation of God in the Old Testament, and an unfolding picture of God as seen by humans. It is not a strictly linear progression, but God does emerge in human perception, and as conveyed through many texts, as a greater, more powerful, more universally active, 'one alone' deity by the end of the Old Testament period than at the beginning. There is nothing methodical about this presentation – it is not ordered, it is not unified, it is not a systematic theology, although many have sought for a system within it. It is a rich picture of the relationship between God, humans and the wider world, a relationship that develops over time, changes in different circumstances and manifests itself in all kinds of literature. And the later, more highly developed picture of God created the conditions for the understanding of God found in the New Testament. In that sense the Old is the precursor to the New – we cannot really understand the New without the Old, nor the God of the New, and the fresh revelation made in Christ, without reference to the Old.

Jesus and the Old Testament

It is uncertain whether Jesus himself made actual reference to the Old Testament, or how far this referencing was done by the disciples, by Paul, by the writers of the Gospels or by subsequent tradition. We can see Jesus as a

A Christian perspective on the Old Testament

fulfilment of many of the relationships described in the Old Testament – for example, Jesus manifests the loyalty of the covenantal God described in Jeremiah 7.23: 'Obey my voice, and I will be your God, and you shall be my people; and walk only in the way that I command you, so that it may be well with you' – and such links have been made by many a preacher on these texts. There is no doubt that the Old Testament was Jesus' Bible and his authoritative text. While proof texts were sought from the Old Testament after the resurrection and in subsequent reflection on his significance, there is still a core element of continuity in the figure of Jesus himself. Later reflection started to make new connections, such as seeing Jesus as king, as the Davidic descendant and Messiah foretold in the older scriptures,[3] or as the innocent sacrificial lamb taken to the slaughter.[4] The writers of the New Testament found themselves expressing new ideas, but in the language and imagery of the old, wanting perhaps to emphasize the essential continuity of events. These Scriptures were their thought-world.

Whether Jesus himself made the same connections is again a matter of dispute. He called himself the 'son of man', a phrase used by both Ezekiel and Daniel, and he may have used 'Messiah' himself also; I refer back to the discussion of Daniel in Chapter 7. Either way, the Old Testament has to be taken seriously by Christians engaging with the New – Scripture has to be taken as a whole. The Old Testament is theologically rich. It contains profound expressions of a just and loving God, creator and redeemer, who acts faithfully on behalf of his people and beyond them to the peoples of the world. It contains both a profound analysis in ethical terms of the nature of righteous and wicked behaviour and the key concept of God's grace and forgiveness of sin. These theological understandings – and many more – not only stand alone in their own right within the context of the Old Testament itself, but also find a new resonance in relation to the New.

Isaiah in the New Testament

The book of Isaiah has always held a central place for Christians. It has even been called 'the fifth gospel' or 'the Romans of the Old Testament' due to its extensive citation in the New Testament (66 times in total). In particular, the argument from prophecy is used to convince readers of the reality of Jesus as a fulfilment of the prophecies uttered in the past, and to convince us that the prophetic role is one of foretelling rather than simply forth-telling (i.e. predicting imminent events). At the centre of this are two famous passages: Isaiah 7.14, 'the young woman is with child and shall bear a son and shall name him "Immanuel"', and Isaiah 9.6, 'For a child has been born for us, a son given to us; authority rests upon his shoulders; and he is named Wonderful Counsellor, Mighty God, Everlasting Father, Prince of Peace.' Both of these passages have their own contexts in Isaiah's time, but are taken out of those contexts in the words of the ancient prophet and applied to the coming of Jesus. They are used in services of Nine Lessons and Carols[5] as part of the prediction of Christ from the pages of the Old Testament.

One could perhaps accuse the writers of the New Testament of doing much the same as Dawkins or Hitchens – extracting a passage to set it in an entirely new context. Dawkins takes many Old Testament stories out of context and places them in the service of trying to discover a foundation or direction for modern morality. That these passages fail to provide such a foundation is inevitable in the selection – had he chosen other extracts, he might have been more successful. For the writers of the New Testament it is essential to use carefully chosen passages to back up what is

A Christian perspective on the Old Testament

being said about Jesus. It is a question of authority – grounding the experience of the present in the prediction of the past.

I have discussed elsewhere[6] the original context of these two particular verses (7.14 and 9.6) from First Isaiah and the way they are used in the New Testament. That the original prophet may not have understood the full purport of his utterance is entirely possible – the veiled nature of prophecy lends itself to a fuller interpretation. This reapplication has in fact been done with many passages over the years, both by the rabbis and by Christian writers and many others; all kinds of variants on what was originally meant are explored in a fresh context that entails the application of older words to a new situation. This is what happens in every midrash ever written and every sermon ever preached. This is the nature of a living Scripture.

In the story of Jesus reading from Scripture in the synagogue at Nazareth it is the Isaiah scroll from which he reads. In fact it is Isaiah 61.1–2, part of what we know as Third Isaiah. This is recorded in Luke 4.18 with a verbatim quotation. Of course we may not be able to know for certain whether Jesus spoke these words or whether the Gospel writer, Luke, is drawing on the Old Testament for his own authorial purposes. We may not wish to take the event or its content literally. However, it makes the point that from early times there was a tradition of Jesus using what we know as the Old Testament as his authoritative Scripture. The citation from Isaiah is very apt –

> The spirit of the Lord GOD is upon me because the LORD has anointed me; he has sent me to bring good news to the oppressed, to bind up the broken-hearted; to proclaim liberty to the captives and release to the prisoners.

In its context in Third Isaiah it is one of the passages that echoes Second Isaiah,[7] in this case the servant song

(Isa. 42.1, 7, 9). Many see the passage as the nearest thing to a prophetic call in this third section of Isaiah, if indeed it is a separate prophet with a separate call. It is easily applicable to the work of Jesus and his message, and that application is what Luke takes up. Jesus was seen by many as a prophet, and so one could argue that this identification with an ancient prophet is deliberately made here. Unsurprisingly, Marcion left out of his Gospel all the opening events of Luke's Gospel, including the tale of the young boy Jesus debating with the elders in the Jerusalem Temple (Luke 2) and this story in Luke 4. The consensus is that Marcion's Gospel begins with 'the descent of Jesus to Capernaum'.[8]

The Gospel of John at its midpoint quotes twice from Isaiah (John 12.37–41). The first quotation, 'Who has believed what we have heard? And to whom has the arm of the Lord been revealed?' is from chapter 53 (v. 1), a small part of one of the suffering-servant passages;[9] the second is from chapter 6, 'Make the mind of this people dull, and stop their ears, and shut their eyes, so that they may not look with their eyes and listen with their ears, and comprehend with their minds and turn and be healed' (6.10), another part of the call where we are given a summary of the future reception of the prophet's message. John's version is slightly different but conveys the essence of these passages.[10]

John adds a comment: 'Isaiah said this because he saw his [Jesus'] glory and spoke about him' (12.41), a direct claim that Jesus' coming was foretold. The prediction relates to the rejection of Jesus despite the many miracles he performed. In the same way the prophet Isaiah received God's call and yet was widely disregarded, as if God had decided in advance that the words would fall on deaf ears (Isa. 6.9–10). It is a statement as much about God's intention as about the suffering of the prophet

A Christian perspective on the Old Testament

(and so of Jesus too) in the rejection he must face. God sends his prophet/his son but the world does not 'know' him.[11] These are just a few of the many citations of Isaiah in the New Testament.

For scholars, the book of Isaiah naturally falls into three parts because different historical contexts are revealed for each section (see Chapter 7). This is rarely conveyed in the pulpit. Many a member of a church congregation might have wondered why there is a strange mixture of judgement and hope in Isaiah (although of course many prophecies do contain these two elements). In Isaiah, though there are editorial links between the first two 'sections', the tone of each part is very different, as are the priorities. Second Isaiah contains some inspiring passages of unreserved hope that seem far distant from First Isaiah. There may or may not have been a Third Isaiah, but we use this distinction in a literary way to distinguish a third section of material that seems to belong to yet another context, or possibly more than one context, and which points to an ever-distant hope of renewal and restoration.

Turning to Second Isaiah, and to Isaiah 53, the final part of this climactic last servant song is read by Philip in Acts 8.26–35. In this tale the apostle Philip meets an Ethiopian eunuch who is reading Isaiah. It is interesting in itself that a foreigner is reading the Israelite Scriptures. Philip rather cheekily asks him, 'Do you understand what you are reading?' and the eunuch asks for guidance. The passage is Isaiah 53.7–8, describing the servant as a sheep led to the slaughter and helpless as a lamb in the face of its shearer. The servant is unable to speak out, denied justice, humiliated and robbed of his life. Philip immediately connects this characterization with Jesus – he is the very same sheep or lamb, a victim of the torture heaped upon him by others. In the context of Isaiah 53 it is not clear who is being described. Is it the prophet himself, an unknown suffering figure of the future, a new Moses?[12] It is as if the prophet is seeing something through a dim glass – is he foretelling the risen Christ and his sacrifice? Is he forth-telling an event soon to come in Israel's life? Or is he simply recounting a vision that he has had and leaving future generations to decipher its meaning? This elusive language is taken up by the New Testament writers to make an easy identification with Jesus.

Understanding the ways in which Jesus and the New Testament writers used the Old Testament gives us an insight into why we read the Old Testament in the way we do in church today. However, I would make a plea for a wider appreciation of the Old Testament in its own right and on its own terms. It is fruitful to read it in its own context, as a witness to its own time. Its rich literature, history and theology is a goldmine of inspiration for all who dip into its pages. Walter Brueggemann in *Texts under Negotiation: The Bible and Postmodern Imagination* helpfully suggests that in a postmodern age we need to find fresh and challenging, even subversive interpretations of texts. He believes that Church interpretation has tended to trim and domesticate the text and calls instead for an act of counter-imagination in which texts are used to challenge the reader and engender the possibility of real change and growth.[13]

Christian exposure to the Old Testament

As Christians, most of our exposure to the Old Testament in church comes through hearing a passage read out alongside one from the New Testament. The pairing of such texts is usually done thematically, so that we get a pick and mix of stories or theological themes from the Old Testament that fit with whichever part of the Christian year we are in.

A Christian perspective on the Old Testament

So, for example, at Christmas we sometimes hear Genesis 1, in which God speaks the word and each of his creative acts come to be. This is read out alongside the prologue to John's Gospel, telling of 'the Word' (v. 1) that is Jesus Christ having existed 'in the beginning' (v. 2) alongside God, without whom 'not one thing came into being' (v. 3). If an Old Testament text is actually preached on – and that can be quite a rare occurrence – it is generally one which aligns itself fairly naturally with the central tenets of the New Testament, and it will often be brought into conjunction with a New Testament text and the two preached on in tandem. In many ways this is a natural way for Christians to read the Old Testament, and I am not criticizing this approach per se. In fact it is very much how Jesus himself used the Scriptures – in a selective way that illuminated what he had to say and how he understood his mission – and how the writers of the New Testament also handled these authoritative texts. As I have said before, selection of texts is an entirely natural practice – we simply have to be careful our selection does not produce a one-sided picture.

As a result some texts get a good airing and others none at all. In a Christian context the lectionary helps us to pick and choose, but there is a danger that this method can lead to over-sanitization: the difficult texts are left out, while others are reinterpreted in the service of a dominant Christian exegesis, probably based on the Gospel reading for the day. While for Christians this kind of lens is appropriate, it does tend to nurture the idea of the Old Testament as a 'supplement where applicable' rather than trying to understand it and engage with it on its own terms. Some texts are primitive, others more sophisticated; many are positive, some are negative. But they are all overridingly realistic, dealing with human life in all its messiness, its joyfulness and its brutality. We are in as much danger if we simply select the positive ones that will feed into our need for moral encouragement as we would be engaging only with the negative texts, in the New Atheist way. If we simply look for ethical principles in the text we reduce the rich offering of narratives, prayers, laments, songs, laws and all manner of other genres to one purpose alone. This is where the New Atheists have got it wrong – we don't look at the Old Testament simply for moral instruction. The Old Testament is a contradictory set of texts – sometimes it will make a moral judgement, sometimes it just leaves a story hanging in the air for us to interpret as we will. Forging our own path of morality and our own sense of what the proper boundaries are for our lives is something that is nourished by reading about the dilemmas and decisions of others, even if those characters existed in centuries long before us. This is where the Old Testament can nourish and revitalize us. And yet we always need to contextualize and hence relativize our moral response to such texts.

The Old Testament, then, is often read in bite-size chunks but not really understood. It is a problem of scope – there is a huge body of texts to cover here, too much for the limited space available. As I have said already, the Old Testament is like a large jigsaw puzzle in which one is constantly finding new pieces. I have attempted to draw out some of its diversity and occasionally to go into more detail to show the rewards of engaging both with the overview and also in depth with particular texts. One needs some background knowledge of the timeline of the Old Testament and of its different books and genres to begin to engage with it. A key aspect of this engagement is an understanding of how ideas develop. Ideas do not arise in a vacuum – they unfold through shared experience and through the historical circumstance of successive events. We can understand the Old Testament only if we grasp

A Christian perspective on the Old Testament

the point that it covers a broad span of time, in which the relationship between God and humans unfolded in many different ways and situations. The narrative of salvation history is an essential framework for comprehending its scope, and yet it is supplemented by many texts that are not so historically orientated but rather add ideas and insights through a variety of genres (such as the genre variation in the Writings, as described in Chapter 6). However, this point about development over time is an important one that most people fail to realize as they hear an extracted passage in the pew. While one piece of the jigsaw puzzle read on one day may well be self-contained and hold its own particular message, wider appreciation of it can only be achieved if it is then placed with the other pieces in an unfolding arrangement.

Then there is the problem of context. We have seen how reading a text out of context can be misleading in the extreme. And yet to understand the overall context of the Old Testament takes years of study and reflection. Furthermore, texts are living – new contexts arise for them all the time, they are not time-bound in their place in the Old Testament – and yet some understanding of the culture that generated those texts is helpful. Of course texts vary in their genre – some texts have a timeless quality that makes them easily quotable and easily applicable, while others are very particular or so specific to a narrative as to make them relatively indigestible to the modern mind. We need to have an eye to their original context and to the culture that produced them. We have to consider that the culture was male-dominated, approved of slavery, was unafraid to exact harsh punishment and was legalistic.

There is also the point that the texts were ideologically driven at the time of writing. They had matters to emphasize and a picture to paint which may be lost to us now. Postmodern studies have helpfully drawn out this point about ideology – in a sense we all read texts (just as we write them) with an agenda, and we cannot get away from that fact. And yet reading ideologically can be immensely rewarding. Huge strides in understanding have been achieved in feminist studies, for example, in the identification of female voices in texts, in considering the 'gaps' – what is not said as well as what is – and in unashamedly applying this hermeneutic, with suspicion, to all texts, whether they lend themselves to this kind of interpretation or not. We might then attempt a feminist reading, or a liberationist one, or any other kind of modern 'reader-response', and by doing so may well discover all kinds of previously hidden fruits. Yet we are still brought back to the point that the texts were generated in a very different culture from ours, one that often seems alien – and that, particularly when we come up against less palatable texts, is the explanation for difficulties in interpretation and especially for modern application in the moral sphere.

We are not going to find sustenance in all that we read (that point is clear from Chapters 1–5!) – and yet for different generations of readers of the Bible, different texts speak in ever-new contexts. And that process continues.

From the academy to the pulpit

It has often been said that preachers have been afraid to introduce the findings of modern biblical scholarship into the pulpit. Perhaps it is hardly surprising in recent years, given some of the radical propositions biblical scholars have made. Prospective clergy study the findings of modern theology and Bible study, usually at theological colleges or on training courses, but rarely do they give their

A Christian perspective on the Old Testament

congregation large doses of it. The main reason for this – quite apart from the impracticality of having to explain the background information – is that the questioning and perceived dryness of biblical studies, with its emphasis on authors, redactors and the shaping of texts, has little to say to faith, spirituality and its nourishing.

This has been going on for years. When in Britain the Bishop of Durham, David Jenkins, dared to preach some of the findings of biblical studies (e.g. that the virgin birth may not have happened literally) he became notorious. And yet these findings were 'old hat' in scholarly circles, even then.

Even more so today. How easy would it be to introduce the findings of the minimalists into one's Sunday sermon? How easy would it be to introduce extra-canonical material and talk about the relativity of the 'canon'? How nourishing is it to speak of sources, dates and authors, when what people want to hear is the gospel message of hope in a difficult world?

There has then been a mismatch between the academy and the Church when it comes to the Bible, a gap that has been widening for a long time. Recent moves towards reclaiming the Bible in its 'final form' and putting an emphasis on its theological cohesion have assisted in mending some bridges, but it is a slow start. It has helped to highlight 'the text in front of us' as a whole rather than attempt to fragment it. The reader-response movement has also helped congregations to understand what authoritative readings are and how there is nothing wrong in an overtly Christian reading, or a reading that looks to the Bible for different reasons – moral ones even (as does Dawkins).

How far should congregations be protected from some of the more radical utterances of biblical scholars? For we should not assume that these utterances are the product of faith; there is often an atheistic or agnostic agenda at work within biblical scholarship,[14] deliberately pointing us away from a faith-orientated approach. This makes the gap wider. Should preachers then only turn to scholarship that reflects more traditional views? If that is the case, there is a danger of being out of date. What is top of the agenda – some kind of factual objectivity about history, theology, authors and sources, or the nourishment that Scripture gives to faith? Perhaps there are more questions here than answers.

Preaching the Old Testament

A reluctance among many clergy to preach on the Old Testament, especially on a Sunday morning at the main service of the day, is evident. There is often no space for the Old Testament on such occasions and the old problem of its perception as less than edifying emerges. I have had many discussions with clergy on this point, and I have seen a vast range of opinion expressed on the topic. One clergyman said he brought the Old Testament 'in somewhere' every week, but I suspect he was the exception rather than the rule!

As touched upon earlier, another issue is that even if the Old Testament is preached upon, resources from scholarship are not always used. So here is another ever-widening gap between the Church and the academy. While the publishing trade still brings out many useful textbooks, introductions and other resources, a fear that biblical scholarship might in some way undermine faith persists. This has been exacerbated by the more radical offerings of scholars in recent times, as we saw in the last chapter, and is reflected in scholarly material that is often afraid to take an overtly 'faith-orientated' line in the interest of academic integrity and the desire to air as many sides of an issue as possible.

A Christian perspective on the Old Testament

There needs to be more common ground between academic biblical studies and the training of the clergy – studying the Old Testament in theological colleges and on clergy courses is not simply for interest alone, it needs to be mediated through sermons and Bible studies into the wider Church and the world (cf. 2 Tim. 3.15–17). Clergy need to be given time to read and reflect on their Scriptures – an overworked clergywoman once asked me if I could recommend just 'one book' on the Old Testament that she might read 'this year'. That was all she had time for and could afford.

These kinds of attitude lead to a vicious circle, in that clergy are reluctant to bring scholarly findings to the people in the pew and so churchgoers seldom gain an insight into the 'original context' that helps to unpack difficult texts. While some biblical scholarship has sought to undermine many of the givens of traditional interpretation, there is no doubt in my mind that a deep and real engagement with the Old Testament and a conveying of that engagement to Christians everywhere are realistic goals.

Of course, as we have seen, not all texts are relevant or even instructive. Yet many are much more than instructive in their rich poetry or theological profundity – such is their number, though, that even they are not read systematically or regularly. The Old Testament contains a very rich fund of material and there is a need to dig deep within it to find relevance. Some themes in the Old Testament are not addressed at all in the New, and yet at the same time we really can't fully understand the New without reference to the Old. In this respect we are short-changing congregations if we do not give them the wider Old Testament context and a taste of its material. It is a context of changing ideas and situations, of changing literary output and of changing theological ideas, most notably about the relationship between

God and humanity and its diversity of material reflects these changes.

I hope that I have shown in this book what a rich diet the Old Testament offers. In the face of attack, its worst aspects can be highlighted and quickly dismissed, but with a more patient, sustained engagement its riches start to emerge. The Old Testament is a complicated set of texts, varied, contradictory but above all realistically reflecting life in all its messiness. It can be our friend, even if a rather challenging and contrary one at the end of the day.

Notes

1 From Dawkins to Marcion: countering scepticism and atheism

 1 Richard Dawkins, *The God Delusion* (London: Black Swan, 2007; originally published by Bantam Press in 2006), p. 51. Winner of the Galaxy British Book Award, author of the year 2007.
 2 Dawkins, *The God Delusion*, p. 283.
 3 Marcion, *Antitheses*. No longer extant.
 4 Adolf Harnack, *Marcion: The Gospel of the Alien God*, trans. J. E. Steely and L. D. Bierma (Durham, NC: Labyrinth Press, 1990 [publ. German 1921]).
 5 Eric A. Seibert, *The Violence of Scripture: Overcoming the Old Testament's Troubling Legacy* (Minneapolis, MN: Fortress Press, 2012).
 6 Sam Harris, *The End of Faith: Religion, Terror, and the Future of Reason* (New York: W. W. Norton, 2004). See also Sam Harris, *The Moral Landscape: How Science Can Determine Human Values* (London: Bantam, 2010); Daniel Dennett, *Breaking the Spell: Religion as a Natural Phenomenon* (New York: Viking Penguin, 2006); Christopher Hitchens, *God Is Not Great: How Religion Poisons Everything* (London: Atlantic Books, 2007); and see also discussion between Dennett and McGrath in Robert B. Stuart, *The Future of Atheism: Alister McGrath and Daniel Dennett in Dialogue* (London: SPCK, 2008).
 7 Dawkins covers a great deal of ground in this chapter, notably on pp. 268–93, which deals with the biblical material.
 8 Dawkins, *The God Delusion*, p. 270.
 9 Dawkins, *The God Delusion*, p. 275.
10 Phyllis Trible, *Texts of Terror: Literary-Feminist Readings of Biblical Narratives* (London: SCM Press, 1992). This was a ground-breaking book for both feminist interpretation and the

highlighting of the cultural violence against women in many Old Testament texts.

11 Dawkins, *The God Delusion*, p. 277.
12 Dawkins, *The God Delusion*, p. 279.
13 Dawkins, *The God Delusion*, p. 280.
14 Dawkins, *The God Delusion*, p. 281.
15 Dawkins, *The God Delusion*, p. 284.
16 Dawkins, *The God Delusion*, p. 284.
17 Dawkins once wrote an article outlining some of the good points of Jesus' ethical teaching: 'Atheists for Jesus', *Free Inquiry* 25:1 (2005), 9–10.
18 St Augustine, *The City of God* and *Confessions*. These are his most famous works.
19 Dawkins, *The God Delusion*, pp. 284–5.
20 Dawkins, *The God Delusion*, p. 287.
21 Dawkins, *The God Delusion*, p. 268.
22 Dawkins, *The God Delusion*, pp. 268–9.
23 Dawkins, *The God Delusion*, p. 270.
24 Alister McGrath (with Joanna Collicutt McGrath), *The Dawkins Delusion? Atheist Fundamentalism and the Denial of the Divine* (London: SPCK, 2007).
25 Alister McGrath, *Why God Won't Go Away: Engaging with the New Atheism* (London: SPCK, 2011). Other books of a similar nature include John C. Lennox, *Gunning for God: Why the New Atheists Are Missing the Point* (Oxford: Lion Hudson, 2011); David Bentley Hart, *Atheist Delusions: The Christian Revolution and Its Fashionable Enemies* (Ann Arbor, MI: Sheridan Books, 2009); and Keith Ward, *Why There Almost Certainly Is a God: Doubting Dawkins* (Oxford: Lion Hudson, 2008).
26 McGrath, *The Dawkins Delusion?*, p. 57.
27 McGrath, *The Dawkins Delusion?*, p. 58.
28 McGrath, *The Dawkins Delusion?*, p. 58.
29 McGrath, *The Dawkins Delusion?*, p. 58.
30 McGrath, *The Dawkins Delusion?*, p. 58.
31 Christopher Hitchens, *God Is Not Great*. Unlike Dawkins, Hitchens at least devotes a whole chapter to the Old Testament

and another to the New (even though he titles the latter 'The Evil of the "New" Testament').

32 Hitchens, *God Is Not Great*, p. 103.
33 Hitchens, *God Is Not Great*, p. 98.
34 Hitchens, *God Is Not Great*, p. 98.
35 Hitchens, *God Is Not Great*, p. 97.
36 Hitchens, *God Is Not Great*, p. 102.
37 Hitchens, *God Is Not Great*, p. 98.
38 Hitchens, *God Is Not Great*, p. 99.
39 Hitchens, *God Is Not Great*, p. 100.
40 Of course, this is only the case in the Exodus 20 version of the account of the Ten Commandments; see Chapter 4.
41 Hitchens, *God Is Not Great*, p. 103.
42 Such as I. Finkelstein and N. A. Silberman, *The Bible Unearthed: Archaeology's New Vision of Ancient Israel and the Origin of Its Sacred Texts* (London: Simon & Schuster, 2001).
43 Hitchens, *God Is Not Great*, p. 103.
44 Hitchens, *God Is Not Great*, p. 104.
45 Hitchens, *God Is Not Great*, p. 104.
46 Hitchens, *God Is Not Great*, p. 104.
47 Hitchens, *God Is Not Great*, p. 107.
48 Hitchens, *God Is Not Great*, p. 103.
49 Hitchens, *God Is Not Great*, p. 107.
50 Hitchens, *God Is Not Great*, p. 110.
51 Hitchens, *God Is Not Great*, p. 113.
52 Hitchens, *God Is Not Great*, p. 117.
53 Hitchens, *God Is Not Great*, p. 120.
54 McGrath, *Why God Won't Go Away*, p. 9.
55 McGrath, *Why God Won't Go Away*, p. 18.
56 McGrath, *Why God Won't Go Away*, p. 19.
57 See pp. 118–20 on Lewis, and pp. 120–2.
58 Tertullian, *Adversus Marcio* and Irenaeus, *Against Heresies* are the most significant works, although there are chapters on Marcionism as a heresy in other works of the period, e.g. Epiphanius in *Panarion*. Justin Martyr's work countering Marcion has not survived, although we roughly know its

contents through other writers and from Justin Martyr's own *Apologies*.
59 These examples come from Tertullian (*Adversus Marcio* II), who also listed as examples of Marcion's account of God's inconsistency the seven-day circumvention of Jericho which contravened Sabbath observance (Josh. 6.14–15), and ideas about repentance which are inconsistent with the case of Nineveh, where wholesale repentance of a foreign people is acceptable (in Jonah 3—4).
60 Judith M. Lieu, *Marcion and the Making of a Heretic* (New York: CUP, 2015), p. 355. I am grateful to Professor Lieu for a useful email exchange about Marcion.
61 Sebastian Moll, *The Arch-heretic Marcion*, WANT 250 (Tübingen: Mohr Siebeck, 2010), p. 78.
62 Ignatius, *Magnesians* 9.2.
63 Justin Martyr, *Apologies*.
64 Harnack, *Marcion*.

2 The character and scope of the Old Testament: countering a bad press

1 Richard Dawkins, *The God Delusion* (London: Black Swan, 2007), p. 268.
2 How many centuries there were in the biblical period is much debated – the recent 'low chronology' scheme (Finkelstein) has made the dating later than traditional reconstructions, due to a redating of archaeological layers (see Chapter 6). Traditional models of biblical chronology are based both on archaeology and on comparison with ancient Near Eastern chronology, notably with Egyptian dynastic periods.
3 Dawkins, *The God Delusion*, p. 268.
4 See John Barton, *People of the Book: Authority of the Bible in Christianity* (London: SPCK, 2012); *Holy Writings, Sacred Text: The Canon in Early Christianity* (Louisville, KY: Westminster John Knox Press, 1998).

5 A good example is Ecclesiastes; see Katharine J. Dell on the canonization of Ecclesiastes in Chapter 1 of *Interpreting Ecclesiastes: Readers Old and New* (Winona Lake, IN: Eisenbrauns, 2014).
6 See discussion in Chapter 1 of Katharine J. Dell, *Opening the Old Testament* (London: Wiley-Blackwell, 2008).
7 The book of Ruth is also moved to take its place after the Judges and before 1 Samuel in recognition of historical chronology.
8 Alister McGrath (with Joanna Collicutt McGrath), *The Dawkins Delusion? Atheist Fundamentalism and the Denial of the Divine* (London: SPCK, 2007), p. 58.
9 McGrath, *The Dawkins Delusion?*, p. 58.
10 Increasingly these are available electronically: examples include Accordance and Bibleworks. Daily readings of the Bible include *Guidelines* (which I co-edited for ten years) and *New Daylight*, published by the Bible Reading Fellowship.
11 Dell, *Opening the Old Testament*. See also the review of it by John J. Collins, 'Book of the Month: Open the Bible a Little', in the *Expository Times* 120:6 (2009), 282–3, who took its strength – the aim of sampling texts and arguments as a prelude to reading a more in-depth Old Testament introduction – as a weakness and, in doing so, misrepresented its purport.
12 *The Postmodern Bible* by a selection of ten authors calling themselves the 'The Bible and Culture Collective (including George Aichele, Fred W. Burnett and Elizabeth A. Castelli (one of four editors)) rather than simply one was a pioneer in this 'method' revolution.
13 Described by Paul Ricoeur as 'the hermeneutical circle'. See the helpful discussion of Ricoeurian hermeneutics and other hermeneutical approaches in John Barton, *Reading the Old Testament* (London: DLT, 1996).
14 John Barton, *Ethics in Ancient Israel* (Oxford: OUP, 2014) shows how ethical concerns were of key importance to writers of texts (as they are to readers of texts).
15 Following Martin Noth, *The Deuteronomistic History* (Sheffield: JSOT Press, 1981) [publ. German, 1st edn 1943; 3rd edn 1957].

16 See an attempt in Dell, *Opening the Old Testament*, pp. 74–5. There are one or two errors in the chronology, as mentioned in John Day's otherwise positive review in the *SOTS Book List* (2009), p. 93 – notably that Joel the prophet should not be dated to 810–750 BCE, his dates being largely unknown (somewhere between the ninth and fifth centuries BCE); that Sennacherib's siege of Jerusalem dates not to *c.* 704 but 701 BCE; and that both Belshazzar and Jeremiah are wrongly described as kings.

17 A recent example is Francesca Stavrakopoulou's BBC television series, *The Bible's Buried Secrets* (2011), in which she follows the 'low chronology' where possible.

18 A recent example is Walter Brueggemann in his *Theology of the Old Testament: Testimony, Dispute, Advocacy* (Minneapolis, MN: Fortress Press, 1997).

19 Ezra seems to have had a concept of 'the law' as an entity, e.g. Ezra 7.10.

20 See discussion in Katharine J. Dell, 'God, Creation and the Contribution of Wisdom', in R. P. Gordon (ed.), *The God of Israel* (Cambridge: CUP, 2007), pp. 60–72.

21 See Dell, 'God, Creation and the Contribution of Wisdom'.

22 Sung at five different Jewish festivals throughout the liturgical year (with some variation in different Jewish traditions).

23 The title used by Dawkins for his book about evolutionary biology, *The Blind Watchmaker* (London: 1986; Penguin Books, 1991).

3 Meeting Dawkins head-on: texts in Genesis

1 Walter Brueggemann, *Texts under Negotiation: The Bible and Postmodern Imagination* (Minneapolis, MN: Fortress Press, 1993).

2 Since Julius Wellhausen in his *Prolegomena zur Geschichte Israels* (Berlin: G. Reimer, 1883), or possibly earlier.

3 Dawkins suggests 'scrumping' as an appropriate word as it specifically refers to apples. More common in that part of the world, however, are grapes, pomegranates, figs, even apricots.

4 Richard Dawkins, *The God Delusion* (London: Black Swan, 2007), p. 284.
5 Dawkins, *The God Delusion*, p. 287.
6 Dawkins, *The God Delusion*, p. 287.
7 See Stephanie Dalley, *Myths from Mesopotamia: Creation, the Flood, Gilgamesh and Others* (Oxford: OUP, 1991).
8 Irving Finkel, *The Ark before Noah: Decoding the Story of the Flood* (London: Hodder and Stoughton, 2014), discusses a previously unknown Babylonian tablet that provides a fascinating parallel to many of the details of the Flood story. See my review in *The Times Literary Supplement* 5787 (28 February 2014).
9 Dawkins, *The God Delusion*, p. 269.
10 Dawkins, *The God Delusion*, p. 269.
11 Dawkins, *The God Delusion*, p. 270.
12 Dawkins, *The God Delusion*, p. 271.
13 Abraham's dates are much debated. Traditional timelines would place him *c.* 1925 BCE, but many have doubted his historical existence and seen the tales as a literary construction, perhaps of the stories of a number of tribal ancestors; or have dated him later.
14 E.g. the angelic intermediary in the story of Manoah in Judges 13. There are many examples.
15 Dawkins, *The God Delusion*, pp. 271–2.
16 See my article on 'Hospitality in the Old Testament' in *RGG* (English version), originally published as 'Gastfreundschaft im AT', in *Religion und Geschichte und Gegenwart*, 4th edn (2000), p. 475.
17 E.g. Judges 15.17: 'When he [Samson] had finished speaking, he threw away the jawbone and that place was called Ramath Lehi', i.e. 'place of the jawbone'.
18 This could be a description of an earthquake.
19 Dawkins, *The God Delusion*, p. 272.
20 These cycles may well have circulated within the tribe and stories about other tribal members might have been attributed to Abraham, or stories otherwise unassociated with him may have become associated at a later stage.

21 See discussion in scholars such as Hermann Gunkel, in his commentary on *Genesis*, HAT 1 (Göttingen, 1907) or more recently Robert Alter, *The Art of Biblical Narrative* (London: Allen and Unwin, 1981).
22 Cf. other delaying tactics in Genesis 24.55; 34.13–17, in these cases by brothers.
23 The episode foreshadows Israel in Egypt, when the lives of their men are endangered and the women are spared, and when, after the plagues have run their course, they escape with the wealth of the Egyptians.
24 Dawkins, *The God Delusion*, pp. 274–5.
25 Dawkins, *The God Delusion*, p. 275.
26 Dawkins, *The God Delusion*, p. 275.
27 J. L. Crenshaw, *Whirlpool of Torment: Israelite Traditions of God as an Oppressive Presence* (Atlanta, GA: SBL, 2008), p. 9.
28 Dawkins, *The God Delusion*, p. 274.

4 Homing in on Hitchens (and Dawkins): Exodus, Numbers and legal texts

1 Christopher Hitchens, *God Is Not Great: How Religion Poisons Everything* (London: Atlantic Books, 2007), p. 98.
2 Hitchens, *God Is Not Great*, p. 99.
3 Hitchens, *God Is Not Great*, p. 100.
4 Hitchens, *God Is Not Great*, p. 100.
5 Hitchens, *God Is Not Great*, p. 100.
6 Richard Dawkins, *The God Delusion* (London: Black Swan, 2007), p. 282.
7 The Hittites had suzerainty treaties whereby a benevolent suzerain gave support to a vassal in return for obligations and services rendered. These treaties would be read in public and renewed frequently. It is possible that the Ten Commandments are in a form that would have been reiterated as a reminder of the relationship between God and Israel, although whether the Israelites saw themselves as in such an obligated relationship with God is a debatable point.

8. Albrecht Alt in his *Essays on Old Testament History and Religion* (Oxford: Blackwell, 1966 [publ. German 1953]) believed that the apodictic form indicated native Israelite law, which contrasts with casuistic law as found in the Book of the Covenant (Exod. 20—23) and in the law codes of other cultures, for example the Code of Hammurabi from Babylon.
9. Julius Wellhausen, *Prologomena to the History of Israel*, 1883.
10. See discussion in E. W. Nicholson, *God and His People: Covenant and Theology in the Old Testament* (Oxford: Clarendon, 1986).
11. There are some additions to verses in the Ten Commandments that may indicate later shaping (as seen in the differences between the two accounts in Exod. 20 and Deut. 5), but there is nothing in the moral instructions that Moses might not have uttered. However, I am not advocating a Mosaic dating here, simply pointing out the uncertainties of assigning a date to such material, be it early or late.
12. G. Von Rad in *Old Testament Theology*, vol. 1 (Edinburgh: Oliver and Boyd, 1965 [publ. German 1960]) argued for this cultic use for the Ten Commandments and for other summary statements of faith as part of a 'theological credo', but it is unlikely that these laws originated there, even if that forms a later context for their use.
13. Anthony Phillips, *Ancient Israel's Criminal Law: A New Approach to the Decalogue* (Oxford: Blackwell, 1970).
14. Alt, on the other hand, had believed that no special penalties for infringement of the commandments were listed because it was implied that God himself would act against the wrongdoer.
15. Ronald E. Clements, *Deuteronomy*, Old Testament Guides (Sheffield: JSOT Press, 1989).
16. Hitchens, *God Is Not Great*, p. 101.
17. Dawkins, *The God Delusion*, p. 277.
18. E.g. Num. 14.18; Jer. 32.18; Joel 2.13; Jonah 4.2; Neh. 9.17; Pss. 86.15; 103.8; 145.8; Nahum 1.3.
19. Mary Douglas, *Purity and Danger: An Analysis of Concepts of Pollution and Taboo* (1966; new edn, London: Routledge, 2005).
20. Dawkins, *The God Delusion*, p. 278.

21 This was the view of Anthony Phillips in *Ancient Israel's Criminal Law*.
22 See M. E. J. Richardson, *Hammurabi's Laws: Text, Translation and Glossary* (Sheffield: SAP, 2000).
23 Dawkins, *The God Delusion*, p. 281.
24 This is a quotation from David T. Lamb's book, *God Behaving Badly: Is the God of the Old Testament Angry, Sexist and Racist?* (Downers Grove, IL: IVP, 2011), which I highly recommend as addressing many of the same issues as this book.
25 Hitchens, *God Is Not Great*, p. 106.
26 Dawkins, *The God Delusion*, p. 280.
27 For this view see Mark Smith, *The Early History of God: Yahweh and the Other Deities in Ancient Israel* (San Francisco, CA: Harper & Row, 1990).

5 Countering Dawkins: texts in the 'histories'

1 See Martin Noth, *The Deuteronomistic History* (Sheffield: JSOT Press, 1981) [publ. German, 1st edn 1943; 3rd edn 1957]. His theory that there is one overarching history from Joshua through to 2 Kings has held the field for a long time in scholarly circles. It has been challenged, however, in recent times by H. Spieckermann, *Juda unter Assur in der Sargonidenzelt*, FRLANT 129 (Göttingen: Vandenhoek & Ruprecht, 1982), who finds a basic Deuteronomistic history core in Samuel–Kings, but argues that Judges may well have been added at a later stage, followed by the book of Joshua.
2 Richard Dawkins, *The God Delusion* (London: Black Swan, 2007), p. 280.
3 Dawkins, *The God Delusion*, p. 280.
4 Dawkins, *The God Delusion*, p. 280.
5 Kathleen Kenyon, *Digging up Jericho* (London: E. Benn, 1957); *Excavations at Jericho* (London: British School of Archaeology in Jerusalem, 1960–83).
6 Cited in J. Hartung, 'Love Thy Neighbor: The Evolution of In-group Morality', *Skeptic* 3:4 (1995), pp. 86–99, and then Dawkins, *The God Delusion*, pp. 289–91.

7 See G. von Rad, *Old Testament Theology*, vol. 1 (Edinburgh: Oliver and Boyd, 1965) [publ. German 1960].
8 See other texts on the ark, such as 1 Samuel 6.
9 Phyllis Trible, *Texts of Terror: Literary-Feminist readings of Biblical Narratives* (London: SCM Press, 1992).
10 Dawkins, *The God Delusion*, p. 276.
11 Many women remain unnamed in the Old Testament. Naming is a very important matter and one that is often a female role when a child is born.
12 Women's roles include dancing, rejoicing, mourning and so on. See A. Brenner and F. van Dijk-Hemmes, *On Gendering Texts: Female and Male Voices in the Hebrew Bible* (New York: Brill, 1993). The role of women as celebrants of male victory is attested to in the songs of Miriam (Exod. 15.21) and Deborah (Judg. 5).
13 W. Brueggemann, *Revelation and Violence: A Study in Contextualization* (Milwaukee, WI: Marquette University Press, 1986), and many other books.
14 Dawkins, *The God Delusion*, p. 273.
15 Dawkins, *The God Delusion*, p. 273.
16 It is thought that the cycles of stories in Judges probably had some oral or written existence before they came to be incorporated in the wider 'Deuteronomistic history'. The amount of information about each judge varies, probably depending on how much was available to the author/editor/compiler.
17 In Greek tradition (such as Homer's *Odyssey*) cannibalism is the chief crime.
18 Cheryl Exum, *Fragmented Women: Feminist (Sub)versions of Biblical Narratives* (Sheffield: JSOT Press, 1993), argues that male fear of female sexuality lurks beneath the surface of this story. Susan Niditch in *Judges*, OTL (Louisville, KY: Westminster John Knox Press, 2008) suggests that the man who defeats his enemy metaphorically rapes him so that the latter becomes feminized.

19 I preached upon it myself at Oriel College, Oxford in 2012, and those of the congregation that I spoke to (except the chaplain) had never heard it before.
20 See David M. Gunn, *Judges*, Blackwell Bible Commentaries (Oxford: Blackwell, 2005) for some fascinating comment about the reception history of texts such as this one in Judges.

6 The Writings: a neglected corner of the Old Testament

1 Creation accounts from Babylonia include the *Enuma Elish* and the Epic of Gilgamesh.
2 'J', the Jahwistic source (using Yahweh for God), was originally dated by Wellhausen at the time of the united monarchy; however, that was questioned in the mid-1970s by H. H. Schmid, *Der Sogennante Yahwist* (Zurich: Theologischer Verlag, 1976) and others, who argued for the exilic period as its origin.
3 This is the part of the canon on which I have written most extensively and so I have kept my discussion here brief and refer the reader to my work.
4 J. J. Collins in a review of *Opening the Old Testament* criticized me for putting more stress on the moral aspect of wisdom than on the Prophets or the law. Maybe that simply reflects my bias, but the point I thought I was making is that in this literature there is an equally important source of ethics, extrapolated from everyday experience passed down from one generation to another. See discussion in Katharine J. Dell, *Opening the Old Testament*, (London: Wiley-Blackwell, 2008), Chapter 3.
5 See Katharine J. Dell, *Seeking a Life That Matters: Wisdom for Today from the Book of Proverbs* (London: DLT, 2002).
6 See Katharine J. Dell, *The Book of Proverbs in Social and Theological Context* (Cambridge: CUP, 2006); *Get Wisdom, Get Insight: An Introduction to Israel's Wisdom Literature* (London: DLT, 2000).
7 Psalm 104 is often characterized as a wisdom psalm because of its close connections with the genre. Categorization, however, is a subjective enterprise.

8 Katharine J. Dell, 'God, Creation and the Contribution of Wisdom', in R. P. Gordon (ed.), *The God of Israel* (Cambridge: CUP, 2007), pp. 60–72.
9 See William P. Brown, *Character in Crisis: A Fresh Approach to the Wisdom Literature of the Old Testament* (Grand Rapids, MI: Eerdmans, 1996), and his recent *Wisdom's Wonder: Character, Creation, and Crisis in the Bible's Wisdom Literature* (Grand Rapids, MI: Eerdmans, 2014).
10 I have written extensively on Job and Ecclesiastes and so have chosen not to prioritize them here (for a change!).
11 See A. Brenner and F. van Dijk-Hemmes, *On Gendering Texts: Female and Male Voices in the Hebrew Bible* (Leiden and New York: Brill, 1993).
12 Unless 'Yah' is Yahweh in Song of Songs 8.6, where 'a raging flame' has sometimes been translated 'flames of Yah', i.e. part of the divine name, Yahweh.
13 See Katharine J. Dell, 'Old Testament Theology in Ecological Focus', in S. Fischer and M. Grohmann (eds), *Weisheit und Schöpfung: Festschrift für James Alfred Loader zum 65. Geburtstag*, Wiener Alttestamentliche Studien 7 (Frankfurt am Main: Peter Lang, 2010), pp. 59–77.
14 Psalm 119 is an acrostic psalm, in which each section basically uses words that begin with each letter in the Hebrew alphabet in turn. The section referred to here has the Hebrew letter נ ('nun'/'n') on the acrostic. This material was originally published in *Lectionary Homiletics* (June–July 2011), as were a few other of my worked examples (also in *Lectionary Homiletics*, October–November 2012 and February–March 2013).
15 This may have its origins in bird imagery (Deut. 32.11; Isa. 31.5), or from the cherubim in the sanctuary symbolizing God's presence, as in Pss. 36.7; 57.1.
16 It is written in Aramaic, as the stories are, and it also links thematically with Nebuchadnezzar's dream in chapter 2.
17 Eric Heaton, *The Book of Daniel: Introduction and Commentary* (London: SCM, 1956).

18 Other variants of these more general suggestions have also been made, such as that he is representative of Judas Maccabeus, who led a successful revolt, and that the vision marks God's approval of Maccabean victory. Of course the vision may have been used for such political ends, but this is unlikely to have been its sole reference.

7 The Prophets: a more convincing source of morality?

1 See the pioneering commentary by Brevard Childs, *Isaiah*, OTL (Louisville, KY: Westminster John Knox Press, 2001), where he takes a canonical approach to the whole book.
2 Particular parallels are texts from Mari on the Euphrates, a city state that rivalled the power of Babylon in its time. The letters reveal much about the nature of prophecy there, and this has been used as a vital parallel for understanding Israelite prophecy, notably in its calls for social justice and morality.
3 I am thinking in particular of the work of Robert P. Carroll on Jeremiah, in which he argued for a disappearing historical figure under the layers of text and editings in the book that bears his name. See R. P. Carroll, *From Chaos to Covenant: Uses of Prophecy in the Book of Jeremiah* (London: SCM, 1981).
4 This chapter (Amos 9) is often seen as a later addition because of its hopefulness. However, should we simply excise the hopeful parts of prophecies quite so readily?
5 There is a good discussion of the significance of 'the land' for Israel in David T. Lamb, *God Behaving Badly: Is the God of the Old Testament Angry, Sexist and Racist?* (Downers Grove, IL: IVP, 2011), pp. 76–81.
6 See the fascinating book by Renita Weems, *Battered Love: Marriage, Sex and Violence in the Old Testament Prophets* (Minneapolis, MN: Fortress Press, 1995).
7 Jeremiah similarly complains at his prophetic role, but nevertheless fulfils it (Jer. 1); Ezekiel obediently eats a scroll that tastes as sweet as honey (Ezek. 3).

8 See Katharine J. Dell, *Opening the Old Testament* (London: Wiley-Blackwell, 2008), pp. 164–6 for discussion of Isaiah 6.
9 There is a second introduction in 2.1, which might suggest that the whole of Isaiah 1 is a compilation of original prophecies by a later hand; and a third in Isaiah 13.1.
10 It was wider ancient legal practice to use impartial elements as witnesses – see R. E. Clements, *Isaiah 1—39*, NCB (London: Marshall, Morgan and Scott; Grand Rapids, MI: Eerdmans, 1980).
11 A strong intertextual resonance also helps to establish links between these books.
12 The instruction mode here resembles that of the wisdom literature, especially in Proverbs 1—9, which contains a series of instruction texts.
13 Perhaps the Assyrian invasion of 701 BCE.
14 The so-called 'servant songs' are four passages where the servant is an individual figure rather than a communal one that can be identified with Israel. The passages are Isaiah 42.1–4; 49.1–6; 50.4–9; and 52.13—53.12, and many suggestions have been made as to the identity of the servant, who remains enigmatic.
15 This is echoed in language used of John the Baptist in the New Testament (e.g. Matt. 3).

8 Back to the Pentateuch and historical books: the power of story

1 See discussion of this theme in Katharine J. Dell, *Opening the Old Testament* (London: Wiley-Blackwell, 2008), pp. 152–5.
2 See Dell, *Opening the Old Testament*, pp. 138–41.
3 See in particular the Earth Bible series edited by Norman Habel.
4 I am quoting myself here in Dell, *Opening the Old Testament*, p. 60. I stand by that evaluation despite criticism of it in the review by John J. Collins in the *Expository Times*, mentioned above. It is the point at which the salvation history as related in the Old Testament starts, with notionally historical figures as opposed to the mythical character of Genesis 1—11.

5 Although the Old Testament itself makes no differentiation between Noah and other figures from the past who are mentioned, particularly from exilic times onwards, e.g. Ezekiel 14.14, 20, where he is named along with Job and Daniel.
6 Albrecht Alt argued that these were different Jacob cycles. See Alt, 'The God of the Fathers', in *Essays in Old Testament History and Religion*, trans. R. A. Wilson (Oxford: Blackwell, 1966), pp. 133–69.
7 This theme of protection is taken up in the New Testament. In Hebrews 13.5, for example, God says, 'I will never leave you or forsake you.'
8 I am citing here the language used by Andrew Lloyd Webber and Tim Rice in their excellent musical, *Joseph and the Amazing Technicolor Dreamcoat*, based on the Joseph story.
9 For example, the early American settlers entering the 'promised land' of the USA used the language of Exodus – see Charles Brock, *Mosaics of the American Dream: America as New Israel, a Metaphor for Today* (Oxford: Bayou, 1994).
10 See Dell, *Opening the Old Testament*, pp. 193–200.
11 See David T. Lamb's superb explanation of the reasons for God's anger in this story in *God Behaving Badly: Is the God of the Old Testament Angry, Sexiest and Racist?* (Downers Grove, IL: IVP, 2011), pp. 27–33.
12 See Dell, *Opening the Old Testament*, pp. 80–5.
13 A particular critic of the Hebrew Bible's own telling of the story of David is Joel Baden who, in *The Historical David: The Real Life of an Invented Hero* (London: HarperOne, 2013), reconstructs David as a revolutionary mercenary who seized the crown of a non-existent kingdom, building it up from nothing.
14 See Dell, *Opening the Old Testament*, pp. 89–95.

9 Questioning the history of Israel: scepticism within the academy

1 Christopher Hitchens, *God Is Not Great: How Religion Poisons Everything* (London: Atlantic Books, 2007), p. 103.
2 Hitchens, *God Is Not Great*, p. 102.

3 Hitchens, *God Is Not Great*, p. 102.
4 The term 'Hebrew Bible' is generally preferred in modern biblical scholarship as it has a neutrality that 'Old Testament' lacks ('old' suggests the need for something 'new', which is not appropriate for Jewish readers).
5 General Charles George Gordon (1833–85), who wrote *Reflections in Palestine* (London: Macmillan and Co., 1883). Hitchens describes him as a 'biblical fanatic' (p. 103).
6 W. F. Albright, *The Archaeology of Palestine and the Bible* (New York: Fleming H. Revell, 1932).
7 Hitchens, *God Is Not Great*, p. 104.
8 Hitchens, *God Is Not Great*, p. 102.
9 Hitchens, *God Is Not Great*, p. 107.
10 Walter Brueggemann, *Texts under Negotiation: The Bible and Postmodern Imagination* (Minneapolis, MN: Fortress Press, 1993).
11 A line followed by, among others, K. Whitelam, in *The Invention of Ancient Israel: The Silencing of Palestinian History* (London: Routledge, 1996).
12 G. Barkay, 'The Iron Age II–III' in A. Ben Tor (ed.), *The Archaeology of Ancient Israel* (New Haven, CT: Yale University Press, 1992), pp. 302–84, at p. 302. The Iron Age covers the period from 1200 to 500 BCE, but there are arguments about its various levels and their relative dating.
13 Israel Finkelstein is essentially an Israeli archaeologist rather than a biblical scholar and records his detailed findings in archaeological books and journals. His view on the monarchy is found in 'The Archaeology of the United Monarchy: An Alternative View', *Levant* 28 (1996), 177–87. He was interviewed by Francesca Stavrakopoulou in her television series *The Bible's Buried Secrets* in the episode 'Did King David's Empire Exist?'
14 Y. Yadin, an Israeli archaeologist whose best-known work was at Masada and Hazor.
15 Barkay, 'The Iron Age II–III', pp. 306–7.
16 John Bright, *A History of Israel* (Philadelphia, PA: Westminster Press, 1959). This book ran to four editions and was highly influential in the field.

17 Whitelam, *The Invention of Ancient Israel*.
18 See also William Dever, *The Lives of Ordinary People in Ancient Israel: Where Archaeology and the Bible Intersect* (Grand Rapids, MI: Eerdmans, 2012). Dever has emerged as the most vociferous anti-minimalist.
19 Francesca Stavrakopoulou, *The Bible's Buried Secrets*, BBC TV series, 2011.
20 I. Finkelstein and N. A. Silberman, *The Bible Unearthed: Archaeology's New Vision of Ancient Israel and the Origin of Its Stories* (London: Simon & Schuster, 2001).
21 Finkelstein and Silberman, *The Bible Unearthed*, pp. 178–9.
22 Kenneth A. Kitchen, *On the Reliability of the Old Testament* (Grand Rapids, MI: Eerdmans, 2003), p. 464.
23 It was labelled 'minimalist' by its detractors, but that name rather than 'The Copenhagen School' has stuck.
24 Philip Davies, *In Search of 'Ancient Israel'* (Sheffield: JSOT Press, 1992). Also *Scribes and Schools: The Canonization of the Hebrew Scriptures* (Louisville, KY: Westminster John Knox Press, 1985).
25 See James Barr, *History and Ideology in the Old Testament: Biblical Studies at the End of a Millennium* (Oxford: OUP, 2000).
26 T. L. Thompson, *The Bible in History: How Writers Create a Past* (London: Jonathan Cape, 1998).
27 I heard Philip Davies, for one, say in a conference talk that he did not like the label.
28 Lester Grabbe, *Ancient Israel: What Do We Know and How Do We Know It?* (London: T&T Clark, 2007), p. 142.
29 For an excellent book on what we can still say about the pre-exilic period, see John Day (ed.), *In Search of Pre-Exilic Israel*, JSOTS 406 (London and New York: T&T Clark International, 2004).

10 A Christian perspective on the Old Testament

1 Matthew Richard Schlimm, *This Strange and Sacred Scripture: Wrestling with the Old Testament and Its Oddities* (Grand Rapids, MI: Baker Academic, 2015), p. 205.

2 Schlimm, *This Strange and Sacred Scripture*, p. 206. These categories relate to his different chapters on the violence, sexism and legalism of the Old Testament.
3 Walter Zimmerli, *Old Testament Theology in Outline* (Atlanta, GA: John Knox Press, 1978), characterized the Old Testament as 'a book of expectation, a book that is open to the future' (p. 240).
4 Cf. the fourth servant song of Deutero-Isaiah in Isaiah 52.13— 53.12.
5 The Festival of Nine Lessons and Carols was invented by Eric Milner-White, then chaplain, at King's College, Cambridge in 1918. It was in fact adapted from an order of service from Truro Cathedral (before the present cathedral was built) in 1880, devised by E. W. Benson, later Archbishop of Canterbury.
6 Katharine J. Dell, *Opening the Old Testament* (London: Wiley-Blackwell, 2008), pp. 167–9. I have also discussed in that book the significance of the suffering servant figure for an understanding of Jesus' role (pp. 161–2), so I refer the reader there.
7 This is a common phenomenon in Third Isaiah (Isa. 55—66).
8 Judith M. Lieu, *Marcion and the Making of a Heretic* (New York: CUP, 2015), p. 197.
9 Cf. Isaiah 51.9 for imagery of the 'arm of the Lord'.
10 Cf. their citation in Matthew 13.15 and Acts 28.27.
11 See J. F. A. Sawyer, *The Fifth Gospel: Isaiah in the History of Christianity* (Cambridge: CUP, 1996).
12 Scholarly suggestions are very numerous – see discussion in Katharine J. Dell, 'The Suffering Servant: Jeremiah Revisited', in Katharine J. Dell, G. I. Davies and Y. V. Koh (eds), *Genesis, Isaiah and Psalms: A Festschrift to Honour John Emerton For His Eightieth Birthday* (Leiden and Boston: Brill, 2010), pp. 119–34. Here I suggest that the image is modelled on a recently known prophet – Jeremiah – although it has a more far-reaching application.
13 For more discussion see Dell, *Opening the Old Testament*, pp. 179–90.
14 Francesca Stavrakopoulou, author and presenter of *The Bible's Buried Secrets* and a professional academic in the field, for

example, is a self-confessed atheist but has great respect for the Bible (see her Wikipedia entry at <https://en.wikipedia.org/wiki/Francesca_Stavrakopoulou>), and has spoken about this publicly on radio and television.

Further reading

John Barton, *What Is the Bible?*, London: SPCK, 1991.
Walter Brueggemann, *Texts under Negotiation: The Bible and Postmodern Imagination*, Minneapolis, MN: Fortress Press, 1993.
Walter Brueggemann, William C. Placher, Brian K. Bount, *Struggling with Scripture*, Louisville, KY: Westminster John Knox Press, 2002.
Eryl Davies, *The Immoral Bible: Approaches to Biblical Ethics*, London: T&T Clark, 2010.
Ellen Davis, *Getting Involved with God: Rediscovering the Old Testament*, Cambridge, MA: Cowley, 2001.
Katharine Dell, *Shaking a Fist at God*, London: HarperCollins, 1996.
Katharine J. Dell, *Seeking a Life That Matters*, London: Darton, Longman and Todd, 2002.
Katharine J. Dell, *Opening the Old Testament*, Oxford: Wiley Blackwell, 2008.
John Goldingay, *Theological Diversity and the Authority of the Old Testament*, Grand Rapids, MI: Eerdmans, 1987.
David Bentley Hart, *Atheist Delusions: The Christian Revolution and Its Fashionable Enemies*, Ann Arbor, MI: Sheridan Books, 2009.
David T. Lamb, *God Behaving Badly: Is the God of the Old Testament Angry, Sexist and Racist?*, Downers Grove, IL: IVP, 2011.
John C. Lennox, *Gunning for God: Why the New Atheists Are Missing the Point*, Oxford: Lion Hudson, 2011.
Tremper Longman III, *Making Sense of the Old Testament: Three Crucial Questions*, Grand Rapids, MI: Baker, 1998.
Alister McGrath (with Joanna Collicutt McGrath), *The Dawkins Delusion? Atheist Fundamentalism and the Denial of the Divine*, London: SPCK, 2007.

Further reading

Alister McGrath, *Why God Won't Go Away: Engaging with the New Atheism*, London: SPCK, 2011.

Matthew Richard Schlimm, *This Strange and Sacred Scripture: Wrestling with the Old Testament and Its Oddities*, Grand Rapids, MI: Baker Academic, 2015.

Eric A. Siebert, *Disturbing Divine Behavior: Troubling Old Testament Images of God*, Minneapolis, MN: Fortress Press, 2009.

Phyllis Trible, *God and the Rhetoric of Sexuality*, Philadelphia, PA: Fortress Press, 1978.

Keith Ward, *Why There Almost Certainly Is a God: Doubting Dawkins*, Oxford: Lion Hudson, 2008.

Christopher J. H. Wright, *The God I Don't Understand*, Grand Rapids, MI: Zondervan, 2008.

Index of biblical references

Genesis
1 45, 54, 127, 133, 213
1—2.4a 50, 53, 55
1—3 38, 46, 49–55
1—11 50, 59, 73, 122, 235 n4
1.9–13 50
1.24–31 50
1.27b 38
2—3 54
2.2–3 51
2.4b–3 51
2.21–24 38
3.4 163
3.9 23
3.13 169
4 167
6—9 46, 55–60
6.9 71
9 58, 164–5
9.18–27 38
9.20 67
11.1–9 163–4
11.6 163
12 72, 165
12.1–9 69, 70
12.10–20 69
15 69
16 109
18 56
18.1–8 63
18.16–33 65
18.25 65
19 7, 60–8, 111
19.2–3 63
19.5 62
19.7–8 62
19.12b 66
19.24 66
20 70, 71
20.1–18 69
21 73
22 71
22.7 73
22.18 74
24.55 228 n22
25.27–34 170
26 71
26.6–11 69
27 170
27.29–35 170
28.10–19 166–8
29.15–18 168–70
29.17 169
29.19 168
29.20 169
29.21 169
29.25 169
34.13–17 228 n22
37—50 170
38 66
38.18 130
41.42 130
48.15–16 167

Exodus 171
2 12, 98
3.12 167
12.35–36 23
15.20 105
15.21 231 n12
20 7, 76, 78, 223 n40, 229 n11
20—24 185
20.8–11 81
20.17 15
21—24 98
21.1–16 169
21.2 38
22.15 168
22.21 63
23.9 63
31.7 91
31.13 91
32 8
32—34 84
32.10 86
32.12 89
33 86–7
33.2 15
33.19 87
34 86–8, 89
34.6 87, 88
34.6–7 86
34.7 87
34.14 88

Leviticus 98
18.1 12, 98
18.7–8 67
18.21 72
18.22 38
19 98
19.33–34 63
20 90
20.2 12, 98
25 12, 98
26.46 43

Numbers 98
6.24 167, 205
12.3 15, 92
14.13–20 89
14.18 229 n18
15 91

243

Index of biblical references

20 133
21.9 23
21.29 137
25 89
31 8, 16, 92

Deuteronomy 171
4 102
4—11 83
5 7, 78, 229 n11
6.4 97
7 38
8.2 72
8.16 72
10.17–19 12, 63, 97
13.6 105
13.10 93
15.12–18 169
17.5 93
20 8, 95
20.17 95
21.18–21 93
21.21 93
22.23–29 64
22.29 168
23.1 92–3
24.17–19 63
26.5–11 63
30.11–20 96
31 173
31.28 156
31.30 172
32.1 156
32.1–2 173
32.1–4 172–3
32.3–5 173
32.11 233 n15
33 173
34 96
34.4 96
34.7 94
34.7b 96

Joshua 7, 40, 99–103, 171, 230 n1
1.5 167
6 8, 102–3
6.2 102
6.14–15 224 n59
6.21 99
6.26 103
17.3 106

Judges 7, 40, 103–14, 225 n7, 230 n1, 231 n16
5 231 n12
6.16 167
11 8, 103–8
11.1 103
11.5–6 106
11.9 106
11.24 106
11.31 104
11.34 105
11.35 105
11.37 105
11.39–40 106
13 227 n14
13—16 173–5
15.14 107
15.17 227 n17
16.7 174
16.12 174
16.14 174
16.22 175
17.6 110
18.1 110
19 7
19—20 108–14
19.1 110
19.2 110
19.3 110
19.16–30 108
19.22 111
19.27 111
19.29 109
20.6 111
21.1–13 105

Ruth 39–40, 121, 137–8, 225 n7
2.12 138
3.9 138

1 Samuel 29, 40, 225 n7, 230 n1
4–5 114, 175
6 231 n8
8.4–20 175–8
8.12–15 177
11.7 112
11.14–15 175–8
11.14–16 178
14.45 105
16—17 171
18.27 179
21.4–5 182
25.44 180

2 Samuel 29, 230 n1
3 180
3.14 179
3.16 180
6.1–5 178–80
6.12–19 178–80
7.12 22
11.1–15 181–3

1 Kings 29, 144, 155, 230 n1
1—11 126
4.32 125
12 86
14.25–28 193
16.24 197

Index of biblical references

2 Kings 29, 144, 155, 230 n1
3.26–27 105
23.21–30 114

1 Chronicles 29, 121, 139, 183–4

2 Chronicles 29, 121, 139, 183–4
3.1 73

Ezra 29, 121, 139
7.10 121, 226 n19

Nehemiah 29, 121, 139
9.17 229 n18

Esther 121, 138–9
4.14–16 138
9.22 139

Job 46, 121, 123, 128, 129, 136, 233 n10
1—2 167
1.9 72
38.26–27 128

Psalms 5, 121, 122, 131–6, 140
36.7 233 n15
57.1 233 n15
74 132
77 135–6
77.3 135
77.15 135
86.15 229 n18
89 141
91.4 138
91.11–12 167
103.8 229 n18
104 132, 232 n7
104.9 127
104.11–12 128
110 141
119 132–5, 136, 233 n14
119.105 133
119.106 133
119.107 134
119.108 134
137 131
145.8 229 n18
147 132, 137
147.1 132

Proverbs 5, 121, 123
1 134
1—9 127, 235 n12
1.1 125
1.7 125
1.18 71
3.12 71
4 133
4.1 71
4.3–4 71
4.7 124
8.24–31 127
10.1 125
10.1—22.16 123
16.1 124
16.1–11 124–6
16.2 124
16.3 124
16.4 125
16.6 125
16.8 125
16.9 125
16.10 126
16.11 126
16.12–15 126
21.6 134
24.21 123
26.14 123
28.15 123

Ecclesiastes 121, 123, 128, 129, 225 n5, 233 n10
1.4–11 128
3.2 128
9.9 137

Song of Songs 38, 121, 129–31
8.6 233 n12
8.6–7 130

Isaiah 29–30, 47, 122, 145
1 235 n9
1—39 145, 154–8
1.1–20 155–8
1.1–2a 155
1.2b 156
1.3 156
1.4 157
1.5–8 157
1.8 157
1.9 157
1.10 157
1.10–17 158
1.15 158
1.16–17 158
1.18 158

Index of biblical references

1.18–20 158
1.19 158
1.20 158, 159
2.1 235 n9
6 210, 235 n8
6.10 210
7.14 208
9.6 208
12.41 210
13.1 235 n9
20 155
24—27 155
25.8 161
30.15 154
31.5 233 n15
36—39 155
40 159
40—55 145, 148, 158–61
40.2 159
40.4 159
40.6 159
40.7 210
40.9 159
40.10 159
40.10b 159
42.1 210
42.1–4 235 n14
42.9 210
44.1–6 160–1
44.2–3 160
44.4 160
44.6 160
44.28 145
45 145
45.18–19 160
45.22 149
45.23b 161
49.1–6 235 n14
49.6 148
50.4–9 235 n14
51.9 239 n9
52.13—53.12 235 n14, 239 n4
53 210, 211
53.7–8 211
55—66 239 n7
61.1–2 209
66.18 38

Jeremiah 145, 234 n3
1 234 n7
7.9 80
7.23 207
8.18–19 151
8.21 151
9.1 151
22.24 130
32.18 229 n18
36.4 44

Lamentations 121, 136–7
3.22–24 136

Ezekiel 145
3 234 n7
14.14 236 n5
14.20 236 n5
16 149, 156
30.13 77
37 151
37.11–14 152

Daniel 121, 139–43, 144
2 233 n16
7.7 140
7.8 140
7.9–10 140
7.13 142
7.13–14 140
7.17–18 140
7.19 140
7.21 141

Hosea 151
2.16 150
2.18 150
2.19 150
3.1 149
4.2 80

Joel
2.13 229 n18

Amos
4.1 146
5.6–7 146, 147
5.10–15 146
9 148–9, 234 n4

Jonah 56, 152–4
1.16 153
2.7 154
3—4 224 n59
3.10 153
4.2 229 n18

Micah 47

Nahum
1.3 229 n18

Zephaniah
2.3 185

Malachi
3.1 22

Sirach
49.11 130

Matthew 5
1.5 103
3 235 n15
5.17 13
10.19 83

Index of biblical references

13.15 239 n10
21.12 205
22.36–40 83
22.37–39 23
24.37–39 60

Mark
2.27 92
3.17 32
11.15 205
29.32–34 60

Luke 4, 20, 21
2 210
4.18 209
7.26 22
16.29 22
17.27 60
18.20 83
18.31 22

24.44 30

John
1.1–14 213
2.14 205
3.16 74
12.37–41 210

Acts
8.26–35 211
17.6 97
28.27 239 n10

Romans 20
5 54
8.31–32 74
10.4 20
13.9 83

1 Corinthians 20

2 Corinthians 20

Galatians 20
3.13 20
4.22–31 21

Ephesians 20

Philippians 20

Colossians 20

1 Thessalonians 20

2 Thessalonians 20

2 Timothy
3.15–17 219

Philemon 20

Hebrews
11.7 60
11.32–34 107–8
13.5 236 n7

1 Peter
1.19–20 74

2 Peter
3.5–7 60
21.4 161

Revelation
1.13 143
14.14 143

Index of authors and subjects

Abimelech 70, 71
Abraham 7–8, 60, 68–74, 165; chronology 227 n13; historical existence 61; intercedes for Sodom 65; trust in God 74
'acts of God' 58
Adam and Eve 50
aetiology 37, 59, 198–203; *see also* origin stories
allegories 31–2; *see also* morality tales; parables
Ammon 68
Amos 146–9
ancestral storytelling 165–6
angels 61–2, 64, 166–7
anger, of God 88–90, 205
archaeological evidence 196–8, 203
archaeology 188–9, 192–5, 198
ark of the covenant 178–80
atheism 6
atonement 54, 85, 159
authority of canon 29, 43

Baal, worship of 86, 89, 147, 149
Barkay, Gabriel 192–3, 194
Bathsheba 181–2
Bethel 147, 166, 167–8

bias: within biblical texts 183–4; of readers 37–9, 203, 216
Bible: as chaotic 27–8; contradiction within 38; genres 30–1, 185–6; as God inspired 30; as historical record 30–1, 39, 191–2; as human construct 27–8; literary production 31–3, 39; as propaganda 200; *see also* canon of Scripture
biblical archaeology 192–5
biblical interpretation 32–3, 39, 191, 209
biblical scholarship 27–8; agenda of 217–18; and the Old Testament 187–8; in preaching 216–18; sociological approach to 195
biblical texts: bias 183–4; explanations of natural disasters 57–8; parochial in outlook 16–17, 38, 190–1; prehistory 30–1; reliability as evidence 192; selectivity 36–7, 46–7, 113–14, 208–9, 213
Bright, John 195
Brueggemann, Walter 212

Index of authors and subjects

Cain 167
canon of Scripture 28–30, 33, 190; *see also* Old Testament: canon
Carroll, Robert P. 199
Catholic canon 29
child sacrifice 72, 98, 104–5
children, status of 71–2, 91
chronology 193, 194, 196, 201–3, 224 n2, 226 n16
Clements, R. E. 82–3
clergy, attitude to Old Testament 218–21
concubines, status of 109
contemporary nations *see* nations, other than Israel, writings of
context: Abraham, wife as sister 69–71; Dawkins' lack of understanding of 8; God's actions 5–6; golden calf 85; Prophets 146; Sodom and Gomorrah 62–3, 66; Ten Commandments 77–8; walls of Jericho 101; *see also* cultural context; historical context; literary context
Copenhagen School, The *see* minimalist scholarship
covenants 44–5, 58, 73, 149–59, 164–5
creation 45–6, 122–3; accounts 50–2, 54–5, 59; doctrine of 164–5; myths 114; in Proverbs 126; in Psalms 127–8; 'seven-day' story 52–3
Creator-God 22, 54–5, 123, 128–9, 150
cultural context 9, 12, 33–5, 101
Cyrus, King 145

Daniel 140–1
David 44, 178–83, 196
David and Bathsheba, in Chronicles 183
Davies, Philip 199–201
Dawkins, Richard: biblical contextual understanding 8; on biblical interpretation 33; character assassination of God 3; on ethics in the Bible 3–4, 114; on fate of foreigners 95; *The God Delusion* 3, 27; on God's anger 89–90; on golden calf 84; on human sin 57; on Jesus Christ 9; on Joshua 99–101; on Levite's concubine 108–9; on nature of Bible 27–8; on near-sacrifice of Isaac 71–2; 'New Atheist' 6; on Old Testament God 3–5; on Sodom and Gomorrah 62; on Ten Commandments 77
death penalty 90–4
debt, jubilee for 98
Delilah 174–5

Index of authors and subjects

Demiurge 4, 21, 23
Dennett, Daniel 6
diversity as punishment 164
divine revelation, human perception of 35–6, 48, 98, 206
divine/human relationship 33, 35–6, 44–5, 48, 58, 61, 78, 149–50, 167, 206

Ehrmann, Bart 19
Eliezer 69
Epiphanius 20
Esau 170
eschatological visions 140–1
Esther 138–9
ethics: Dawkins' view 3–4, 114; Hitchens' view 14–15; in proverbs 123; in Scripture 34, 38–9; *see also* morality
evidence, nature of 191–2
Exile, the 42
exilic writings 122–3, 136
exodus, the 41, 171–2
explanation stories 55, 111–12, 163–4
Ezekiel 151–2
Ezra 185

faith, nourished by Scripture 217–18
Finkelstein, Israel 193–4, 197–8
First Isaiah 145, 154–5, 209

Flood, the 46, 50, 55–60
folk tales 69–70
food laws 88
foreigners, fate of 95; *see also* hospitality to strangers
forgiveness 87
'fulfilment in' motif 5, 207, 208–9

Galatians, Marcion amended version 21
Garden of Eden 50
genealogies 165–6, 184
genocide 101
genres in Bible 30–1
Gentiles, gospel to 4
Gibeah 111, 112
Gideon 167
God 7–8, 87; anger of 88–90, 205; concern for Israel 148–9; as destructive 65–6; 'fear of' 72; hidden 135; jealousy of 88–90; judgement of 65–6, 147–8; as King of Israel 176; as lawgiver 133; nationalistic view of 41, 90, 172; nature of 124–5, 136–7, 157, 160–1; obedience to 66, 71–3, 85, 104; of the Old Testament 3–5, 13, 205–6; pathos of 150–1; as protector 167; in Proverbs 124–5; relationship with humanity 33, 35–6, 44–5, 48, 58,

251

Index of authors and subjects

61, 78, 149–59, 167, 206;
revelation of 35–6, 48,
98, 206; as role model 11;
stories of power 64; trust
in 74, 136, 154–5
golden calf 8, 84–8
good and evil 53–4, 59–60, 65
Grabbe, Lester 201–2

Harnack, Adolf 4, 24
Harris, Sam 6
Hebrew Bible 21, 29, 121, 145
high chronology 193
historical books (of the Old
Testament) 29
historical context 85, 215
historicity 32–3; of
Pentateuch 94–5
Hitchens, Christopher: on
biblical punishments 92–3;
on biblical scholarship
188–90; on ethics in the
Bible 14–15; on golden
calf 84–6; on historicity
of Pentateuch 94–5;
on Jesus Christ 18; on
nature of Bible 28; 'New
Atheist' 6; on the New
Testament 17–18; on the
Old Testament 13–17; on
parochial nature of Bible
16–17, 38, 190–1; on Ten
Commandments 76–7,
78–9
holy war 101–2
homosexual rape 64, 108, 111

hope 158–60
hospitality to strangers 63,
97–8, 108–9, 110–11
humanity: pride of 164;
relationship with God 33,
35–6, 44–5, 48, 58, 61, 78,
149–59, 167, 206

idolatry 84–6, 88, 147
Ignatius 23
inherited sin 87
inter-tribal warfare 112, 113
Isaac 7, 69, 170;
near-sacrifice 71–5
Isaiah (book): authorship
of 145; hope in 158–60;
judgement in 156–8;
themes 154–5; use in
preaching 211
Isaiah (prophet) 154, 208–11
Israel: in exile 42; God as
King of 176; God's concern
for 148–9; monarchy 110,
112, 125–6, 175–8, 196–8;
salvation of 159, 160; as
separate nation 184–5;
sins of 147–8, 157–8
Israel, kingdom of 196
Israelite society 79–80, 90–1

Jacob 166, 168–70
Jacob's ladder 166–8
Jenkins, David 217
Jephthah 103–4, 106–7
Jephthah's daughter 8, 103–6,
107

Index of authors and subjects

Jeremiah 136, 150–1
Jericho, walls of 40–1, 99–102
Jesus' Bible 30, 207
Jesus Christ: atonement for original sin 54; authority derived from the Old Testament 47–8, 209–10; and Daniel's vision 143; Dawkins' view of 9; death as sacrifice 74–5; 'fulfilment in' motif 5, 207, 208–9; Hitchens' view of 18; image of self 207; and the Jewish law 21, 91–2; moral teaching 9; parallel with Isaac 74–5; parallel with Isaiah 210–11; person of 5; rejection of 210–11; superseding God of Old Testament 20–1; and the Ten Commandments 83–4
Joab 181–2
Jonah 152–4
Joseph, tribe of 147
Joseph's coat 170–1
Joshua 7, 8, 167, 173
judgement 150–1, 154; God's 65–6, 147–8; in Isaiah 156–8
Judges 7
justice 65–6; *see also* social justice
Justin Martyr, St 20, 23–4

kingship *see* monarchy in Israel

Kitchen, Kenneth 198

Laban 168–70
lament 135–6
languages, phenomenon of 163–4
laws 31; authority of 43; as moral guide 133–4; of the Old Testament 9, 11, 15, 23–4; in Psalms 132–4
Leah 168–70
lectionaries 36, 47, 213
legal texts 97–8
Lemche, Nils Peter 199
Levi, tribe of 85
Levite's concubine 7, 108–11
Lewis, C. S.: *Mere Christianity* 18
liberation 171–2
life after death 152
literary artistry 100
literary context 85–6, 189–90
living Scripture 209
Lot 7–8, 60, 62–5, 111
Lot's daughters 67
Lot's wife 66
love, nature of 130–1
'love thy neighbour' 98
low chronology 193, 224 n2, 226 n17
Luke, Gospel of 4; Marcion amended version 21

McGrath, Alister: critique of Dawkins 11–13; critique

Index of authors and subjects

of Hitchens 18–19; on cultural context 34; on 'good' laws 97–8
magic, rejection of 59
maiming 90
Marcion 4, 205; *Antitheses* 20; canon of Scripture 28; dismissing the Old Testament 19–21; dualism 22–4; and the 'New Atheists' 24–5; tailoring texts 21–2, 33
marriages 130–1, 185
Matthew, Gospel of 5
maxims 31; *see also* laws; morality
Megiddo 194
Megilloth 121
mercy 65–6, 136–7
Messiah 143, 207
Mezquita 47
Michal 179–80
minimalist scholarship 198–203
miracles 100
Moab 68
monarchy in Israel 110, 112, 125–6, 175–8, 196–8
monotheism 90, 149, 166–7
morality 133, 148, 214; of Abraham 71; in Flood narrative 56–7; modern 8; in prophetic books 146, 161; proverbs as source of 123; in Scripture 11, 114–15; in wisdom literature 129; *see also* ethics
morality tales 170–1, 181–3; *see also* allegories; parables
Mosaic covenant 44
Moses 8, 15–16, 167; as author of Pentateuch 189; as author of Ten Commandments 80–1; and golden calf 84, 85, 86; intercession for the people 87, 88–9; and promised land 96; song of 172–3
myths 31–2, 59, 100, 153, 163

Naomi 138
nationalism 41, 90, 172
nations, other than Israel, writings of 189–90
natural disasters, explanation for 11, 56, 57–8
nature of God 124–5, 136–7, 157, 160–1
nature of love 130–1
Nehemiah 185
'New Atheists' 6–7, 24–5
New Testament: canon 28–9; covenant 45; as jigsaw puzzle with Old 47–8; morality 9
Noachic covenant 44, 58, 164–5
Noah 7, 50; *see also* Flood, the
Nuzi culture 69

Index of authors and subjects

obedience, to God's will 66, 71–3, 85, 104

Old Testament: canon 28–30, 39–42, 121–2; Christian engagement with 205, 213–14; culture of 215; as evolving story 214–15; genres 185–6; as ideology 199, 215–16; Jesus' authority within 47–8, 209–10; as jigsaw puzzle with New Testament 47–8; legalism 97–8; as parochial in outlook 16–17, 38, 190–1; in preaching 211, 218–20; as propaganda 200; as quirky friend 204; as source of morality 7–8; use in modern worship 212–13; view of God 205–6

Omri, King 196

Omride dynasty 197–8

oral traditions 32–3, 74, 94, 102

origin stories 53–4, 68, 85

original sin 9–10, 53–4

parables 163–4; *see also* allegories; morality tales

Paul, St, writings of 4, 20–1

Pentateuch 7, 15; authorship of 189; historicity of 94–5

Philip and the Ethiopian eunuch 211–12

Phillips, Anthony 81–2

poetry 31, 44

polygamy 168–70

polytheism 149–50

post-exilic writings 184–5

preaching: the Old Testament 211, 218–20; using biblical scholarship 216–18

predestination 124–5

pride of humanity 164

promised land 87, 151–2, 167, 172; invasion of 95, 101–2

propaganda, Bible as 200

prophecy 144; authority of 44; to Gentiles 153; hope in 158–60; role of 5, 22; in surrounding cultures 145–6

prophetic books 146; authorship of 144; canon 145; morality in 146, 161

Prophets 5, 22, 23, 29

prophets, historical figures 144, 146

prostitutes, status of 109

prostitution 149

Protestant canon 29, 39

proverbs 31, 123–4; authority of 43

Proverbs (book) 5; creation in 127; as manual for life 126

Psalms (book) 5; creation in 127–8; law in 132–4; reflecting Old Testament 131–2

psalms, authority of 43

Index of authors and subjects

punishments 90–4, 148, 150–1, 157
Purim 139
purity 93, 158

Rachel 168–70
Rahab 102–3
rainbows 56, 165
rape: homosexual 64, 108, 111; laws against 64
readers of biblical texts 37–9, 203, 216
recompense 138
redaction 33, 144, 155
redactors 43, 44, 81, 177, 189, 191–2, 217
reductionist scholars 189
repentance 153–4
resurrection 152
retribution 138
revenge, acts of 98
rewards 148
righteousness 125
'ritual decalogue' 87
Ruth 137–8, 184

Sabbath 51, 81; keeping of 9, 13, 76, 82, 184; laws 91–2
sacrifices 102, 104–5; *see also* child sacrifice
salvation, of Israel 159, 160
Samson 174–5
Samuel 175–8
Sarah, as Abraham's sister 69–71, 73
Saul, King 23, 112–13

Schlimm, Matthew: *This Strange and Sacred Scripture* 204
Scripture: as nourishment to faith 217–18; as a whole 207–8
seals 130
Second Isaiah 145, 158–60, 209–10, 211
secular humanism 6
Seibert, Eric 4
selectivity, biblical texts 36–7, 46–7, 113–14, 208–9, 213
Septuagint 29
servant song 210
Shishak 193–4
Silberman, N. A. 197–8
sins 125; inherited 87; of Israel 147–8, 157–8
social justice 146–9, 158, 161
sociology, approach to biblical studies 195
Sodom and Gomorrah 60, 68, 111
Solomon, King 43, 125
'son of man' 142–3, 207
Song of Songs 130–1
Stavrakopoulou, Francesca 196, 226 n17, 239 n14
stories 31; exceptional subject matter 109–10; myths 59; repetition within 69–70; theological 61; *see also* explanation stories; origin stories; symbolic stories

Index of authors and subjects

storytelling 73–4, 109–10, 169–70; ancestral 165–6; in the Pentateuch 162–3
'suffering servant' motif 159, 210, 211–12
symbolic stories 50, 52–3, 55–60, 109–10
symbolism 31–2

Tamarin, George 100–1
tattoos 130
Ten Commandments 14–15, 228 n7; Christian context of 83–4; chronology 229 n11; as contract 77–8; as man-made 76–7; as moral code 79–80; part of covenant relationship 78, 79; presupposition for laws 82; provenance of 80–1
Tertullian 20
thanksgiving 132
theology 39, 61
Third Isaiah 145, 209–10
Thompson, Thomas L. 199, 201
Torah 7, 29
Tower of Babel 163–4
Trible, Phyllis 8
trust, in God 74, 136, 154–5

universalism 149, 153, 158–9, 160, 167, 184
Uriah 181–2
Uta-Napishtim 55

virgin birth 217
visions 151–2
vows, solemn 104, 105, 113

watchmaker-creator 48
Whitelam, Keith 195
wisdom 126, 127
wisdom literature 42, 123; morality in 129
women, status of 63–4, 66, 67–8, 91, 105–6, 111, 112, 113, 131, 138, 231 n11, 231 n12
worship: Christian 113–14; corrupt 158; use of Old Testament in 212–13
Writings 5, 29, 121–2
written traditions 94; in contemporary cultures 189–90

Yahweh 79, 90, 98, 106, 149–50, 166–7

zealots 10–11

www.ingramcontent.com/pod-product-compliance
Lightning Source LLC
Chambersburg PA
CBHW022004220426
43663CB00007B/953